the **information** store

📞01603 773114
email: tis@ccn.ac.uk

21 DAY LOAN ITEM

the last date stamped above

ed for overdue items

 CITY COLLEGE NORWICH

Children in Charge series

Children in Charge
The Child's Right to a Fair Hearing
Edited by Mary John
ISBN 1 85302 368 X
Children in Charge 1

Children in Our Charge
The Child's Right to Resources
Edited by Mary John
ISBN 1 85302 369 8
Children in Charge 2

The Participation Rights of the Child
Målfrid Grude Flekkøy
ISBN 1 85302 489 9 pb
ISBN 1 85302 490 2 hb
Children in Charge 4

of related interest

A Voice for Children
Speaking Out as Their Ombudsman
Målfrid Grude Flekkøy
ISBN 1 85302 118 0 pb
ISBN 1 85302 119 9 hb

Children in Charge 3

A Charge Against Society
The Child's Right to Protection

Edited by Mary John

Jessica Kingsley Publishers
London and Bristol, Pennsylvania

First published in the United Kingdom in 1997 by
Jessica Kingsley Publishers Ltd
116 Pentonville Road
London N1 9JB, England
and
1900 Frost Road, Suite 101
Bristol, PA 19007, U S A

Copyright © 1997 Jessica Kingsley Publishers

Library of Congress Cataloging in Publication Data
A CIP catalogue record for this book is available from the Library of Congress

British Library Cataloguing in Publication Data
A charge against society: the child's right to protection. – (Children in charge; 3)
1. Children – Services for 2. Child Care
I. John, Mary
362.7

ISBN 1-85302-411-2

Printed and Bound in Great Britain by
Cromwell Press, Melksham, Wiltshire

Contents

List of Figures vii

Editor's Acknowledgements ix

Part One: Protecting Whom?
1. Protecting Children or Reinforcing Dependency?
The Research Issues 3
Mary John

Part Two: Intrapsychic or Structural Approaches?
2. The International Resilience Project 19
Edith Grotberg

3. Systems Abuse 33
Judy Cashmore

Part Three: Childhood Put at Risk
4. Child Soldiers 51
Rachel Brett

5. Children's Labour in Mexico
Rights, Protection and Violation 64
Araceli Brizzio de la Hoz and Manuel Martinez Morales

6. A Safe Haven
Do International Standards and National Laws Protect Unaccompanied
Refugee Children in the UK Today? 77
Louise Williamson

7. Marginality and Extermination in Brazil
From Uneasiness to Well-Being 88
Janina Gonçalves

8. Teenage Sexuality World-Wide 98
David Treharne and Wendy Thomas

9. School Exclusion in the UK
An Entitlement at Risk? 107
Vanessa Parffrey

10. Children as Witnesses in the Crown Court 126
Etta Mitchell

Part Four: Family – A Safe Haven?

11. Domestic Violence and Child Contact Arrangements
Children's Right to Safety 135
Marianne Hester and Chris Pearson

12. Working With Children Who Have Been Abused 149
Ann Catchpole

13. Protecting Children or Policing Innocence?
The Role of the Mother After Disclosure
of Child Abuse in the UK 160
Sheila Townsend

Part Five: Young People Responding to a Changing Culture

14. Violence and Young Minds 171
Stephen Flood and Peter Wilson

15. Protection Through the Prevention of Exploitation
The North Devon Project on Drugs 187
Will Palin

16. Teaching Hieroglyphs with Authority
The Roles of Primary School Teacher, the Pupil, School Culture
and Local Community in Rural Mozambique 195
Mikael Palme

17. Truancy
The Greenstreet Detached Truancy Project 217
Tuaneri Akoto

Part Six: Strengthening the Human Spirit

18. The Truth of Single-Parent Families 233
Children from single-parent families

19. The Rights of the Child
in a Paediatric Oncology Unit 238
Penelope Cousens and Michael Stevens

20. Learning Rights
A Fundamental Prerequisite
for Protecting Oneself and Others 246
Gael Parfitt

The Contributors 262
Subject Index 266
Author Index 273

List of Figures

5.1	Postcard of daily life in a Mexican village near Jalepa	65
9.1	Number of exclusions in one area of one LEA, UK	112
9.2	Patterns of exclusion over a short-term period	112
9.3	Number of exclusions: one area of a local administrative area: UK	113
9.4	Number of exclusions: one area of a local administrative area: UK	113
9.5	Barchester unit: a joint social service/education resource	114
9.6	Feelings of six excluded children	117
9.7	Views of 12 staff in exclusion units	120

Editor's Acknowledgements

Many of the papers included in this collection were first presented in their original form at the 'World Conference on Research and Practice in Children's Rights; a Question of Empowerment?' held at the University of Exeter in September 1992. Other papers have been inspired by that gathering or report on work that has been developed within the spirit of concerns expressed there. It is only appropriate, therefore, to make acknowledgement here of the support that we received in holding that Conference, held as it was at a time when Children's Rights were not very much on the public agenda in the United Kingdom despite the ratification of the UN Convention by the UK the previous December and the setting up of the Children's Rights Development Unit.

A number of individuals and organisations had the vision to support what, at the time, seemed a high risk venture. Such individuals need to be thanked for inspirational support. The Assistant Director of Education for Devon County Council, Dr Paul Grey, supported us in concrete and facilitative ways and continued to further the cause of the implementation of the UN Convention of the Rights of the Child imaginatively within the County Council before he left to become Director of Education in Surrey in March, 1996. The Conference Manager, Ron Delve, Co-ordinator Hillary Olek and Graphic Designers Michael and Amanda Still held a risky undertaking together and ensured its success. The Conference Committee — made up of colleagues from various Departments in the University: Postgraduate Medical School, Department of Child Health, Psychology Department, Sociology Department, Law Department, School of Education, Department of Continuing and Adult Education — all demonstrated true interdepartmental co-operation and colleagues from the Dartington Social Research Unit of the University of Bristol, from the Faculty of Education at the University of Plymouth and the local Social Services Department reinforced that with real inter-institutional commitment of a high order and continued after the Conference with input into the discussions of the publication possibilities for the Conference papers. There remains only one regret which is that my original Co-Conference organiser, Christina Sachs, from Exeter University Law Department, was taken ill fairly early on in the preparations and, although she did manage to attend some of the Conference, sadly she died before the fruits of that Conference could be harvested. We remember her life and work on behalf of children and families with affection and gratitude.

No acknowledgements of the birthing process of this collection would be complete without mention of the children and young people who acted as midwives to much of the work and many of the ideas that have emerged. First, the work of ten Cornish Schools and their 350 pupils who contributed in a dramatic form their views and feelings about certain Articles of the UN Convention of the Rights on the Child. To them, their adult allies, their teachers and the overall organiser, Rhys Griffith, my thanks for having raised our consciousness in such stimulating ways. To the Young People's Evaluation Panel (Louise Pilcher, Joanne Kestevan, Louise Bridges, Kirstie Randall, Chris Hodder, Natalie Whitelock, Matthew Hendy, Molly Walker, Nicola Gregory, Felicity Thomas, Richard Partridge, Niki Dada, Vicky Maund, Alice Craven, Liz Beardsall, David Mance, Liz Palmer, Charlotte Murphy, Will Woodward and Rachel Bolt) who made the aim of children's participation meaningful, I remain indebted for all they taught us about listening to young people. To their schools – Kings School, Ottery St Mary; Mount St Mary Convent, Exeter; Sands School, Ashburton and the teacher/chauffeurs who believed that what these young people were doing mattered – my appreciation.

The Conference was financially supported by the Bernard Van Leer Foundation, the Elm Grant Trust, the Trustees of Westhill College Birmingham, University of Plymouth Faculty of Education, the School of Education of the University of Exeter, the University of Exeter Research Fund, Devon County Council Education Department and the Social Services Department, the Disabled Young Adults Centre, Cow and Gate Ltd, John Wyeth and Brother Ltd and Milupa. To them, my sincere thanks.

My gratitude to the individual contributors to the chapters in this volume is warm and sincere. They have all been inspiring to work with and it is my hope that their work, albeit that much of it is ongoing, will inspire others who work with children in similarly creative and imaginative ways. Having expressed my appreciation for contributions of various kinds to the process of the development of this volume and the two that have preceded it, I wish to make specific acknowledgements for the generous permission I have received from the Bernard Van leer Foundation and Dr Edith Grotberg for permission to reprint the extract on the International Resilience Project. I would like to thank the many colleagues who have assisted me in the task of bringing this final volume to completion: in particular, Penny Towsend, formerly Co-ordinator of the Devon Youth Council, whose great insight and skill I have benefited from in her services to me as expert adviser, editorial assistant and mentor. I acknowledge the support of the technical and administrative staff within the School of Education, Michael Still as an editorial assistant in the early stages of the work and my secretary, Angela Garry, for protection from the encroaching world, editorial and secretarial support, wizardry in all forms of new technologies and an unfailing good will when this preoccupation with children's rights began to encroach upon her own rights!

Finally, but by no means least, my heartfelt thanks to my husband, Theodore, for his support during the delivery of these three volumes – triplets which have been more demanding of him than any other multiple birth in his lifetime in obstetrics!

PART ONE

Protecting Whom?

CHAPTER ONE

Protecting Children
or Reinforcing Dependency?
The Research Issues

Mary John

I loathe my childhood and all that remains of it.

(Sartre 1964)

Thus wrote Jean Paul Sartre, reminiscing about his precocious childhood spent in provincial France before the First World War. His father died early so he was brought up in his grandfather's home in a world, even then, eighty years out of date. He writes about an illusion-ridden childhood which was dominated, in his view, by a false conception of life, ideas and literature. He takes stock of its effect on his work and thinking and demonstrates elements of childhood resilience in conditions of adversity, a theme which forms the focus of this volume.

But what does 'remain' of childhood and in what sense is any childhood 'up to date' and in touch with the changing world? *Freedom's Children* (Wilkinson and Mulgan 1995) reports on a year-long research project which claims to have undertaken one of the most thorough analyses of a generation's attitudes (18–34 year olds) and experience ever undertaken in the UK. It revealed that:

> The values of young people in Britain today have been profoundly shaped by prosperity and peace, education, travel and communications and by an inheritance of freedoms...There is a steady shift towards what some commentators call 'post material values'. Our map of British values shows how values are fragmenting, as younger age groups move towards more 'modern' values such as autonomy and authenticity. Our survey evidence describes the swing away from tradition and authority, and rising tolerance... We show how men's values are becoming more feminine and how women are becoming more masculine, attached to

risk, hedonism and living on the edge. In particular, women in the youngest age groups are taking far more pleasure in violence – more even than young men. Thirteen per cent of 18–24-year-old women agree that 'it is acceptable to use physical force to get something you really want'. We expect female violence to become a major issue in the years ahead. (p.11)

This leaves one wondering which particular features of childhood experience and a changing culture have left such an ominous legacy. For all of us, our childhoods have a considerable effect upon our present thoughts and, indeed, our present disposition. How have we survived these childhoods, what scars do we bear from them, what inner strengths have we developed, what vulnerabilities? How have these experiences affected the way in which we view the world?

Is it possible in a world which is changing rapidly, and often not in ways which nurture children, to 'protect' our young people from some of life's more stressful experiences? Of course we cannot. If we do, we do it at the risk of usurping the growth of independence and autonomy which will eventually make them full citizens and participants in the democratic process. It is this tension that is explored in the chapters that follow.

We counterpose the way in which systems ostensibly set up to serve the best interests of the child and protect them from dangers sometimes themselves create such aversive conditions that they do just the opposite with work with children, some of it peer-led which strengthens them to deal with life as they construe it and as it matters to them. We will, therefore, be contrasting systemic or paternalistic approaches with child-centred or intra-psychic ones which strengthen the child's ability to protect themselves.

What does 'remain', in Sartre's words, of some children's childhoods; what effects does it have in their adult lives; what shadow does it cast across their future and for how long?

A CHANGING WORLD – DAMAGED CHILDHOODS?

The collapse of political regimes has revealed some of the desperate situations that have been children's lot within those regimes and sometimes the changes themselves have exposed children to new dangers, new uncertainties and new risks or meant that old traditions are increasingly out of step for the world that they live in and the world that they will grow into as adult members.

Mikael Palme's chapter on education in post-civil war Mozambique illustrates this well. Not only is the educational system out of touch with the real needs of the indigenous cultures but it is also driven by outside agencies, the givers of aid, the donor community who shape what should be the aspirations of the system. So now, although the terrible dangers of the war are over, the educational system itself, by its disjunction with the needs of the people, threatens the appropriate development of the child and places some of those children in very ambiguous positions relative to their own culture. Palme documents the many dilemmas and the real failure to have any insight into the meaning of education within a changing culture.

As counterpoint, although in an entirely different cultural context, we have chosen to include in this collection some examples of local action which demonstrate children running some of their own projects. What is important about such projects is that the young people have started from the world as they know it. The Greenstreet Project (Tuaneri Akoto's chapter) starts from what young people found aversive about attending school, what made them truant and tried, through the various activities of the peer group, to develop not only important life skills but their own sense of self worth. It locates them with a place in the society in which they live – skills and feelings about themselves which they see as relevant to that life.

Returning to the broad theme of political upheaval and childhood, Eastern Europe suddenly revealed to Western eyes some of the tragedies of childhood under their former totalitarian regimes. Coupled with the collapse of totalitarian regimes has been the rise of nationalism – as, for example, in the former Yugoslavia, where the suffering of children has been horrific and unremitting. They have certainly not been protected or rescued yet this has been a war which has been conducted in Europe under the full glare of media publicity. The huge numbers of child orphans and refugees at the end of the 15 years of civil war in Mozambique has added to our professional concerns about the long-term effects of these harrowing experiences on young lives. Children, not only in Mozambique but closer to home in Belfast, have seen parents and siblings slaughtered before their eyes. Moreover, in wartime, children are now deliberately targeted as a means of terrorising the enemy: for evidence of this one need look no further than the harrowing reports of the International War Crimes Tribunal established by the UN Security Council to investigate the violations of humanitarian law in former Yugoslavia (National Children's Bureau 1994). In peacetime, children are just as deliberately neglected by governments who spend a combined total of £350 billion on military programmes while over one billion people struggle to survive on less than £1 a day (Sivard 1993).

Whilst war is clearly a devastating and harrowing experience, Rachel Brett, in Chapter 4 outlines projects trying to keep children out of armed conflict, whether as child soldiers or as civilians. Nevertheless, it is not the only mortal risk children face. In 1993, UNICEF estimated that whilst 500,000 children died as a result of war, as many as 12.4 million died as a result of poverty, disease and malnutrition. Poverty is not just a matter for the developing world, although the example we use here is from Brazil. It is true to say that even the wealthiest countries have poor records as far as child neglect is concerned. The Fordham Institute for Innovation in Social Policy – using a combined measure of infant mortality, government spending on education, teenage suicide and income distribution – concluded that in the United States and the United Kingdom children are worse off today than they were in 1970 (Miringoff and Opdycke 1992). So how, if at all, can we protect children and rehabilitate them after trauma?

A group of psychologists in post-apartheid South Africa have pooled their ideas to provide psychological perspectives on the effects of adversity (Dawes and Donald 1994). As one would expect, these notions are complex and difficult to generalise. The birth of the new South African society has provided a useful opportunity for reflecting on childhood as a developmental phase and, indeed, on the impact adversity might have on the quality of that childhood:

> It could…be said that our history has been characterised by our failure as a nation to nurture our children. It comes as no surprise that we are reaping the bitter fruits of that historical failure. Current concern about 'marginalised youth' or the 'lost generation' is a belated response to a problem which has been evolving since the 1970s and which adults have been ignoring all along. But even more disconcerting is the tendency of significant opinion-formers to blame the young people alone for the situation they find themselves in. The solutions proposed to deal with the problem also indicate a lack of understanding of the nature of the problem and its origins. Proposals for militarisation programmes or calls for community service for youth are likely to complicate an already complicated problem area. (Ramphele 1994, p.v)

In looking at what modern developmental psychology has to offer in understanding the psychological consequences of adversity, Rose (1990) criticises the discipline for ignoring the moral base of notions of 'optimal' childhoods which form the basis for actually constructing and policing modern childhoods. He extends this criticism to the ways in which the discipline 'invents' children's needs and naturalises what are socially determined aspects of development. If one accepts these criticisms, it becomes clear that modern childhood is considerably shaped by psychology itself. Of course, such power can be used in positive and negative ways as everyday discourse is coloured by the discipline. Rose and others like him have drawn our attention to the assumptions and power which lies behind much everyday knowledge which has informed, in so many ways, psychological understanding of the consequences of adversity. It becomes clear in this work that it is important not to confuse the psychological and moral bases of positions that are adopted in advocating what is best for children. In the context of South Africa, research is often either inadequate or insufficient – partly to do with the social political history of the country. More research which is creative and insightful and mindful of children needs to be undertaken everywhere to help understand the consequences of the many hardships children suffer.

Another significant way in which the world is changing is increasing urbanisation. Cristina Szanton Blank, reporting on the UNICEF Urban Child

Project (Szanton Blank 1994), makes it clear that whilst we are aware that since the early 1970s the recession has severely threatened the welfare of vulnerable groups both South and North and many trends have been documented, the complex ways in which these trends have affected the well-being of our young populations have only begun to be understood. She sees difficulties in demonstrating 'how existing world conditions and social transformations are creating a relatively unhealthy, disheartened and troubled population of young people who are growing up with more severe problems of social adjustment than ever before.' (p.2). In her view, this social deterioration is chronic in the developing world, although it is not clearly recorded. The Urban Child Project reports on field work in five nations – Brazil, the Philippines, India, Kenya and Italy – documenting the desperate situations facing street children. Gonçalves, in Chapter 7 exposes the context of some of this suffering in Brazil.

Gonçalves and Palme both indicate the influence of the financial situation: whether that is, as in the case of Brazil, the consequence of a huge foreign debt or, as in Mozambique, the effect of donor agencies on the nature of provision. Both aid and the globalisation of capital have had dire consequences for the health, well-being and education of children.

There are topics we have not included which develop the theme of adversity further, for example missing children or children who run away. We have not included child prostitution and sexual trafficking in children, nor have we included the various kinds of other abuses, for example satanic and ritual abuse of children. There are some losses which are not simply of childhood innocence but of a beloved parent. We have not included work with children on grief and bereavement, which does work towards making children more resilient and able to cope. We have, in looking at damage to childhood in a changing world, tried to balance this with interventions which aim at trying to strengthen the child.

THE CHILD'S RIGHT TO PROTECTION AS OUTLINED IN THE UN CONVENTION ON THE RIGHTS OF THE CHILD[1]

As has been indicated earlier in this series, the United Nation's Convention on the Rights of the Child is made up of 54 Articles which are conventionally thought of as clustering around three aspects of rights, namely: Participation, Provision and Protection. The previous two volumes (*Children in Charge* and *Children in Our Charge*) dealt respectively with research and practice as it concerned participation and provision. In the present collection, our concentration is on work that relates to respecting, in various ways, the child's rights to protection. Essentially, the 'Protection' Articles relate to rights which require adults to care for children by protecting them from psychological, emotional,

---

1   UNGAOR 1991.

physical and sexual maltreatment. In this collection, we look at indirect ways in which such maltreatment may come about, as, for example, in the implementation of systems designed to protect children which, in their manifestations and operations, do entirely the reverse. We have, therefore, included material on what Judy Cashmore in Chapter 3 has dubbed 'Systems Abuse'. The Articles which specifically relate to the issue of 'Protection' in the Convention are Articles 2, 16, 19, 22, 32, 33, 34, 35, 39 and 40.

If we pause for a moment and look at each of these in turn, it will be helpful in providing some insight into the climate that has been provided by the Convention. Although U N Conventions often are criticised for having no teeth unless they are incorporated in some way into each national legislature of the signatories, such manifestos are important in providing us with some insight into the climate of the times in terms of what is currently thought that, in an ideal world, a child's life should be. The drafting process involved many countries and many consultations and the alacrity with which many countries have ratified the Convention is some indication of a commonality of ideals here. This book, however, sadly documents the many areas in which even signatory states still fail to measure up to their aspirations in protecting and acknowledging the rights of the child to protection in its very many forms. It examines the gaps between the rhetoric and realities, where good intentions are not realised in provision, economics or, sometimes, in attitudes as they relate to specifics.

Article 2 is a general and comprehensive statement about protection of the child. Briefly stated, it indicates that, without discrimination on any grounds whatsoever, the parties to the Convention (commonly referred to as the States Parties) undertake to respect and ensure the rights set forth in the Convention and furthermore shall take all measures that are deemed appropriate to ensure that the child is protected against all forms of discrimination or punishment on the basis of status, activities, expressed opinions, or beliefs of the child's parents, legal guardians, or family members.

Article 16 refers largely to the child's rights to privacy and it may well be thought in the material written by children from single parent families (Chapter 17) that at times they experience such breaches of privacy and experience discrimination as a result of the exposure of their family circumstances about which they feel sensitive. This Article specifically states that no child shall be subjected to arbitrary or unlawful attacks on his or her honour and reputation. The way the children have coped with such infringements of their rights in a dignified and intelligent way is chastening in reminding us yet again what skilful operators, in an often threatening social world, such young people can be. This reminder is further reinforced in the work by Penelope Cousens and Michael Stevens (Chapter 19), who talk of how some children who know they are going to die of cancer are able to be sympathetic to and support their parents' grief about this inevitable outcome. Privacy is often a difficult right to respect in the interests of protecting the child. The sensitive work undertaken by Ann Catchpole (Chapter 12) with young children who have been abused shows how a skilled, experienced and sensitive adult can respect the children's wishes for, and indeed rights to, privacy and can take care not to intrude into secrets they do not wish to tell and how, in the course of building up such a respectful trust, the children often feel able to share secrets they can hardly bear to think about. This chapter provides an example of good practice – practice which is not, however, universally so child-centred in other settings in the UK and elsewhere. The extent to which a young person is able to participate in decisions throughout the whole child protection system in the UK and the frequent conflict between the child's wishes and the professional's perception of their best interests is well documented by Schofield and Thorburn (1996).

Van Manen and Levering (1996) point out, however, that childhood secrets are not always painful ones: 'Some secrets are treasures that children covet; like flowers in a forest, these secrets come with the territory of childhood…' but they go on 'Other secrets are imposed on children; sometimes these secrets turn into malignancies and monsters, leaving complex scar tissue on the membranes of personal identity. But what these dark and pathological secrets share with those that are nice or more benign is that the secrets of the past may have their effects in the present. The good deeds and wrongdoings of one generation often live on in successive generations' (p.xx).

Article 19 is quite specific about the responsibility of the States Parties to take all appropriate legislative, administrative, social and educational measures to protect the child from all forms of physical or mental violence, injury or abuse, neglect or negligent treatment or exploitation including sexual abuse, while in the care of parent(s), legal guardian(s). There is much, sadly, in this volume to show how much still has to be done by the signatories of the Convention to protect children from all these threats – ranging from the possibility of death itself, as outlined by Janina Gonçalves writing in Chapter 7 about the broader and appalling context of child extermination in Brazil, to the exploitation and the various hazards experienced by child workers in Mexico (Chapter 5), to concerns expressed by Rachel Brett in Chapter 4 about children's involvement in armed combat, to work on child sexual abuse and the educational process itself, which Vanessa Parffrey (Chapter 9) describes as rendering vulnerable children more vulnerable still. This Article goes on to urge the States Parties to establish social programmes to provide the necessary support for the child and those who have care of the child and all the associated structures for prevention, identification, referral, investigation, treatment, follow-up and various aspects of judicial involvement. Whilst the development of such procedures may be laudable, the procedures in themselves can be very stressful indeed for children who have already experienced violence and abuse. Etta Mitchell (Chapter 10) describes, on the basis of direct experience, what is currently being done in the United Kingdom to protect child witnesses in court

– work that is further documented and described by Helen Dent and Rhona Flin (1996). So, whilst there is clearly some need to develop ways of monitoring and controlling ways in which children are abused, there is always the danger that the children themselves might be further damaged in this process. Children have been put through harrowing experiences in court in the name of justice.

A court case in the United Kingdom in 1991, alleging the ritual and sexual abuse of two young girls by various members of their family during black magic rituals, highlighted quite dramatically the need for legal reform when the case collapsed because the prosecution felt they could no longer rely on the 10-year-old child's evidence after she had been in the witness box for four days. It was stated: 'the girl's evidence was so uncertain, inconsistent and improbable... The girl, who clutched a pink rabbit while giving evidence, was shielded by screens as she recounted in a whisper how she was repeatedly raped by her father and thought it was normal as it happened so often. "I just assumed it happened to all girls" she told the court'. This case provided a distressing example of how the examination and cross-examination of children in court was an entirely inappropriate process (*Times* report 1992). Law reforms to stop children having to give live evidence in court have been urged for some considerable time and Etta Mitchell's chapter gives an account of how far this has developed in the United Kingdom.

Article 22 deals with the rights of child refugees, a topic which is developed in Chapter 6 by Louise Williamson. In the Convention the provision is that the child who is seeking refugee status in accordance with applicable international and domestic law and procedures, whether accompanied or not, should receive appropriate protection and humanitarian assistance. Chapter 6 explores the implications of the fact that Article 22 was one of the Articles that was not agreed to by the United Kingdom in the ratification process for unaccompanied child refugees arriving in the United Kingdom.

Aracelli Brizzio de la Hoz and Manuel Martinez Morales, in Chapter 5, illustrate some of the problems associated with child labour as they have experienced them in Mexico. Child labour is an issue specifically addressed by the Convention in Article 32, which concerns itself with 'the right of the child to be protected from economic exploitation and from performing any work that is likely to be hazardous or to interfere with the child's education or to be harmful to the child's health or physical, mental, spiritual, moral or social development.' They explain the pressures the child is often under to work in order to contribute to the support of his family or even to ensure his/her own personal survival. Their chapter provides some further details of the provisions of Article 32 and other associated international and national instruments as they relate to child labour. The incidence of child labour is a global concern as economies get tighter and, as the grip of poverty deepens, everybody, including children, tries to find a means of survival. The extent of child labour, however, is often hard to establish as so much is hidden and covert and being hidden and covert means that children have no rights or union to protect them as workers. There is a form of child labour which is not dealt with in any detail in this volume which has given cause for widespread concern – the trafficking in children for sexual purposes (Article 35 deals directly with the sexual exploitation of children), notably the Philippines with, until recently, a known record of attracting tourists for these purposes. Thankfully there is now some evidence of a clamp-down on such activities with the adult perpetrators and 'customers' being prosecuted. Where poverty prevails, however, it seems relatively hopeless to stamp it out altogether. The Brazilian Centre for Childhood and Adolescence (CNBIA) has recently estimated that there are about 500, 000 girls who have turned to prostitution to earn a living, some of whom are as young as nine years old. The prostitution of young girls in Brazil is seen as the direct consequence of years of economic recession and the low status afforded to women in the country (de Oliviera 1996). With the growth of the tourism industry, selling their bodies has become a way for poor young girls to have access to the dollars of tourists.

In contrast, there can be a betrayal of the child's rights under Article 32 within systems actually designed to benefit children and their welfare and which are commonly regarded as benign. The education system is a case in point. Vanessa Parffrey, in Chapter 9, points out the consequences for children with particular difficulties and disabilities in the new market in education in the UK. The system itself cannot be a source of direct marginalisation but, in the way it is responded to and is operated, can become harmful to the child's health or physical, mental, spiritual, moral or social development. In another cultural context – looking more widely at the harm education policies can do – Field (1995) writes that, according to media reports, for least two decades there has been a rising incidence of the so-called 'adult diseases', that is of the familiar symptoms of work-related stress, among Japanese school-aged children. In 1990, a nation-wide survey of grammar school children showed that 63.2 per cent were suffering from high levels of blood cholesterol, 36.2 per cent from ulcers, 22.1 per cent from high blood pressure and 21.4 per cent from diabetes. It is very disturbing to find this high incidence of such symptoms amongst school-aged children. Moreover, a spokesperson for the leading artificial hair manufacturer Aderansu claims that wig use is increasing among children who are suffering from stress-related baldness caused by the pressures of cram school attendance or bullying in their regular schools. In an educational broadcast on national radio around that time, there had also been a programme on stress-related baldness among women and Field questions whether women who had children at crucial stages of their schooling figured high in these statistics as 'mother and child constitute a labouring team'. She explains:

> There are no child labour laws to protect Japanese two-year-olds from having to trace a path through countless mazes to acquire small-motor co-ordination…from having to curb their sensibilities within the regime

of the workbook before they can ride swings or wash their own faces – for, of course, the point is neither simply to perfect small-motor co-ordination nor to increase vocabulary *per se*, but to produce adults tolerant of joyless repetitive tasks, in other words, disciplined workers. (Field 1995, p.54)

There are no child labour laws either to protect not prodigies but ordinary school children from fourth through to sixth grade, of whom 50 per cent in the capital region attend cram schools, from the routine of rushing home after school, grabbing dinners packed by their mothers, exchanging their school text books for cram school books, spending from 5–9p.m. at the cram school, perhaps staying on for private lessons until 11p.m. and, by the time entrance exams are around the corner, getting home after midnight to tackle school homework with, finally, a short burst of video game playing – such games having been bought as expensive bribes – before going to sleep around 2 a.m. (Arita and Yamaoka 1992). Field points out that although it might appear that the children have no choice in this, not only do they know that this is the only way to get ahead but also that the only way of seeing their friends is to go to the cram school. Whilst ideas about choice and liberalism are necessarily complicated as they relate to children's rights and have indeed been put to the test by Japan's parliamentary democracy over the last few years, Field emphasises that liberal ideology has been formally underlined by the provision of basic rights and, implicitly, by the productivity of the 'free' enterprise which has brought prosperity to substantial sections of Japanese society.

Fukuyama (1995) investigates, the origins of competitiveness, which he sees as the most important issue facing the United States, Britain and other industrial democracies. He looks further at why East Asia has grown as fast as it has over the past two generations and feels that most people have looked in the wrong place by looking at the problems in terms of free market or state interventionist policies. Culture, in his view, lies at the heart of Asian success, so he examines the roots of economic behaviour – not just in East Asia, which is often seen as the principal example of culturally-based economic success, but at contemporary economic systems in North America, Europe and Latin America too. Trust, community and social commitments all turn out to be important. He asserts that the tendency for some democracies towards individualism will be bad for their economies. He sees a the close relationship between moral virtue and *habit* (Editor's italics) manifest in the concept of 'character'.

In the educational regime earlier described by Field, the character building seems to be achieved, if this indeed is what such regimes do build, at considerable cost to the child. In what sense then are we protecting them – are we preparing them for life in the new millennium – as active citizens in the new economies? It is important here to heed Rose's earlier admonition that we must not confuse moral and psychological positions, Fukuyama, in elaborating his point, indicates that whereas it easy to *know* the right thing to do intellectually, only people with 'character' are able to do it under difficult circumstances or challenging circumstances. He refers to Aristotle's view that, in contrast to intellectual virtue, 'ethical virtue' (ethike) is for the most part the product of habit (ethos) and has indeed derived its name, with a slight variation of form, from that word. Aristotle expanded on this by saying 'our moral dispositions are formed as a result of the corresponding activities... It is therefore not of small moment whether we are trained from childhood in one set of habits or another; on the contrary it is of very great, or rather of supreme importance.'[2] These are cautionary words indeed as we look at the lives of children, of what they live through and the resilience that is required of them. What consequences has this for their 'character' in these terms and at what cost can 'character' that favours economic prosperity for the nation be fostered?

Returning to the Articles of the United Nation's Convention as they relate to the protection of the child, Article 33 relates to protecting children from using narcotic drugs and psychotropic substances (as defined in the relevant international treaties) and the prevention of the use of children in the illicit production and trafficking in such substances. In this volume, material on the North Devon Youth project is included which illustrates a form of intervention with drug users which has been very much influenced in its design by peer insight and peer involvement and is, therefore, close to the culture of young people. The starting point has not been to require total abstinence but to start at the point that the young drug user is at and initially aim to reduce some of the more obvious health risks in taking drugs. This means that much of the early activity is involved in containing the problem rather than initially trying to eliminate it. Chapter 8, by Treharne and Harris, argues for a similar approach involving peer education and an acceptance that sexual behaviour is, in a high proportion of cases, a feature of a young person's life. They argue that to see sexual health as part and parcel of reproductive health is not to face up to the realities of young people's lives and, as a result, important aspects of education about sexual health which can often be successfully mediated by the peer group are overlooked.

Article 34 deals with sexual exploitation and sexual abuse, which are aspects of the risks that feature in increasingly pathologised childhoods. In this collection there are three chapters which deal with this subject. Chapter 11, by Hester and Pearson, whilst broadly looking at violence, takes a very different stance from that adopted by Sheila Townsend in Chapter 13 and the reader will question whether it is acceptable to count on the child's intricate understanding and social skills in order to accommodate adult needs, as exemplified

---

2   Aristotle explains in Nicchomachean Ethics Book II i.8. that for people to be truly virtuous, they must habituate themselves to virtuous behaviour such that it becomes second nature and pleasant in itself – or if indeed not pleasurable, nevertheless something which the virtuous can take pride in.

by Townsend with reference to case work with mothers of abused children and the children themselves. Children seem able to do, according to the account provided, some sort of cost-benefit analysis – but should they ever be put in this position and is their resilience possibly overestimated? Some of the material outlined by Hester and Pearson substantiates a case for the protection of children and children's rights to protection over and above parental rights of access. Children's rights which require adults to relinquish rights are always fraught and the child rarely wins out.

The defence needs of some countries overruled arguments from many others that soldiers should not be conscripted below the age of 18, the age at which the young person is no longer 'a child' within the definition of the Convention. Article 38 relates to child soldiers and children in war zones. Rachel Brett outlines some research that is being undertaken in this area.

War, torture, neglect, exploitation and abuse and, indeed, any other form of cruel, inhuman or degrading treatment or punishment have costs in children's lives and well-being. Article 39 provides that countries should take responsibility for the rehabilitation and reintegration of the child in 'an environment which fosters the health, self-respect and dignity of the child.' Article 40 protects the rights of the child who is alleged as, accused of, or recognised as having infringed the penal law 'to be treated in a manner consistent with the promotion of the child's sense of dignity and worth'. Although research has continued to demonstrate that detention does little to prevent re-offending, and often appears to encourage it, it was hoped that 1993 would see the end of penal custody for children – which is outlawed in Article 37 of the Convention indicating that this should only be seen as a last resort. Children, it seems, in some countries remain viewed in some quarters as a threat to the present social order rather than an important investment for the future. In all senses they remain 'a charge' against society.

RESEARCH ON RESILIENCE

Much research has been undertaken on documenting the many injustices and hardships that children suffer around the world. Some of it inevitably leads to 'bad' behaviour. We know little about the effects of many of the kinds of violations on young people's mental health described by Flood and Wilson in Chapter 14. We introduce the collection on a positive note by looking at the work of the International Resilience Project and, throughout the book, take up themes to do with strengthening the human spirit. Whilst our primary aim must be to protect children and their rights, we cannot protect them from all the troubles that life might bring. We therefore need to think carefully about the development of resilience as, perhaps, in a changing hurtful world, this is probably one of the most important aspects of our children's development: a responsible and respectful way of protecting them.

REFERENCES

Aristotle (1975) *Ethica Nicomachea, Nicomachean (Books* I–X*)* Cambridge, Mass: Harvard University Press.

Arita, M. and Yamaoka, S. (1992) 'Karoji Shokogun (The Overworthy Child Syndrome).' *Asahi Journal, March 20,* 11–16.

Dent, H. and Flin, R. (1996) *Children as Witnesses.* London: Wiley.

de Oliviera, S. (1996) *Child Prostitution on the Rise in Brazil.* The ICRI Brazil Project.

Field, N. (1995) 'The child as laborer and consumer: The disappearance of childhood in contemporary Japan.' In S. Stephens (ed) *Children and the Politics of Culture.* Princeton: Princeton University Press.

Fukuyama, F. (1995) *Trust: The Social Virtues and the Creation of Prosperity.* London: Hamish Hamilton.

Miringoff, M. and Opdycke, S. (1992) *The Index of Social Health: Monitoring the Social Well-being of Children in Industrial Countries.* Tarrytown, N.Y: Fordham Institute for Innovation in Social Policy.

National Children's Bureau (1994) *Children Now, 3rd Edition.* London: National Children's Bureau.

Ramphele, M.A. (1994) Foreword to Dawes, A. and Donald, D. *Childhood and Adversity; Psychological perspectives from South African Research.* Cape Town: David Philip.

Rose, N. (1990) *Governing the Soul. The Shaping of the Private Self.* London: Routledge.

Sartre, Jean Paul (1964) *Words.* Translated by Irene Clephane. First published in France in 1964. This translation first published in 1964 by Hamish Hamilton. Taken here from the (1974) Harmondsworth. Penguin Books.

Schofield, G. and Thorburn, J. (1996) *Child Protection: The Child's Role in Decision Making.* London: Institute for Public Policy Research.

Sivard, R.L. (1993) 'World Military Expenditures, 1993.' *World Priorities, Washington DC, 5.*

Szanton Blank, C. (1994) *Urban Children in Distress: Global Predicaments and Innovative Strategies.* Reading: Gordon and Breach.

United Nations General Assembly Official Records (UNGAOR), Resolution 25, 44th Session (1991) *The United Nations Convention on the Rights of the Child.* New York: UN.

van Manen, M. and Levering, B. (1996) *Childhood's Secrets. Intimacy, Privacy and the Self Reconsidered.* London: Teacher's College Press.

Wilkinson, H. and Mulgan, G. (1995) *Freedoms Children: Work, relationships and Politics for 18–34 Year Olds in Britain Today.* London: Demos.

PART TWO

Intrapsychic
or Structural Approaches?

CHAPTER 2

The International Resilience Project[1]

Edith Grotberg

The concept of resilience is not new, although defining it precisely remains a problem. A number of researchers (see further reading) have identified specific factors such as trusting relationships, emotional support outside the family, self-esteem, encouragement of autonomy, hope, responsible risk taking, a sense of being lovable, school achievement, belief in God and morality and unconditional love for someone. But there is insufficient understanding on the dynamic interaction of these factors, their roles in different contexts, their expression and their sources. A child's own genetic make-up and temperament are fundamental to whether he or she will be resilient. That is, a child's vulnerability to anxiety, challenges, stress or unfamiliarity determines his or her self-perception, how he or she interacts with others and how he or she addresses adversities.

Over the last five or so years, a number of international meetings have addressed the construct of resilience. It is the conclusions of these meetings, together with the literature, that have led to the definition of resilience that is used in the International Resilience Project: 'Resilience is a universal capacity which allows a person, group or community to prevent, minimise or overcome the damaging effects of adversity'. The project set out to examine what parents, care givers or children do that seems to promote resilience. It is thus concerned with promoting resilience in children as they develop over time, without the need for some kind of pathology in the family or child. Furthermore, the basic unit for the study is the child in context.

To launch the study, an Advisory Committee made up of international organisations was formed comprising the Civitan International Research Centre, UNESCO, Pan American Health Organisation (PAHO), World Health

---

1 This chapter is reprinted from *A Guide to Promoting Resilience in Children: Strengthening the Human Spirit* by Dr. Edith Gothberg. Both the author and the Bernard Van Leer Foundation have kindly given their permission to publish this extract.

Organisation (WHO), International Children's Centre (ICC), International Catholic Child Bureau (ICCCB) and the Bernard van Leer Foundation. The Advisory Committee's role was to provide suggestions and criticisms to the International Resilience Project. Participants from 30 countries joined the project and the findings are based on the data submitted between September 1993 and August 1994 by the first 14 countries to reply (Lithuania, Russia, Costa Rica, Czech Republic, Brazil, Thailand, Vietnam, Hungary, Taiwan, Namibia, Sudan, Canada, South Africa and Japan). The international perspective helps us to learn what different cultures are doing to promote resilience: Do they draw on the same pool of resilience factors? Do they vary in which factors are combined to address adversity?

The instruments used by the researchers in the different countries were: fifteen situations of adversity to which adults and children were asked to respond; three standardised tests; actual experiences of adversity reported by respondents together with their own reactions to these situations and a checklist of fifteen statements that indicate resilience in a child as below:

Checklist for children

- The child has someone who loves him/her totally (unconditionally).
- The child has an older person outside the home she/he can tell about problems and feelings.
- The child is praised for doing things on his/her own.
- The child can count on her/his family being there when needed.
- The child knows someone he/she wants to be like.
- The child believes things will turn out all right.
- The child does endearing things that make people like her/him.
- The child believes in power greater than seen.
- The child is willing to try new things.
- The child likes to achieve in what he/she does.
- The child feels that what she/he does makes a difference in how things come out.
- The child likes himself/herself.
- The child can focus on a task and stay with it.
- The child has a sense of humour.
- The child makes plans to do things.

A total of 589 children participated as well as their families and caregivers: 48 per cent were girls and 52 per cent boys. Just over half the children were aged from 9 to 11 years, the remainder were aged six years or under. The findings suggest that every country in the study is drawing on a common set of resilience factors to promote resilience in their children. Adults and older children use more resilience promoting supports, inner strengths and interpersonal skills than younger children in promoting resilience in the children. Overall, less than half the respondents are using resilience promoting behaviour and even those respondents vary individually in use of the factors, largely depending on the situation. Socio-economic level contributed very little to variations in responses.

It is not possible to determine cultural variations by country because the numbers of respondents per country are too small. However, it is clear that there are relationships between culture and resilience factors. Some cultures rely more on faith than on problem-solving in facing adversity. Some cultures are more concerned with punishment and guilt while others discipline and reconcile. Some cultures expect children to be more dependent on others for help in adversity rather than becoming autonomous and more self-reliant. The parents in some countries maintain a close relationship with their children while others 'cut off' their children at about age five. The resilient children manage this kind of rejection; non-resilient children withdraw, submit and are depressed.

In the International Resilience Project the children were not studied independently from their settings. In promoting resilience, any work with children must similarly be in the contexts of their families, their schools, their communities, and the larger society. Even though much could be said about promoting resilience in parents, in teachers, in communities and in societies, the project focused on promoting resilience in children. These parents, teachers, communities and societies are essential to promoting resilience in children, so attention is centred on the child, but in his or her setting. The construct of resilience and the factors that contribute to it continue to be discussed at local, national and international fora, while development projects in different countries are using the concepts to inform and elaborate their own work.

WHY BOTHER WITH RESILIENCE?

'My father gets drunk. He said he was going to kill my mother and me. My mother put me with friends and ran away. I don't know where she is.' (6-year-old boy)

'I have to go to the hospital a lot because I have so many illnesses. I don't know if I will ever get well.' (10-year-old girl)

'I saw my father get stabbed by a neighbour who was mad at him.' (6-year-old girl)

'I am very short and people tease me at school all the time.' (11-year-old boy)

Day in and day out, children all over the world face situations like the ones described above. Some face stresses such as divorce or illness while others confront catastrophe – war, poverty, disease, famine, floods. Whether such experiences crush or strengthen an individual child depends, in part, on his or her resilience. Resilience is important because it is the human capacity to face, overcome and be strengthened by, or even transformed by, the adversities of life. Everyone faces adversities; no one is exempt. With resilience, children can triumph over trauma; without it, trauma (adversity) triumphs. The crises children face both within their families and in their communities can overwhelm them.

While outside help is essential in times of trouble, it is insufficient; along with food and shelter, children need love and trust, hope and autonomy; along with safe havens, they need safe relationships that can foster friendships and commitment; they need the loving support and self-confidence, the faith in themselves and their world, all of which builds resilience. How parents and other caregivers respond to situations, and how they help a child to respond, separates those adults who promote resilience in their children from those who destroy resilience or send confusing messages that both promote and inhibit resilience.

THREE SOURCES OF RESILIENCE

To overcome adversities, children draw from three sources of resilience features labelled: I HAVE, I AM, I CAN. What they draw from each of the three sources may be described as follows.

I HAVE

- People around me I trust and who love me, no matter what
- People who set limits for me so I know when to stop before there is danger or trouble
- People who show me how to do things right by the way they do things
- People who want me to learn to do things on my own
- People who help me when I am sick, in danger or need to learn.

I AM

- A person people can like and love
- Glad to do nice things for others and show my concern
- Respectful of myself and others
- Willing to be responsible for what I do
- Sure things will be all right.

I CAN

- Talk to others about things that frighten me or bother me
- Find ways to solve problems that I face
- Control myself when I feel like doing something not right or dangerous
- Figure out when it is a good time to talk to someone or to take action
- Find someone to help me when I need it.

A resilient child does not need all of these features to be resilient, but one is not enough. A child may be loved (I HAVE), but if he or she has no inner strength (I AM) or social, interpersonal skills (I CAN), there can be no resilience. A child may have a great deal of self-esteem (I AM), but if he or she does not know how to communicate with others or solve problems (I CAN), and has no one to help him or her (I HAVE), the child is not resilient. A child may be very verbal and speak well (I CAN), but if he or she has no empathy (I AM) or does not learn from role models (I HAVE), there is no resilience. Resilience results from a combination of these features.

These features of resilience may seem obvious and easy to acquire; but they are not. In fact, many children are not resilient and many parents and other caregivers do not help children become resilient. Only about 38 per cent of the thousands of responses in the International Resilience Project indicate that resilience is being promoted. That is a very small percentage for such a powerful contribution to the development of children. On the contrary, too many adults crush or impede resilience in children or give mixed messages, and too many children feel helpless, sad and not fully loved. This is not the situation necessarily out of intent; it is more the fact that people do not know about resilience or how to promote it in children.

Children need to become resilient to overcome the many adversities they face and will face in life: they cannot do it alone, they need adults who know how to promote resilience and are, indeed, becoming more resilient themselves.

WHAT IS RESILIENCE?

There are many accounts of children and adults facing and overcoming adversities in their lives in spite of the fact that their circumstances suggested they would be overcome by the adversities. Here are some real experiences people have had. Using the I HAVE, I AM, I CAN model, here is what they did that would promote resilience in the process of overcoming the adversity:

1. A five-year-old boy comes home and tells his mother: 'This big boy keeps bullying me. He hits me and sometimes he kicks me. I tell him to stop and he does for a while and then he starts again. I'm really

scared of him.' The mother can draw on I HAVE features of 'people around me I trust and who love me, no matter what' and 'people who help me when I am in danger'; the I AM features of the child can be strengthened by seeing him or herself as a 'person to be liked and loved' and 'sure things will be all right'; the I CAN features of the child include 'talking to others about things that frighten or bother me' and 'finding someone to help me when I need it'. The interaction between the mother and boy was like this: the mother listened to him and told him how sorry she was and comforted him. Then she said he was right to tell the teacher and he may want to do that every time the other boy bothers him until it stops. She offered to talk to the teacher or to the boy's parents, but wanted her son to develop an increasing sense of being independent and so did not want to insist. The boy felt free to share his feelings and to listen to solutions to the problem. He saw that he is part of the solution and wanted to learn further what he can do.

2. An eleven-year-old girl tells about this experience: 'My cousin and I were hiking in the mountains in the winter. I fell into deep snow and could not get out. I was very frightened.' The girl can draw on the I HAVE resilience feature of 'people who help me when I am in danger', the I AM features of 'willing to be responsible for what I do' and 'sure things will be all right' and I CAN features of 'find ways to solve problems and I face' and 'find someone to help me when I need it'. The interaction between the girl and the cousin was like this: the girl tried on her own to get out of the deep snow and could not. She then called to her cousin who was way ahead and asked her for help. When her cousin came they talked about the fears they were both feeling, but decided they had better get busy and dig the girl out. They succeeded and felt they had had enough excitement for one day, so went home.

Resilience is a basic human capacity, nascent in all children. Parents and other caregivers promote resilience in children through their words, actions and the environment they provide. Adults who promote resilience make family and institutional supports available to children. They encourage children to become increasingly autonomous, independent, responsible, empathic and altruistic and to approach people and situations with hope, faith and trust. They teach them how to communicate with others, solve problems and successfully handle negative thoughts, feelings and behaviours. Children themselves increasingly become active in promoting their own resilience.

Children need these abilities and resources to face many common – and some not so common – crises. When the International Resilience Project asked children and their parents around the world what adversities they had experienced, the answers were numerous. Among those difficulties experienced within the family, in order of frequency, were:

- death of parents or grandparents
- divorce
- separation
- illness of parent or siblings
- poverty
- moving, family or friends
- accident causing personal injuries
- abuse, including sexual abuse
- abandonment
- suicide
- remarriage
- homelessness
- poor health and hospitalisations
- fires causing personal injury
- forced repatriation of family
- disabled family member
- parent's loss of job or income
- murder of a family member.

In addition, children and their parents reported facing the following adversities outside the home:

- robberies
- war
- fire
- earthquake
- flood
- car accident
- adverse economic conditions
- illegal, refugee status
- migrant status
- property damage from storms, floods, cold
- political detention

- famine
- abuse by a non-relative
- murders in neighbourhood
- unstable government
- drought.

THE LANGUAGE OF RESILIENCE

Children facing such situations often feel lonely, fearful and vulnerable. These feelings are less overwhelming for children who have the skills, attitudes, beliefs and resources of resilience. But, before we can begin to promote resilience, we need a shared language with which to describe, illustrate and explain it. The concept of resilience is relatively new for describing the behaviour of people. Some languages do not have a word for it. Castillano (Spanish), for example, has no comparable use of the word 'resilience' but, instead, uses the term '*la defensa ante la adversidad*' (defence against adversity). The same idea can be described by using another word or term. Most people around the world understand the idea of overcoming adversity with courage, skills and faith.

The vocabulary of resilience is more than a set of words that will allow us to talk about this emerging concept. It is a set of tools to use in promoting resilience. Armed with the language necessary to recognise resilience when they see it, adults can help children identify resilient behaviour more easily in themselves and others. They can use the vocabulary to reinforce those feelings and beliefs that support resilience and to guide their own and their children's behaviour. The more concepts they understand, the greater their options for acting in ways that help children meet the crises in their lives with strength and hope. Children who learn the vocabulary are better able to recognise resilience in themselves and others. They become increasingly aware of how to promote it.

The I HAVE, I AM and I CAN categories are drawn from the findings of the International Resilience Project, which identified 36 qualitative factors that contribute to resilience. These can be divided into three major categories, each consisting of five parts:

I HAVE

The I HAVE factors are the external supports and resources that promote resilience. Before the child is aware of who she is (I AM) or what she can do (I CAN), she needs external supports and resources to develop the feelings of safety and security that lay the foundation, that are the core, for developing resilience. These supports continue to be important throughout childhood. The resilient child says:

I have:

- Trusting relationships: parents, other family members, teachers and friends who love and accept the child. Children of all ages need unconditional love from their parents and primary care-givers, but they need love and emotional support from other adults as well. Love and support from others can sometimes compensate for a lack of unconditional love from parents and care-givers.

- Structure and rules at home: parents who provide clear rules and routines, expect the child to follow them, and can rely on the child to do so. Rules and routines include tasks the child is expected to perform. The limits and consequences of behaviour are clearly stated and understood. When rules are broken, the child is helped to understand what he or she did wrong, is encouraged to tell his or her side of what happened, is punished when needed and is then forgiven and reconciled with the adult. When the child follows the rules and routines, he or she is praised and thanked. The parents do not harm the child in punishment and no one else is allowed to harm the child.

- Role models: parents, other adults, older siblings and peers who act in ways which show the child desired and acceptable behaviour, both within the family and toward outsiders. These people demonstrate how to do things, such as dress or ask for information, and encourage the child to imitate them. They are also models of morality and may introduce the child to the customs of their religion.

- Encouragement to be autonomous: adults, especially parents, who encourage the child to do things on his or her own and to seek help as needed, help the child to be autonomous. They praise the child when he or she shows initiative and autonomy, and help the child, perhaps through practice or conversation, to do things independently. Adults are aware of the child's temperament, as well as their own, so they can adjust the speed and degree to which they encourage autonomy in their child.

- Access to health, education, welfare and security services: the child, independently or through the family, can rely on consistent services to meet the needs the family cannot fulfil – hospitals and doctors, schools and teachers, social services and police and fire protection, or the equivalent of these services.

I AM

The I AM factors are the child's internal, personal strengths. These are feelings, attitudes, and beliefs within the child. The resilient child says:

I am:

- Lovable and my temperament is appealing: the child is aware that people like and love him or her. The child does endearing things for others that help make him or her lovable. The child is sensitive to the moods of others and knows what to expect from them. The child strikes an appropriate balance between exuberance and quietness when responding to others.

- Loving, empathic and altruistic: the child loves other people and expresses that love in many ways. He or she cares about what happens to others and expresses that caring through actions and words. The child feels the discomfort and suffering of others and wants to do something to stop or share the suffering or to give comfort.

- Proud of myself: the child knows he or she is an important person and feels proud of who he or she is and what he or she can do and achieve. The child does not let others belittle or degrade him or her. When the child has problems in life, confidence and self-esteem help sustain him or her.

- Autonomous and responsible: the child can do things on his or her own and accept the consequences of the behaviour. There is the feeling that what he or she does makes a difference in how things develop and the child accepts that responsibility. The child understands the limits of his or her control over events and recognises when others are responsible.

- Filled with hope, faith and trust: the child believes that there is hope for him or her and that there are people and institutions that can be trusted. The child feels a sense of right and wrong, believes right will win, and wants to contribute to this. The child has confidence and faith in morality and goodness and may express this as a belief in God or higher spiritual being.

I CAN

The I CAN factors are the child's social and interpersonal skills. Children learn these skills by interacting with others and from those who teach them. The resilient child says:

I can:

- Communicate: the child is able to express thoughts and feelings to others. He or she can listen to what others are saying and be aware of what they are feeling. The child can reconcile differences and is able to understand and act on the results of the communication.

- Problem solve: the child can assess the nature and scope of a problem, what he or she needs to do to resolve it and what help is needed from others. The child can negotiate solutions with others and may find creative or humorous solutions. He or she has the persistence to stay with a problem until it is indeed solved.

- Manage my feelings and impulses: the child can recognise his or her feelings, give the emotions names and express them in words and behaviour that do not violate the feelings and rights of others or of himself or herself. The child can also manage the impulse to hit, run away, damage property, or behave otherwise in a harmful manner.

- Gauge the temperament of myself and others: the child has insight into his or her own temperament (how active, impulsive and risk-taking or quiet, reflective and cautious he or she is, for example) and, also, into the temperament of others. This helps the child know how fast to move into action, how much time is needed to communicate and how much he or she can accomplish in various situations.

- Seek trusting relationships: the child can find someone – a parent, teacher, other adult or same – age friend – to ask for help, to share feelings and concerns, to explore ways to solve personal and interpersonal problems or to discuss conflicts in the family.

Each of the I HAVE, I AM and I CAN factors suggests numerous actions children and their care-givers can take to promote resilience. No one child or parent will use the entire pool of resilience factors, nor need they. Some use many; others use few. However, the larger the pool of possibilities before them, the more options children, parents and care-givers have, and the more flexible they can be in selecting appropriate responses to a given situation.

STRENGTHENING THE HUMAN SPIRIT

At different ages, children rely more or less heavily on their I HAVE, I AM and I CAN resources. As children grow, they increasingly shift their reliance from outside supports (I HAVE) to their own skills (I CAN), while continually building and strengthening their personal attitudes and feelings (I AM).

Just as the resilience skills used by children vary at different ages, so must parents and other care-givers vary resilience-promoting language and behaviour to match the child's developmental stage. Children develop over time at different rates and so some information may be appropriate for younger or older children not necessarily within their chronological age group. One common factor for all age groups, however, is that the child is the test for whether or not you are promoting resilience faster than he or she can handle, whether the child is comfortable with what you are doing, understands what you are doing or is learning what you are teaching and encouraging. The response of the child is the touchstone for the effectiveness of what the parent or other care-giver is doing to promote resilience in the child.

FURTHER READING

The following are references to some of the research that has informed the work of the International Resilience Project.

Arindell, W.A., Hanewald, G.J. and Kolk, A.M. (1989) 'Cross-national constancy of dimensions of parental rearing styles: The Dutch version of the Parental Bonding Instrument (PBI).' *Personality and Individual Differences 10*, 9, 949–956.

Block, J.H. and Block, J. (1980) 'The role of ego-control and ego-resiliency in the organisation of behaviour.' In W.A. Collins (ed) *Minnesota Symposia on Child Psychology: Development of Cognition, Affect, and Social Relationships.* Hillsdale, NJ: Erlbaum Associates.

Bronfenbrenner, U. (1979) *The Ecology of Human Development.* Cambridge, MA: Harvard University Press.

Brooks, R. (1992) 'Self-Esteem During the School Years.' *Paediatric Clinics of North America 39*, 3.

Garbarino, J., Kostelny, K. and Dubrow, N. (1993) *No Place to be a Child.* Lexington, MA: D.C. Heath and Co.

Garmezy, N. (1985) 'Stress-resistant children: the search for protective factors.' In J.E. Stevenson (ed) *Recent Research in Developmental Psychopathology, Journal of Child Psychology and Psychiatry Book Supplement.* Oxford: Pergamon Press.

Garmezy, N. (1987) 'Stress, competence, and development: continuities in the study of schizophrenic adults, children vulnerable to psychopathology, and the search for stress-resistant children.' *American Journal of Orthopsychiatry 57*, 2, 159–174.

Gordon, E. and Song, L.D. (1994) 'Variations in the experience of resilience.' In M. Wang and E. Gordon (eds) *Educational Resilience in Inner-City America.* Hillsdale, NJ: Erlbaum Associates.

Grotberg, E. (1994) 'Coping with adversity.' *Civitan Magazine*, February-March, 10–11.

Grotberg, E. (1993) 'Promocion de la "defensa ante la adversidad" en los ninos: Nueva aproximacion.' *Medicina y Sociedad 10*, 1–2, 24–30.

Grotberg, E. (1993) *Promoting Resilience in Children: A New Approach.* University of Alabama at Birmingham: Civitan International Research Centre.

Grotberg, E. and Badri, G. (1992) 'Sudanese children in the family and culture.' In U.P. Gielen, L.L. Adler and N.A. Milgram (eds) *Psychology in International Perspective.* Amsterdam: Swets and Zeitlinger.

Hiew, C.C. and Cormier, N. (1994) *Children's Social Skills and Parental Relationship in Promoting Resilience.* Presented at the Annual conference of the International Council of Psychologists, Lisbon, Portugal, July 1994.

Kagan, J. (1991) *Temperament and Resilience.* Presented at the Fostering Resilience Conference, Washington, DC: Institute for Mental: Health Initiatives.

Kaufman, J., Cook, A., Arney, L., Jones, B. and Pittinsky, T. (1994) 'Problems defining resilience: Illustrations from the study of maltreated children.' *Development and Psychopathology 6*, 115–147.

Kotliarenco, M.A. and Duenas, V. (1993) *Vulnerabilidad versus 'resilience': Una propuesta de accion educativa.* Trabajo presentado en el Seminario: Pobreza y desarrolio humano: Legitmidad y validez del diagnostico y evaluacion convencional. Santiago, Chile, Noviembre 1992.

Loesel, F. (1992) *Resilience in Childhood and Adolescence. A Summary for the International Catholic Child Bureau.* Geneva, Switzerland, November 26 1992.

Loesel, F. and Biesener, T. (1990) 'Resilience in adolescence: A study on the generalisability of protective factors.' In K. Hurrelmann and F. Loesel (eds) *Health Hazards in Adolescence.* New York: Walter de Gruter.

McCallin, M. (1993) *Living in Detention: A Review of the Psychosocial Well-Being of Vietnamese Children in the Hong Kong Detention Centres.* Geneva: International Catholic Child Bureau.

Mrazek, D.A. and Mrazek, P.J. (1987) 'Resilience in child maltreatment victims: a conceptual exploration.' *Child Abuse and Neglect 11*, 357–366.

Osborn, A.F. (1990) 'Resilient children: A longitudinal study of high achieving socially disadvantaged children.' *Early Childhood Development and Care 62*, 23–47.

Parker, G., Tupling, J. and Brown, L.B. (1979) ' A parental bonding instrument.' *British Journal of Medical Psychology 52*, 1–10.

Rutter, M. (1987) 'Psychosocial resilience and protective mechanisms.' *American Journal of Orthopsychiatry 57*, 316–331.

Rutter, M. (1991) *Some Conceptual Considerations.* Presented at the Fostering Resilience Conference, Washington, DC, Institute for Mental Health Initiatives.

Segal, J. and Yahraes, H. (1988) *A Child's Journey.* New York: McGraw Hill.

Shure, M.B. (1991) *Resilience as a Problem-Solving Skill.* Presented at the Fostering Resilience Conference, Washington DC, Institute for Mental Health Initiatives.

Sparling, J. (1992) *A Program of Screening and Intervention in a Romanian Orphanage.* Sixth International Conference on Children at Risk, sponsored by University of Colorado and Pan American Health Organisation, Santa Fe, NM.

Staudinger, U., Marsiske, M. and Baltes, P. (1993) 'Resilience and levels of reserve capacity in later adulthood: Perspectives from life-span theory.' *Development and Psychopathology 5*, 541–566.

Truant, G.S., Donaldson, L.A., Herscovitch, J. and Lohrenz, J.G. (1987) 'Parental representations in two Canadian groups.' *Psychological Reports 61*, 1003–1008.

Wade, C. (1993) 'The impact of gender and culture on our conception of psychology.' *The General Psychologist 29*, 3.

Wang, M., Haertel, D. and Walberg, H. (1994) *Educational Resilience in Inner-City America*. Hillsdale, NJ: Erlbaum Associates.

Werner, E. (1994) 'Risk, resilience, and recovery: Perspectives from the Kauai longitudinal study.' *Development and Psychopathology 5*, 503–515.

Werner, E. and Smith, R.S. (1982) *Vulnerable but Invincible: A Longitudinal Study of Resilient Children and Youth*. New York: McGraw Hill.

Wolin, S.J. and Wolin, S. (1993) *The Resilient Self*. New York: Villard Books.

CHAPTER 3

Systems Abuse[1]

Judy Cashmore

While child abuse generally refers to the abuse of children within their own families, it is now recognised that children can also be abused and neglected by the very systems that are supposed to care for them and protect them. Systems abuse is broadly defined as the abuse or neglect that children suffer at the hands of systems involved in their care, education, health and welfare. It is significant for several reasons. First, it goes beyond the usual focus of abuse – the family – to encompass broader institutional and societal arenas. Second, the recognition that children can be harmed by the intervention of the state into their family life is likely to be a significant factor in the determination of the threshold for state intervention. If intervention is seen as having a positive effect with few, if any, harmful effects, it is likely that the threshold for intervention will be relatively low. If, however, there is evidence that intervention is unlikely to achieve a net gain for children in terms of keeping them safe and enhancing their development, then the threshold for intervention is likely to be higher and the grounds for intervention more serious. In essence, there is an expectation that the state should not intervene if it has nothing to offer or if its intervention does more harm than good. This expectation is formalised in some legislation which, for example, states that no action should be taken if guarantees that the children will be better off cannot be met. Third, systems abuse is important because it brings with it an acknowledgement of the need for the state to be accountable to children and families for providing the required services for children and their families and for ensuring that its intervention is helpful, not harmful.

---

1   This chapter draws upon work for the Systems Abuse Inquiry, commissioned in Australia by the New South Wales Child Protection Council and represents the opinion of the authors, not necessarily those of the NSW Child Protection Council.

WHAT IS SYSTEMS ABUSE?

Gil (1982) was one of the first to provide a clear definition of abuse as a result of state intervention or lack of intervention. He identified three types of abuse – institutional abuse, programme abuse and system abuse. Gil defined 'institutional abuse' as abuse that is a result of 'any system, programme, policy, procedure or individual interaction with a child in placement that abuses, neglects, or is detrimental to the child's health, safety, or emotional and physical well-being, or in any way exploits or violates the child's basic rights (p. 9).' It is, therefore, restricted to the abuse of children in out-of-home care. 'Programme abuse', Gil defined as abuse that occurs when 'programmes operate below accepted service standards or rely upon harsh and unfair techniques to modify behaviour'. Finally, Gil defined 'systems abuse' as abuse that is 'perpetuated not by a single person or agency, but by the entire child care system stretched beyond its limits' (Powers, Mooney and Nunno 1990).

The current definition of systems abuse used in this chapter combines these three forms of abuse outlined by Gil and defines it as the preventable harm done to children in the context of policies or programmes which are designed to provide care or protection. Such abuse may result from what individuals do or fail to do, or from the lack of suitable policies, practices or procedures within systems or institutions. In fact, a large proportion of the examples and the 'causes' of systems abuse relate to *neglect* rather than to abuse. This neglect is the result of a lack of appropriate services, either because they do not exist, are inadequate, inaccessible or not properly co-ordinated.[2]

Whereas Gils' three separate forms of abuse tend to focus on the location or the responsibility for the abuse, the current definition is less concerned about location and sees the resourcing issue underlying Gils' definition of systems abuse as one of the 'causes' of systems abuse. Under this definition, responsibility for systems abuse lies mainly at the institutional level, although the individual and societal levels are also implicated. Indeed, we argued in the Systems Abuse Report that:

> A focus on the institutional level should not allow individuals to evade responsibility for their own poor practice (Thomas 1990). Neither should it obscure the socio-political context in which societal institutions operate nor the inappropriateness of using institutions to make up for societal problems. Although this broader context is not the focus of this study, its effect is large. It sets the constraints on institutions, particularly in terms of the resources that they have to work with, the mandate they

---

2   This is similar to the situations outlined by Herbert and Mould (1992) as requiring advocacy for children: when needed services are not accessible; are not available; are not appropriate; are not effectively provided; or when the voice of a child is not being heard (p. 118).

are given and the strategies they can adopt. (Cashmore, Dolby and Brennan 1994, p.12)

SOME CHARACTERISTIC FORMS AND EXAMPLES
OF SYSTEMS ABUSE

Systems abuse can take a number of different forms, ranging from a failure to provide appropriate services through to direct physical, emotional or sexual abuse within an institution. In its simplest, but probably least recognised form, systems abuse may occur when children's needs are simply not considered. In effect, children are 'invisible'. This may be because of conflicting political priorities or interests or as a result of adult ignorance. Agencies making decisions which affect children may not have children's needs on their agenda or there may be no body of information indicating when problems arise for children. As a result, their needs may be overlooked (Cashmore, Dolby and Brennan 1994). For example, the needs of the children of prisoners to see their parents, especially when they have travelled some distance to do so, may be forgotten when their parents are punished for misbehaviour in prison by withdrawal of their visiting privileges. As a second example, child witnesses may have difficulty coping with the intimidating presence of the accused and the sometimes incomprehensible language of the courtroom. The needs of these children are often only barely acknowledged in the adult criminal court system.

Two further examples of children's needs being overlooked may be termed 'pass the parcel' and 'pillar to post'. 'Pass the parcel' or 'not my responsibility' occurs when service provision is fragmented or poorly co-ordinated. For example, when children have multiple problems, such as severe emotional disturbance, substance abuse and learning difficulties, different services may deal with one problem but not see the child's overall needs. 'Pillar to post' refers to the movement of children from one service provider to another with no overall or long-term recognition of their needs (Cashmore, Dolby and Brennan 1994). Probably the best example is the series of moves which children in substitute care often experience, being moved from one placement to another as a result of placement breakdowns which, in many cases, may have been avoided by better assessment and earlier response to the child and the substitute carers.

More commonly, essential services may not be provided or they may be inadequate, inappropriate or inaccessible. For example, services may be inappropriate or inaccessible because of cultural differences, because children, young people and their carers do not know they exist or how to access them, because of geographic constraints, or because entry to programmes or services is based on criteria that children with multiple needs cannot meet.

Perhaps a more worrying example of systems abuse is the abuse or neglect that children may suffer in institutions such as child care, out-of-home care placements or schools. Community trust and expectations that children in these institutions should be safe and cared for have been severely shaken by widespread allegations of physical and sexual abuse in child care settings, schools, children's homes and in church settings in England, Ireland, Canada, the United States, and, most recently, in substitute care in New South Wales in Australia. Even more disturbing than the allegations themselves have been the attempts by those in authority in a number of cases to prevent those allegations being heard (Overton 1992/3; Rindfleisch and Rabb 1984; Westcott 1991).

WHY DOES SYSTEMS ABUSE OCCUR?

There are a number of reasons why systems abuse occurs and continues to be overlooked. Some of these are a result of political and administrative decision-making and management whereas others are inherent in the nature of bureaucracies and organisations and include the tendency to become closed off from the outside world and to value regulations for their own sake rather than consider the welfare of those they are supposed to serve (Cashmore, Dolby and Brennan 1994, p.35).

Lack of resources

Perhaps the most obvious cause of systems abuse is the lack of resources that generally besets welfare and children's services. These areas frequently do not draw the resources they need because neither their client body nor their workers have much political power nor the means to galvanise support for increased resources. The problem has, however, intensified recently as the demand for child protection and substitute care and other children's services has far outstripped the available resources in most Western countries (Cashmore and Castell-McGregor 1996; Morrison 1996; US Advisory Board on Child Abuse and Neglect 1990).

The first and most direct effect is a lack of services, inadequate or pressured services and long delays and waiting times for those services that are available. That, in turn, may result in stringent 'gate-keeping' to ensure that services can manage their work-loads. While this may be important for workers to help them maintain quality of service, it is detrimental to children whose needs or multiple needs would cause too great a burden on the service. It is damaging to children to be labelled as having a problem when services to assist the child and their family are not available; identification of problems without the provision of services is no solution.

A lack of resources and a shortage of services has other indirect effects. It means that workers have to carry high case loads that do not allow them to work effectively. High case loads also prevent workers from having the time to review their decisions and ways of working or to follow up cases to ensure that appropriate action has been taken. Working under these conditions can be quite debilitating to staff and is likely to result in poor job satisfaction and high staff turnover, disrupting the continuity of work and further undermining attempts to follow through with cases.

Resources alone, however, are neither the only problem nor the sole solution. Poor collaboration within and across agencies, inadequate skills and training and lack of attention to children's views all contribute to systems abuse.

Lack of co-ordination

When the various agencies that provide services for children do not provide a co-ordinated response, children may miss out on services by 'falling between the gaps' of the services or they may receive a less efficient and less helpful response. In some cases it may lead to 'overservicing' when children are subjected to multiple assessments or interviews because the various agencies have different perspectives, requirements and methods of intervening. For example, children who are suspected of being abused may be interviewed separately by the police, child protection workers and various legal and medical professionals. While the task of identifying, prosecuting and responding to child abuse certainly requires the skills of various professionals, the effect on children of being subjected to various interviews and having to outline the details of what happened to them can be deleterious (Spencer and Flin 1990; Whitcomb 1992). In addition to the benefit of appropriate collaboration in providing a fuller and more accurate picture to assist proper decision-making, collaboration may also help the workers involved by providing support and allowing the burden of decision-making to be shared. This requires policies and practices which encourage collaboration, workers who have an understanding of their own and others' roles and responsibilities, and the development of informal networks based on trust and some shared values.

There are, however, a number of barriers to 'working together' and it cannot be assumed that organisational policies to do so will be translated into practice. The barriers include differences in professional and organisational priorities, power and training, concerns about confidentiality and different expectations about accountability, and supervision and responsibility for decision-making (Morrison 1996, p.130). Moreover, when workers in one organisation believe that those in another lack the skills, training or resources to respond effectively, it is unlikely that they will refer children and their families to them. This is quite often the case in relation to notifications of abuse to the statutory authority or social welfare departments. Despite mandatory notification, for example, it is well recognised that some doctors and teachers are very reluctant to notify suspected abuse because they believe that the child will not only be no better off but may be harmed by ineffectual intervention. Furthermore, when organisations are severely stretched and failing to meet the demands on their services, workers within that organisation who are concerned that the costs of collaboration outweigh its benefits to them may undermine attempts to introduce collaborative policy and practice.

As Hallett (1993) and others have pointed out, inter-agency collaboration is not a panacea and should be used and evaluated as a means to an end, not an end in itself. The end goal must be better outcomes for children. Although setting up the necessary organisational machinery is important, and so too are workers' perceptions that they are working well together, the real measure of success is what collaboration achieves for children and their families (Morrison 1996). While collaboration is important, it is not enough. As Hallett pointed out: 'Co-ordination will not mask underlying problems such as lack of professional skill, ambiguous legislation, organisational inertia, professional resistance or lack of resources. It is important to avoid investing co-ordination with the power to change things it can't change' (1993, p.4).

Lack of skills and training

A consistent concern in the literature, and one that emerged from the Systems Abuse Inquiry in New South Wales, was the joint problem of inadequate training and supervision and the lack of specialist workers. In the related areas of child protection investigations and assessments, and service delivery and the legal process, inadequately trained and poorly supervised staff contribute to systems abuse. In both child protection and substitute care work in Australia there has been a widespread move towards generic or 'all purpose' staff, who lack specialist training and who, at the same time, have to try to manage competing priorities because of high case loads. The results are investigations which lack evidentiary cogence, quick case closure and referral to other agencies and children in substitute care whose placements are not properly monitored and managed.

In service delivery too there is commonly a shortage of skilled staff able to work with children with disabilities or emotional disturbance, especially those in substitute care. It is ironic, and a clear indication of the value of children in society, that those who have most contact with children in substitute care and in juvenile justice institutions – foster carers and residential care workers – generally have lower status, receive lower remuneration and are more poorly trained than those who have less direct contact with children. This is cause for concern because there is considerable evidence that inadequate training, low status, limited career opportunities, occupational isolation and long working hours contribute to the abuse of children in care (Powers, Mooney and Nunno 1990; Shaughnessy 1984; Westcott 1991) (Cashmore, Dolby and Brennan 1994, p.52).

Despite its higher status, the legal profession also lacks the specialised skills that are necessary to interview and obtain evidence from children, especially young children. Their lack of understanding of children's language and development, and of the way children disclose abuse (Sorenson and Snow 1991) is evident in the type and complexity of questions lawyers ask children in court (Perry *et al.* 1995; Walker 1993) and in their often unreasonable expectations of a child's ability to report what happened. Unfortunately, cases involving children – where children are the alleged victims, the subjects of a protection order or the alleged offenders – generally do not bring prestige to the lawyers involved and, in some jurisdictions, are seen as a legitimate 'practice' area for inexperienced lawyers. The requirement that lawyers practising in these areas needed any specialised training and knowledge of the law beyond their general qualification to practice law has, for example, only recently been introduced in New South Wales.

Inadequate supervision and staff support

Child protection work and the provision of substitute care both suffer from a lack of appropriate supervision and support for the workers and service providers (Reder, Duncan and Gray 1993; Steinhauer 1991). To work effectively, child protection workers need to have structured opportunities to reflect on practice, judgements, feelings and prejudices – opportunities that are generally not available when resources are scarce and case loads too high (Morrison 1996). Even if they are given the opportunity, however, workers are unlikely to express their concerns unless they feel supported and safe about doing so. In the words of one worker:

> Where I think it all went wrong is that...if you were in a hierarchy one down, you were in the lowerarchy (sic), you won't say half the stuff you want to say, because it could be used against you and, indeed, may be. Especially when the case blows up and people are looking for scapegoats. You don't dare say half the stuff, like 'I don't feel competent to be in this case because it's beyond me, or "I'm really scared to go out and visit that family".' (MacKinnon 1992, pp.273–274)

Staff support is, however, very important because workers who are stressed and uncared for are less able to care for others. They are also more likely to require stress leave or to leave their job, so contributing to a lack of continuity for children and their families. As Morrison points out: 'Staff care exists when organizations attend to their staff's needs for identity, esteem, efficacy, meaning, belonging, and growth. Without this, staff will not be able to go on day after day listening and responding to the pain, disruption, grief, loss, and violence that is child abuse' (1996, p.138).

Similarly, foster carers need support so that they continue to care for the children in their care and minimise placement break-downs (Berridge and Cleaver 1987; Cavanagh 1992; Steinhauer 1991). Unfortunately, they often do not get it. Once again this is because workers are over-loaded, have more urgent demands on their time and may also fail to recognise fully the important role of the foster carer and the need to respond before problems escalate and force a change in placement.

Lack of voice for children

Perhaps one of the main factors that allows systems abuse to continue is our inability as adults to give children a voice. Children are often seen as incompetent and unable to participate in decision-making; as objects of concern rather than as persons in their own right with rights. Despite Article 12 of the UN Convention on the Rights of the Child, children are not routinely given an opportunity to express their views freely in all matters affecting them. Not all jurisdictions have legislation or practices which allow children to express their views. Changes to policy and practice are generally not reviewed for their impact on the children affected by them. Instead, there is still a general expectation that parents will act on behalf of their children, although they may be unable, or in some cases unwilling, to do so. Where children are in substitute care or otherwise living away from home and have little contact with their parents, it is assumed that those who are acting *in loco parentis* will act in their best interests. Unfortunately, this is not always the case and such abuse often remains hidden from public scrutiny because of structural isolation and concern about the reputation of the service provider. Abuse in care has recently become a major issue in New South Wales following allegations by former 'wards of the state', prompted by revelations about the activities of a departmental employee who used his position to gain information about vulnerable children in care.[3] Research funded by the Department of Community Services, which was coincidentally released at that time, confirmed that there was a disturbing level of abuse in care with approximately one in four young people leaving care between 16 and 18 years of age indicating that they had suffered some form of abuse while in care (Cashmore and Paxman 1996).

Few children are able to advocate on their own behalf and few complain. They may not know what rights they have or who to complain to, and indeed there may be no one who is accessible and able to act on their behalf. Few of the young people who had been abused in care in New South Wales had complained because they did not trust their worker and did not expect that they would be listened to and believed. They also feared retaliation from those they complained about (Cashmore and Paxman 1996). As Lindsay (1991) commented in relation to the 'Pindown' Inquiry in England: 'Children in care have shown extreme reluctance in complaining, doubting, with some justification, that anyone will believe them and fearing, with equal justification,

---

3   This occurred in the current Royal Commission into Police – one particular aspect of that Commission being an investigation of police protection of paedophiles. Subsequent allegations of abuse in care covered the range of abuse suffered by young people who had left substitute care.

victimisation and reprisals if they complain against those who can exercise so much power and control over their lives' (p. 437).

Children, especially those in such situations, therefore need powerful advocates who are accessible to children and able to hear what they are saying. It means listening to children, understanding their verbal expressions and their behaviour, and not assuming that, as adults, we always know what is best for children and what they need and want. Underlying this is respect for children as people with rights. As Minow (1990) pointed out, children's rights should not be interpreted as a threat to adult or parental rights, which causes conflict which would not otherwise exist, but as an instrument which merely makes public existing conflict, inviting resolution. Furthermore, Minow argues that 'the image of rights as damaging and weighty instruments that should be reserved for adults must be challenged in light of the damage suffered by children who have been denied them' (p.304).

PREVENTING AND COMBATING SYSTEMS ABUSE: CHILD-ORIENTED SYSTEMS

Outlining the features and causes of systems abuse provides an important starting point for preventing and combating systems abuse. For example, understanding that various factors – such as a lack of resources, poor co-ordination of services, inadequate training and supervision and poor staff support, and the lack of a voice for children – contribute to systems abuse indicates that each of these 'causes' should be targeted in counteracting systems abuse. But this is not enough. It is also important to have a clear view of what the goal is. The goal is to improve the well-being of children and prevent systems abuse. This is necessary because it provides a focus and a means of measuring whether or not the desired outcomes (aspects of improved well-being for children) are being achieved. These measures then provide the benchmarks for the necessary monitoring and review processes to ensure that progress is made towards the goal.

What might such a child-oriented system look like? What are the essential features of such a system? How do we move beyond the rhetoric of the 'children's best interests' to the reality of children's lives, taking into account the variation in their circumstances and requirements? In the Systems Abuse Inquiry, we posited that such a system would take account of factors that are important in promoting security for children. These apply both to systems and institutions whose aim is to promote their well-being (the health, education and child care, and child protection systems) and also to systems for which this is not the primary aim (criminal justice system). They also apply to families and the role of other institutions could be to provide new and better models of adult-child interactions. They form the basis of standards for the care of children (Cashmore, Dolby and Brennan 1994, p.116).

Attachment theory (Ainsworth *et al.* 1978) provides some clear guidelines for the features of care-giving or services that are likely to promote children's security. They include sensitivity to the child's needs and providing timely, appropriate and accessible intervention. Providing sensitive and appropriate assistance means listening to children and accurately assessing what their needs are, including their need for continuity. It means giving children a voice by giving them age-appropriate information and allowing them the opportunity to express their views or to have an advocate who is able to put those views. It does not necessarily mean acceding to the child's wishes or making children feel they are responsible for the decision.

Being accessible means being available and receptive when the child is ready; too often help is available according to a timetable that reflects the needs of the organisation rather than those of the child (Cashmore, Dolby and Brennan 1994, p.121). That also implies timeliness; responding to the child's sense of time rather than an adult sense of time (Goldstein, Freud and Solnit 1979).

Underlying these requirements is the need to take account of children's need for continuity and stability of care. Failure to do so is perhaps one of the main 'symptoms' of systems abuse and is exemplified by the multiple placements that children in substitute care often experience and by the 'pass the parcel' examples outlined earlier whereby children are passed from one service to another. It is also evident in the marked attrition of children and families being transferred from one service to another. Humphreys (1993), for example, provides a useful exploration of the reasons that children did not receive counselling although they were referred to counselling by departmental workers after being sexually assaulted. Only 60 per cent of the children who were referred for counselling actually attended the first appointment; the others were 'lost in the system' for a variety of reasons. Complex intake procedures, poor referral procedures (including the use of telephone rather than written referrals), poor inter-agency communication and long waiting lists all contributed to children not receiving the counselling services they were referred to. There were few case conferences at which the child's need for counselling and other services was discussed and, in a number of cases, early case closure by the referring service hindered case co-ordination and follow up.

It is important, therefore, that services support children and their families through transitions from one worker to another, from one service to another and on exit from a service or programme. Support through transitions can make the difference between children and families actually receiving the next service or not. It can also assist children leaving a service and provide useful information as to the success of the programme and the need for community supports. This has only recently been recognised in Australia in relation to young people leaving care, a decade or so after research in England (Stein and Carey 1986) had established the need for preparatory and supportive programmes for these vulnerable young people.

MONITORING AND REVIEW PROCESSES

Establishing the principles for child-oriented systems dealing with children is the first step in preventing or counteracting systems abuse. It involves setting standards and constitutes a primary level of prevention. The aim should be to provide consistent, coherent and comprehensive services for children (Cashmore, Dolby and Brennan 1994). Standards, however, must be monitored and reviewed across agencies and services to ensure compliance and to promote the effectiveness and accountability of the system. Monitoring and review mechanisms should provide a means of finding the gaps between policy and practice by encouraging communication between front-line workers and service providers and those who are responsible for developing policy. They should also allow clients to participate in the evaluation and review process.

Unfortunately, it is the welfare and juvenile justice systems, which perhaps have the greatest need for review and monitoring, which most conspicuously lack them (Cashmore, Dolby and Brennan 1994, p.142). In New South Wales, for example, the Children (Care and Protection) Act 1987, now currently under review, has been operating for nearly a decade without any process for reviewing the placements of children in substitute care. Under Article 25 of the UN Convention on the Rights of the Child, children in substitute care are entitled to periodic review of their circumstances but the Children's Boards of Review which were included in the 1987 legislation were never established because of the economic cost. While community visitors regularly visit children in residential institutions, other review mechanisms, such as the accreditation, professional regulation and registration of workers and carers involved in out-of-home care for children, are absent. Furthermore, as the recent revelations in New South Wales concerning paedophilia and the abuse of children in care have made clear, there are still only limited checks on the backgrounds of those who have the closest contact with children and the least supervision – foster carers and carers in residential and group homes and in family day care (Cashmore, Dolby and Brennan 1994, p.142).

These deficiencies obviously need to be addressed and amended by establishing proper monitoring and review mechanisms, instituting checks and accreditation processes for workers and carers, increasing client and community involvement and setting up appropriate research and information systems. Information beyond that required for financial management is necessary to ensure that policy development and resource allocation are based on the needs of children and to evaluate the effectiveness of programmes and services. Moreover, in the absence of relevant information, problems and gaps within the system are likely to continue unrecognised.

COMPLAINT MECHANISMS

At the tertiary level of prevention, appropriate complaint mechanisms are necessary to detect and provide redress in cases where children are abused or neglected by the system. While complaints processes may inform the review and monitoring process and provide useful feedback to management, they are not sufficient by themselves, especially for children and young people, because few complain. They may not know who to complain to or how to do so or may not be willing to complain because they do not expect to be believed. Complaint-handling procedures for children and young people therefore need to pay particular attention to issues of accessibility and advocacy. A number of principles of good practice for complaints procedures for children were outlined by Rosenbaum and Newell (1991). These are briefly summarised by Cashmore, Dolby and Brennan (1994) as follows:

1. The rights of children and young people and the procedures for complaint if these rights are disregarded should be well-publicised to children and young people through appropriate media.

2. The procedures should be accessible to children and young people (e.g. reply-paid envelopes, simple forms, allowing complaints by phone or in person rather than in writing, toll-free phones).

3. Complaints should be accepted from children directly without requiring parental or other adult approval.

4. Where this is in the child's best interests, parents or other adults should be able to make a complaint on behalf of a child if the child gives approval or if he or she is unable to complain directly due to age or disability.

5. The procedure should be speedy and take into account children's perception of time. The complainant should be informed at every stage as to what is happening and should also be able withdraw the complaint.

6. The procedure should be simple and user-friendly (e.g. skilled interviewers should interview children, if necessary, on their own ground).

7. Children should have access to a free, easily accessible, independent and confidential advocacy service which could provide support, advice and assistance.

CONCLUSIONS

Systems abuse is a relatively recently recognised form of abuse. It is defined here as:

> ...the harm done to children in the context of policies or programs designed to provide care or protection. The child's welfare, development or security are undermined by the actions of individuals or by the lack of suitable policies, practices or procedures within systems or institutions. Such abuse may result from what individuals do or fail to do, or from the lack of suitable policies, practices or procedures within systems or institutions. (Cashmore, Dolby and Brennan 1994, p.157)

Understanding the 'causes' of systems abuse is an important first step in prevention and underlines the need to ensure that organisations caring for children have the necessary structures, resources and skills to allow staff to work effectively. In addition, well-functioning systems that are truly child-oriented, rather than those which merely espouse the rhetoric, are essential. The aim must be to promote children's security and development rather than simply trying to avoid abusive practices. This means taking children seriously, giving them a voice, assuring continuity of care and extra help around transition points and attending to their individual needs. It also involves skilled assessment to determine what children's needs are, supporting and being involved with their communities and providing a balance of prevention programmes.

Quality assurance mechanisms, including monitoring and review processes, also constitute an important defence against systems abuse. They are essential to indicate whether appropriate standards are being maintained, to ensure that individual cases of abuse are detected and dealt with and to indicate whether staff and workers have the necessary conditions to work effectively. They need to extend beyond mere economic accountability and to provide an opportunity for client, staff and community participation (Cashmore, Dolby and Brennan 1994, p.154). Few systems, however, currently meet the criteria for being child-oriented, provide the necessary structures or include appropriate monitoring, review and complaints mechanisms.

REFERENCES

Ainsworth, M.D.S., Blehar, M.C., Waters, E. and Wall, S. (1978) *Patterns of Attachment.* Hillsdale, NJ: Erlbaum.

Berridge, D. and Cleaver, H. (1987) *Foster Home Breakdown.* Oxford: Blackwell.

Cashmore, J., Dolby, R. and Brennan, D. (1994) *Systems Abuse: Problems and Solutions.* Sydney: New South Wales Child Protection Council.

Cashmore, J. and Paxman, M. (1996) *Longitudinal Study of Wards Leaving Care.* Sydney: Social Policy Research Centre, University of New South Wales.

Cashmore, J.A. and Castell McGregor, S. (1996) 'The child protection and welfare system.' In K. Funder (ed) *Citizen Child: Australian Law and Children's Rights.* Melbourne: Australian Institute of Family Studies.

Cavanagh, J. (1992) 'Children and young people in out-of-home care: Treating and preventing individual, programmatic and systems abuse.' *Children Australia 17,* 17–25.

Gil, E. (1982) 'Institutional abuse of children in out-of-home care.' *Child and Youth Services 6,* 7–13.

Goldstein, J., Freud, A. and Solnit, A. J. (1979) *Beyond the Best Interests of the Child.* (2nd ed.) New York: Free Press.

Hallett, C. (1993) *Inter-Agency Work in Child Protection and Parental and Child Involvement in Decision-Making.* Seminar No 1, New South Wales Child Protection Council.

Herbert, M.D. and Mould, J.W. (1992) 'The advocacy role in public child welfare.' *Child Welfare, LXXI,* 114–130.

Humphreys, C. (1993) *The Referral of Families Associated with Child Sexual Assault.* Sydney: NSW Department of Community Services.

Lindsay, M.J. (1991) 'Complaints procedures and their limitations in the light of the Pindown inquiry.' *Journal of Social Welfare and Family Law 6,* 432–441.

MacKinnon, L. (1992) *Child Abuse in Context: The Participants' View.* Unpublished Ph. D. thesis, University of Sydney.

Minow, M. (1990) *Making all the Difference: Inclusion, Exclusion, and American Law.* Ithaca: Cornell University Press.

Morrison, T. (1996) 'Partnership and collaboration: Rhetoric and reality.' *Child Abuse and Neglect 20,* 127–140.

Overton, J. (1992/93) 'Child abuse, corporal punishment, and the question of discipline: the case of Mount Cashel.' *Critical Social Policy 36,* 73–95.

Perry, N.W., McAuliff, B.D., Tam, P., Claycomb, L., Dostal, C. and Flanagan, C. (1995) 'When lawyers question children: Is justice served?' *Law and Human Behavior 19,* 609–629.

Powers, J.L., Mooney, A. and Nunno, M. (1990) 'Institutional abuse: A review of the literature.' *Journal of Child and Youth Care 4,* 81–95.

Reder, P., Duncan, S. and Gray, M. (1993) *Beyond Blame: Child Abuse Tragedies Revisited.* London: Routledge.

Rindfleisch, N. and Rabb, J. (1984) 'Dilemmas in planning for the protection of children and youths in residential facilities.' *Child Welfare 63,* 205–215.

Rosenbaum, M. and Newell, P. (1991) *Taking Children Seriously: A Proposal for a Children's Rights Commissioner.* London: Calouste Gulbenkian Foundation.

Shaugnessy, M.F. (1984) 'Institutional child abuse.' *Children and Youth Service Review 6,* 311–318.

Sorensen, T. and Snow, B. (1991) 'How children tell: The process of disclosure in child sexual abuse.' *Child Welfare 70,* 1, 3–15.

Spencer, J.R. and Flin, R. (1990) *The Evidence of Children: The Law and Psychology.* London: Blackstone.

Stein, M. and Carey, K. (1986) *Leaving Care.* Oxford: Basil Blackwell.

Steinhauer, P.D. (1991) *The Least Detrimental Alternative: A Systematic Guide to Case Planning and Decision Making for Children in Care.* Toronto: University of Toronto Press.

Thomas, G. (1990) 'Institutional child abuse: The making and prevention of an un-problem.' *Journal of Child and Youth Care 4,* 1–22.

U.S. Advisory Board on Child Abuse and Neglect (1990) *Child Abuse and Neglect: Critical First Steps in Response to a National Emergency.* Washington DC: US Government Printing Office.

Walker, A.G. (1993) 'Questioning young children in court: A linguistic case study.' *Law and Human Behavior 17,* 59–81.

Westcott, H.L. (1991) *Institutional Abuse of Children – From Research to Policy: A Review.* London: National Society for the Prevention of Cruelty to Children.

Whitcomb, D. (1992) *When the Victim is a Child (Second edition).* Washington D.C.: U.S. Department of Justice.

PART THREE

Childhood Put at Risk

CHAPTER 4

Child Soldiers

Rachel Brett

Children who are not otherwise recognized as full members of the society should not be forced to take on the heaviest of all responsibilities.

(Hammarberg 1990, p.101)

INTRODUCTION

During 1994 and 1995, children under the age of 18 years were fighting in armed conflicts in at least 32 countries in all regions of the world. International law currently prohibits the recruitment into armed forces and participation in hostilities of those under 15 years of age. In most countries, national law sets a higher age, usually 18 years. In many conflicts the provisions of neither national nor international law are respected. The effect of military involvement on those who have not reached physical, mental and emotional maturity has not yet been fully documented but there is a growing body of evidence. The physical effects include not only the deaths and injuries suffered also by adult soldiers but are further exacerbated by the problems which result from the fact that the child is still growing (for example, the need for repeated amputations rather than a single operation and the greater incidence of hearing impairment because of the sensitivity of the child's eardrum). Even at the simplest level, the physical effects also have social and emotional effects on the child – not merely because of a longer expected life span, but also because they are likely to impair the child's social functioning as, for example, in the difficulty of education for those with hearing impairments and of finding job opportunities for the physically handicapped. The psycho-social effects of children's involvement in killings and other acts of war, separation from families and, frequently, involvement in drugs, alcohol and sexual activity (with their related health problems) are more complex, and the consequences of many other aspects of children's involvement remain to be explored.

THE INTERNATIONAL FAILURE

At the time when the text of the draft Convention on the Rights of the Child had been adopted by the UN Commission on Human Rights but not yet by the UN General Assembly, Thomas Hammarberg (then Secretary General of Radda Barnen, the Swedish Save the Children) wrote:

> The most disappointing part of the Convention is the Article dealing with children in armed conflicts. The compromise that came out of the repeated discussions on this very point was a failure. The International Committee of the Red Cross has even found the formulation a step backwards compared to existing humanitarian law. The Article has several shortcomings. It makes the protection of civilians, including children, a matter of feasibility and not of necessity. It is weak on the issue of child soldiers. The Convention sets the age limit for recruitment to combat service as low as fifteen, and thereby indirectly legitimizes the use of fifteen- and sixteen-year-olds as combat soldiers. The problem of child soldiers is acute in several parts of the world. More than twenty-five governments have in recent times used children below sixteen years of age for combat service. A number of guerilla movements have done the same. For instance, those who work with refugee children have been shocked by the traumatic damage that has been done to the young boys who have been into battles...
>
> This Article was weakened during the drafting process, ironically, while more and more delegations began to support the views of the non-governmental groups. The reason for the setback was the pressure from the US delegation. A formulation that 'no child' should take a direct part in hostilities was adopted twice with consensus, with the US delegation included. But suddenly in November/December 1988 that decision was no longer acceptable. The US delegation requested a formulation that only those below fifteen should be protected against war service. As the commission worked in the spirit of consensus the others accepted; the most conservative voice played the tune. (Hammarberg 1990, p.101)

This remained the position when the Convention on the Rights of the Child was adopted and Article 38 enshrines 15 years as the minimum age for recruitment into armed forces and participation in hostilities, although with the caveat that, in recruiting in the 15 to 18 year age range, states 'shall endeavour to give priority to those who are oldest'. In fact, the provision reproduces Article 77 (2) of Additional Protocol 1 (1977) to the four Geneva Conventions of 1949. This was a major setback in the efforts to enhance the protection of children in this area and, in particular, to raise the minimum age for recruitment and participation in hostilities to 18 years in line with the general recognition of 18 as the age of majority.

RAISING THE AGE FOR RECRUITMENT AND PARTICIPATION

The deliberate recruitment of very young soldiers (some as young as 5 years old) by RENAMO in Mozambique and the brutalisation process through which they were put, Iran's employment of young 'martyrs' to clear the minefields in the war with Iraq and museveni's boy soldiers marching in to Kampala were, perhaps, the key factors in bringing the attention of the international community to the disturbing growth in the phenomenon of child soldiers, as well as the diversity of their experiences. The efforts to raise the minimum age for recruitment into armed forces and participation in hostilities to 18 years did not stop with the adoption of the Convention on the Rights of the Child. A dual approach was adopted through the Red Cross Movement and through the United Nations. In 1991, the Council of Delegates of the International Red Cross and Red Crescent Movement adopted a resolution endorsing 18 years as the minimum age and called for a study on child soldiers. The study, undertaken on behalf of the Henry Dunant Institute, resulted in the publication of the book *Child Soldiers* (Goodwill-Gill and Cohn 1994). In this book, the authors distinguish between forced recruitment (entailing the threat of violence or actual violence to the physical integrity of the child or someone close to him or her), coercive or abusive recruitment (that is those situations where there is no proof of direct physical threat or intimidation but the evidence supports the inference of involuntary enlistment) and voluntary recruitment. Why do children volunteer ? The answers are many and relate not only to the fact that today's conflicts are predominantly internal ones which strongly affect the civilian population and therefore also children – both directly and indirectly, physically and emotionally – or to the greater use which can be made of children as soldiers – because of the new generation of lightweight weapons and in the propaganda war which is an essential component of many such conflicts – but they also depend on the individual experience, situation and make-up of the child (including her/his age and developmental stage).

The general objective factors which the authors identify are:

• The militarisation of daily life
• Physical and/or structural violence
• Choosing the less bad alternative.

The subjective factors include:

• Religion, ideology and indoctrination
• Social, community and family values and peer pressure.

Finally, individual feelings of helplessness or vulnerability, the desire for revenge and identity formation may be crucial elements.

In December 1995, as part of its Children in War project, the Council of Delegates of the Red Cross and Red Crescent Movement adopted a plan of action concerning children in armed conflict, which includes a section on child soldiers and the commitment 'To promote the principle of non-recruitment and non-participation in armed conflict of children under the age of 18 years'. Three specific objectives to achieve this are specified by the plan:

1. Promotion of national and international legal standards to this effect, and also the recognition and enforcement of such standards by all armed groups (governmental and non-governmental).

2. Preventing children from joining armed forces or groups by offering them alternatives to enlistment

3. Raising awareness in society of the need not to allow children to join armed forces or groups.

At the same time, the Committee on the Rights of the Child, the expert committee established to oversee the implementation of the Convention on the Rights of the Child, chose to take 'Children in Armed Conflicts' as the topic for its first day of themed discussions (perhaps not surprising given that Thomas Hammarberg had been elected to the committee). This discussion took place on 5 October 1992. Amongst the committee's recommendations were that there should be an optional protocol to the Convention raising the minimum age for recruitment into armed forces and participation in hostilities to 18 years (and one of its members produced a preliminary draft optional protocol to this effect) and that there should be an expert study on ways and means to improve the protection of children from the adverse effects of armed conflict.

The World Conference on Human Rights encouraged the Committee on the Rights of the Child to study the question of raising the minimum age of recruitment and the UN Commission on Human Rights, in resolution 1994/91, agreed to establish a working group to draft an optional protocol. The first session of the working group took place in autumn 1994. At that session, general agreement was reached on a prohibition on compulsory recruitment of under-18s into armed forces and on their participation in hostilities (although the USA, Pakistan and Austria expressed a preference for 17 years for the minimum age for participation in hostilities). However, no agreement could be reached on the issue of volunteers into governmental armed forces as a number of countries, notably the UK, USA, Netherlands and New Zealand, recruit volunteers below the age of 18 years and wish to continue to do so (none of these countries advanced any reason for not raising the minimum age except for their own national practice). This is one of the issues to be given further consideration at the second session of the working group, to be held in January 1996. Another issue not fully resolved is how to deal with the issue of recruitment into non-governmental/opposition forces. There was a general desire by governments to address this crucial question but no final decision was made as to the method by which to do it. A number of other, more technical, issues are still to be resolved.

DEVELOPING A BETTER UNDERSTANDING OF THE ISSUE

The Committee on the Rights of the Child has the power, under article 45 (c) of the Convention, to 'recommend to the General Assembly to request the Secretary-General to undertake on its behalf studies on specific issues relating to the rights of the child'. This was the provision they invoked when they proposed a study on children affected by armed conflict. This proposal was warmly welcomed by the World Conference on Human Rights and was approved by the UN General Assembly in 1993 by resolution 48/157. The UN Secretary-General appointed Graca Machel, former Minister of Education of Mozambique and widow of President Somora Machel, to undertake the study – renamed 'Study on the impact of armed conflict on children'. She is due to submit the study to the UN General Assembly in autumn 1996.

The issue of child soldiers is one of the key elements in the study and the research on it is being co-ordinated by the Quaker United Nations Office, Geneva, with a steering group of other non-governmental organisations (NGOs) and under the auspices of the NGO Sub-Group on Refugee Children and Children in Armed Conflict (this is a sub-group of the NGO Group for the Convention on the Rights of the Child, which is itself the continuation of the NGO group which was so involved with the drafting of the Convention). This Child Soldiers Research Project aims to create a more accurate picture of the size, scope and nature of the phenomenon of child soldiers, including the particular factors which lead to the involvement of children as combatants and, therefore, the development of practical strategies for reducing or eliminating such involvement in the future. Case studies have been, or are being, commissioned from people or organisations working in the field in up to 30 countries in all regions of the world. Ten of these are intended to be in-depth case studies. Some of the information sought may not be obtainable but it is hoped that the case writers will use many different sources and approaches in order to reach the nearest to a comprehensive response. For example, the number of children serving with opposition or rebel armed forces may be unobtainable but the number of children in detention for offences related to armed activity may provide an indication of the numbers, sex and ages involved. The case writers are also encouraged, where possible, to approach parents, teachers, institutional personnel, project workers and community leaders, as well as children themselves and those in or responsible for government and other armed forces. Case writers are also encouraged to include comparative information for adults, for example what proportion of the armed forces are made up of children? how does the number of girl combatants compare with that of adult women soldiers and so on.

For the purposes of these case studies, the following definitions are used:

> *Child:* Anyone under the age of 18 years. Under Article 38 of the 1989 UN Convention on the Rights of the Child, the minimum age for

recruitment, whether compulsory or voluntary, into armed forces, as well as for participation in combat, is 15 years. The same age is stated in the additional protocols to the 1949 Geneva Conventions governing the conduct of armed conflicts. However, the national law may set a different minimum age(s) for compulsory and/or voluntary recruitment. The Graca Machel study has stated that 18 years should be the minimum age for recruitment and participation in hostilities, in line with the general age of majority contained in Article 1 of the Convention on the Rights of the Child. Therefore, the case writer should make distinctions between those below the age of 15 years and those between 15 and 18 years. Where applicable, the age specified in national legislation should also be taken into account. In addition, it may be necessary to consider the situation of those who are now over 18 years but who fell within this age group at the time of their recruitment or service.

Soldier: a member of any kind of regular or irregular armed force or armed group in any capacity. Also, those accompanying such groups – even if not defined/identified as members – other than purely as family members, including, therefore, cooks, porters, messengers and so on. However, distinctions should be made between those who carry arms and participate in combat directly (combatants) and those serving in support capacities. In some cases the roles change over time and such changes and the reasons for them should be recorded.

Recruitment: covers all means by which people become members of armed forces. Compulsory recruitment means the legal enrolment in governmental armed forces. Forced recruitment means the enrolment into any kind of armed force by the threat or use of force on the persons concerned or those close to them, or their property. Voluntary recruitment means where the person concerned chooses of their own free will to enrol in the armed force. Induced recruitment means those situations where there is no proof of direct threat or intimidation but the circumstances suggest that the enrolment is not voluntary.

Armed Forces: means all regular governmental, irregular governmental, government-supported or condoned forces, armed police or internal security forces, armed opposition or rebel groups, militias, self-defence groups, private or other armed units. In writing the case studies, the author should make clear the nature of the armed force or group.

All case writers are asked to provide information on the following areas:

Context

Describe the conflict, including the type of conflict, background, duration, different stages or phases and how it ended (if it has), in order to set the scene for your answers and to facilitate a general understanding of the situation. An overview of other relevant information would also be helpful, for example the percentage of children in the population, the difficulties you have encountered in doing the case study and the nature of your (or your organisation's) work in the country.

Recruitment

This section seeks to identify how many and which children become involved in armed forces, how they become involved, what functions they perform initially and whether this changes over time, with particular attention paid to the effect of gender in relation to all these issues. It therefore includes:

1. *Numbers in armed forces:* This includes a breakdown of ages (lowest age, under 15, 15–18 years) and sex. How does this relate to the number of adults in the armed forces? At what age are children considered to be adults for this purpose? Is this different for girls? Is age the criterion used or is there another definition, for example height? Is there a minimum age for legal recruitment (compulsory or voluntary) under national law? Are those responsible for recruitment aware of the international standards about the minimum age for recruitment?

2. *Type of activities performed:* Does this vary according to age, sex, method of recruitment, type of armed forces, duration of service? Are girls forced/expected/encouraged to render sexual services? Does this vary according to their age and the other functions which they perform?

3. *Type of armed forces in which children are serving, for example governmental, opposition, self-defence forces:* Are there armed forces which have no child soldiers? Were children involved in any peace-time armed forces?

4. *Method of recruitment:* Is it compulsory, forced, voluntary or induced? If voluntary, what were the reasons for volunteering? Were benefits offered to encourage volunteers (financial, other)? Are there situations where the armed groups are considered to be better off than the governmental armed forces? Are some categories of children more vulnerable to recruitment than others? If so, which categories, for example poor, less educated, those from families with problems, children separated from their parents/family (give reasons for separation), certain age group(s), boys/girls, rural/urban, refugees and/or displaced, those in conflict zones, specific ethnic/indigenous or religious groups? To what type of recruitment are they vulnerable and why? Are particular categories targeted for recruitment and, if

so, which ones, why and by whom? Are certain categories not targeted for recruitment and, if so, why?

Treatment in the armed forces

This section seeks to identify how children are treated or affected while they are in the armed forces. The similarities and differences between children and adults, both in treatment and in the effects of their experience, should be addressed. Particular attention should be paid to the affect of age and gender in relation to all these issues.

1. Are families involved in the armed forces in any way, for example cooking for their soldier-family members, caring for wounded family members?

2. *Conditions of work:* Are the children paid and how does this compare with adult soldiers? Does it vary according to age, gender, type or duration of service? Do they get leave or time off for recreation or visits to their family (do adult soldiers)? Are they given training? Does this include training in any skills which might be useful in civilian life? Are they subjected to toughening-up procedures? What punishments are given for disobedience? Do they receive any education? Do they get preferential feeding or other treatment in relation to adult soldiers? Are they subject to abusive treatment, such as provision of drugs, alcohol, the rendering of sexual services, other?

3. *Duration of involvement in armed forces:* How long do children stay in the armed forces? What affects the duration of their service? Do the tasks they perform and the treatment they receive vary with the duration of service?

4. *Numbers killed and injured, and types of injuries:* How many child soldiers (including those in support functions) get killed? How does this compare with the numbers of adult soldiers killed and with the number of child civilians killed? Do the deaths result from different causes? How many child soldiers are injured? What types of injuries do they suffer? How do these compare with the numbers and types of injuries to adult soldiers and to child civilians? Are there injuries which are child specific, for example hearing loss caused by firing automatic weapons? How do age and gender affect numbers and types of deaths and injuries of child soldiers?

5. *Provision of treatment for injured:* Are injured child soldiers provided with medical care? Are they returned to their families for care?

If so, what happens to those without families? Are they abandoned to their own devices? How does their care compare with the provision for injured adult soldiers?

6. Numbers and reasons for demobilisation other than at the end of an armed conflict, for example invalidity, capture, other? Are there circumstances in which organised demobilisation has taken place other than at the end of the conflict?

7. *Treatment on capture:* How are child soldiers treated when captured? Are they treated as prisoners of war? Is any provision made for access (by families or others)? Is any special provision made for them as children, for example education? Are they returned to their families? Are they recruited into the capturing force? Does their treatment differ between different parties to the conflict? Does age, sex, involvement in killings/atrocities, method of recruitment, injuries or other factors affect the way in which they are treated?

Those undertaking in-depth case studies are also asked to cover the following areas, and to include discussions with child soldiers themselves so that their attitudes and concerns on the issues and their views about the factors that contribute to their reintegration to civil society and the difficulties they are experiencing are reflected. Where girls have been involved in the conflict, case writers are also asked to note their special concerns.

Reasons for involvement

This section is intended to identify the factors which decide why children become involved in some conflicts and not in others or change from passive observers/victims into active participants. It should include an analysis of methods of recruitment and involvement, including the reasons for volunteering or circumstances of engagement, and information on any preventive strategies employed to reduce or eliminate recruitment of children – whether by those in authority or by communities, families, the children themselves or others – and their effectiveness. Observations, suggestions and recommendations in relation to actions and strategies to decrease or prevent such involvement in the future should be included. Detailed questions are:

1. Have there been different stages in the conflict? How has this affected the involvement of children? At what stage in the conflict did children first become active participants or have they been involved throughout? Historically, have children always been involved in armed conflicts (if so, from what age) or is this something new or different in size or kind?

2. What specific factors led to the involvement of children, for example shortage of adult soldiers, the attitude of the military/political leadership, ideology, vulnerability of certain groups of children, the need (or perceived need) to support or protect the family, peer group pressure? Was it a policy decision by those in military/political authority? Do families/communities support the involvement of their children, if so why, for example material benefits, ideology/religion/culture?

3. What factors inhibited or prevented such involvement, for example availability of education, ideology, stable family environment, opposition by families (mothers?) or communities, opposition by military/political/religious or other leaders?

4. Were any specific strategies employed to reduce/prevent child recruitment, including volunteerism? If so, what, by whom and how effective were they, for example keeping schools open, sending children away from the area or out of the country, reuniting separated children with families, making financial or material contributions instead, provision of alternative activities for children (e.g. as first aid workers)?

5. How do the military view the involvement of children in their armed forces and their relationship to them? How do they view the involvement of children in opposing armed forces?

The post-service situation

The purpose of this section is to understand the short, medium and long-term effects of children's participation in conflict. In this regard, when answering the following questions it would be most helpful if information describing the situation of former child soldiers could be compared, where appropriate, with that of former adult soldiers and of children who were not actively involved in the conflict.

1. *Education:* What proportion of former child soldiers are attending school? Is their present level of education appropriate to their age? Are special programmes considered necessary to meet their educational needs? If so, why and what form do/will they take? Who will be responsible for their implementation, for example government/military, local/international organisations? In addition to enabling the children to regain the education they lost as a result of their involvement in the conflict, are educational activities also considered to assist in a more general way in re-educating the children to civilian life? How is this accomplished? Do teachers identify any problems working with

child soldiers? Are teachers given support and assistance in their work? Is it considered that they will require any special training to work with former child soldiers? What is the attitude of the former child soldiers to education?

2. *Physical and mental well-being:* Do former child soldiers have any special health problems, for example physical disabilities, sexually transmitted diseases? Are the children considered to behave differently from other children who were not actively involved in the conflict? How do people describe their behaviour? Are these issues specific to certain groups/categories of child soldiers, for example girls/adolescents/children from a particular family/ethnic background? Do these health/social issues create difficulties in their daily lives and affect their successful reintegration? What forms of intervention could help in overcoming these difficulties? Is there any indication that former child soldiers are engaged in criminal/violent activities? In situations where some time has passed since their involvement in the conflict, are there indications of long-term social/emotional consequences for the children, for example family discord, difficulties in assuming their appropriate roles in society?

3. *Employment/Vocational Training:* Do former child soldiers experience difficulties in finding employment? What factors influence this situation? Where children have come from rural homes, do they usually resume their family's traditional means of livelihood? Are vocational training schemes available for former child soldiers? Are they appropriate to local circumstances – availability of necessary materials, opportunities for employment, etc? Are the child soldiers integrated with other children on these training schemes? Are other forms of job training available, for example apprenticeship to local craftspeople/assistance to learn the family's traditional means of income generation? Who initiates and is responsible for these schemes? Do personnel on these schemes identify any special problems working with former child soldiers? Is special training/support available to them in their work with the children?

4. *Community Attitudes and Involvement:* Do the children's families and communities identify any social/economic consequences due to their participation in the conflict? Do they affect their reintegration to civil society? How do they cope with these problems? Are some problems specific to certain groups of

children, for example age/gender-related/family circumstances/knowledge of role played/acts commited by the child during conflict? Is there any community mobilisation to assist the children's reintegration? Who initiated this, parents/teachers/community leaders...? What measures do the community think could be implemented to facilitate the children's social reintegration? Did the families/community support the recruitment of children, and why? Has their attitude changed towards this form of recruitment, and what brought this about? Is there support for recruitment of children only from certain sectors in the community – who, why, and how do other community members cope with this? Do the families/community identify any benefits to themselves or their children as a result of participation in conflict? If so, what are they?

Planning for reintegration

For countries where conflict has ended

Did the parties to the conflict sign a peace agreement? If so, was the participation of children as soldiers recognised/specified in any way in the peace agreement? Did this recognition reflect concern for the effects of militarisation on children per se and the consequent need to assist them to reintegrate to civil society? If so, what is considered to have influenced the decision to incorporate recognition of this particular group of soldiers in the peace agreement? Have former child soldiers received any demobilisation benefits? What form do they take? Are they comparable to those awarded to adult soldiers? Have programmes for rehabilitation/reintegration of former child soldiers been implemented? What form do they take and who is responsible? What factors are considered (a) to assist this process and (b) to hinder programme development? Are any special groups of former child soldiers targeted as in special need of programmes? Who are they and how are they identified? Are any children excluded from the programme? Is the military supportive of/involved in the children's rehabilitation? Are the children monitored in any way? Who is responsible for the monitoring? What issues are prioritised?

For countries where conflict is on-going

Have children actively serving as soldiers been officially demobilised or otherwise ceased participating in the conflict? Who are these children – members of government forces/rebel groups/militias/other? Did these children receive any benefits – demobilisation pay/clothing/tools, etc, to assist them on their return to their families/communities? Is their progress monitored in any way? What factors influenced the end of their participation – a specific policy decision/resistance from families and community/pressure from local/international organisations/changes in the nature of the conflict? Is there any planning now for the future rehabilitation/reintegration of children presently involved in the conflict? Who initiated this planning process and which organisations (governmental/local/ international) are involved? What factors influenced the decision to develop such programmes? What factors are hindering the planning process? What are considered to be the priority issues for the children in addressing rehabilitation/reintegration? Are the children involved in the planning in any way?

PROSPECTS

The Child Soldiers Research Project is due to be submitted to the Machel Study by the end of April 1996 – an impossibly short time-frame for a research project of such ambitious scope! The continuing need for the kind of information and in-depth analysis which the research project aims to produce will be great.

The lack of accordance between the existing national and international law and practice illustrate the fact that merely raising the minimum age for recruitment and participation in hostilities at the international level will not be enough. There is a need for a real understanding of the factors which drive adults to involve children, and children to volunteer for combat, to enable the formation of effective preventive strategies to begin and serious consideration to be given to programmes for the rehabilitation and reintegration into civilian life of these young soldiers. Without such programmes, the prospects for peace in the current and recent conflicts around the globe are doubtful.

REFERENCES

Hammarberg, T. (1990) 'The UN convention on the rights of the child – and how to make it work.' *Human Rights Quarterly 12*, 1, 97–105.

Goodwin-Gill, G. and Cohn, I. (1994) *Child Soldiers.* Oxford: Clarendon Press.

CHAPTER 5

Children's Labour in Mexico
Rights, Protection and Violation

Araceli Brizzio de la Hoz and Manuel Martinez Morales[1]

We are sick of so many mistakes and
so many guilts, but our worst
crime is called
abandonment of childhood.

Neglect the origin of life.
Many of the things we need can wait.
A child can't.

He is making his bones right now,
creating his blood and making his senses.

We should not answer him tomorrow,
His name is NOW.

Gabriela Mistral[2]

INTRODUCTION

The rights and family environment of working children was investigated through an anthropological study in Mexico involving field research for several years.

---

1   English translation by Professor Aubry Reece and Professor Eileen Sullivan, University of Veracruz, Mexico. Special thanks to Lloyd M. Pérez for editing and proofreading the text.

2   Gabriela Mistral is the pseudonym of a celebrated Chilean poet whose real name was Lucia Godoy Alcayaga. She was born in Vicuña, Coquimbo in 1889. She died in New York in 1957. Lucía was a teacher and later a Consular representative of her country in Europe, Brazil and the USA. She soon became famous for her lyrical compositions such as *Sonnets of death* (1915) and *Desolation* (1923) which were dedicated to love and maternity. In 1945 she received the Nobel Prize for Literature and three years later she lived in Xalapa, Mexico. This is one of her poems.

© *Daniel Mendoza A.*

Figure 5.1 Postcard of daily life in a Mexican village near Jalepa

The UN Convention on Children's Rights and the Constitution of Mexico state that persons under 18 years of age are considered minors. In labour, the law establishes differences in regard to minors in, for example, the minimum age to work (which is constantly violated). In our study we have tried to shed some light on some taken-for-granted terms and to put forward some alternatives about children's work, exploitation problems and their rights.

Our objectives were to:

- Define the concepts 'children's work' and 'juvenile's work'.

- Distinguish between *protection* and *violation* of the child's inalienable rights

- Identify some social risks of early involvement of children in the workforce

- Gather opinions about the child's own life

- Analyse why work as a survival strategy violates the child's human rights

- Make some recommendations to try to end the exploitation of children.

Child labour in most Latin American countries has similarities which have emerged during the last two decades. Due to the decrease of the buying power of salaries, the elimination of social subsidies, the increase of unemployment and the reduction of consumption per capita, a large number of Latin American families have had to develop a variety of strategies for their survival. One of them is the participation of women and children in the labour market in activities of the so-called 'underground economy.' These children, whose parents did not enjoy any of the benefits of economic development of their countries during the 50s and 60s, now attract our attention. They are heirs to the historical conditions of poverty and exploitation that have been at the root of the current crisis. This child population is part of a *critical exclusion group* in Latin America.

After the approval of the Convention on the Rights of the Child in 1989 and its ratification by over 144 countries in Asia, Africa, Europe and Latin America, and after 30 other countries have signed their intention of accepting it, in 1992, nevertheless, the overview of the well-being of children is discouraging. Poverty, violence, abandonment and the necessity to work are some of the complex problems that – mainly in the countries named 'The Third World' – are a feature of the majority of children's daily lives. As a result of the widespread call for children's rights, the improvement of different countries' law, and the protection of child workers as expressed by the International Labour Office (ILO) during 1990 and 1991, the debate on whether or not poor children should work as their only source of survival should have ceased. However, disagreements about what kinds of assistance are to be provided still persist.

OUR STUDY

One of the major obstacles identified by studies and programmes on the problems of child workers is, without doubt, the diversity of criteria and ideologies of researchers and some authorities. We wish to propose a few methodological considerations which have emerged from our reflections on, and fieldwork with, child workers and their families. We will try to establish the delicate boundary between protection and violation of the child's rights. We will cite some evidence of the risks of working at too tender an age and we will consider the opinions expressed by working street-children in Mexico City.

Should we protect children so that they do not have to work prematurely or should we protect their work because of their own and their families' economic needs? In order to reply to these questions let us clarify some terms:

Work is not a social task

The concept of work as applied to minors lends itself to ambiguous interpretations and popular opinion frequently confuses it with tasks which are part of the socialisation process. There is also ambiguity in the terms child, adolescent, youngster and minor. These acquire different values and meanings depending on their cultural context, historical references and the discipline in which they are cited. Thus, Pedagogy, Medicine, Anthropology and Law, to mention a few, have different views and so a study on the topic inevitably becomes more complex. In addition, this confusion seems to arise partly from traditional cultural reminiscences that exist in rural mediums within ethnic groups that have a closed economy (i.e. auto-consumption.) Nevertheless, the problem which concerns us exists in the final decade of the 20th Century, a period in which market economy predominates, linked to an international context.

In traditional societies, progressive or gradual efforts to incorporate the child into productive work and into the family were geared towards preparing the child for his or her future social role in the group or community. The benefits of such an involvement were the self-development of the individual. In this context, these socialising tasks in the learning period during childhood were related to the gradual participation in the family group, school and community. Such socialising tasks are *common to all children*. This process, which begins at birth and ends with death, has as its primary objective the transmission and development of standards and cultural values which, at an early age, provide the foundation for the harmonious bio-psychosocial development of individuals.

In contrast to this, we have the activities which comprise *child labour*. Such activities are focused toward the production and commercialisation of *goods*, as well as the offering of services in an unequal relationship (oppression by gender, subordination by age and exploitation by social class). These activities, which interfere with opportunities for play, freedom of movement and spontaneity, and pervert the course of childhood, *are undertaken only by poor children* whose families receive insufficient income to subsist. Social inequality forces such children to perform any remunerative activity available in order to survive.

Child labour is not juvenile labour

In Mexico (where the Child's Right Convention was ratified on 21 September 1990) the political Constitution of the country in Article 123 part III explicitly states: 'the utilization of labour of children under 14 years of age is prohibited.' The use of the labour of anyone under 14 is prohibited, but the child is not prohibited from working. Those above this age and under 16 years old shall work a maximum of six hours per day. The same prohibition is stated in Article 22 of the Federal Labour Law. Moreover, Article 173 stipulates that 'the labour of someone over 14 years of age but under 16 years is subject to special ways of protection and vigilance in terms of work inspection'.

It can be gathered from this that there is a clear distinction between prohibition and protection, which permits us to attempt the following definitions:

> We define child labour as any activity done by individuals under 14 years of age for a third person (employer or client) in a subordinate capacity in exchange for a remuneration which permits them to fulfil certain vital needs regarded as unrenounceable rights of the child... And we deem

"juvenile labour" (minor) to be any activity, psychological or intellectual, which is done by individuals over 14 years of age and under 16 years of age for employers or clients in the category of subordinates according to the Mexican Federal Labour Law and Human Rights. (Brizzio 1986)

RISKS OF EARLY INCORPORATION INTO THE WORKFORCE

There is a general agreement among both the findings of individual researchers and the research produced by the ILO regarding the undesirability of the early incorporation of children into the workforce because of the health risks involved. The specific risks connected with this practice are: the possibility of contracting a disease, bone deformities, stunting of growth and mutilation or death due to accidents on the job.

The following case history illustrates the most extreme of these risks – death:

Age: 7.

Sex: Male.

Treated in the emergency department for symptoms including distended abdomen, vomiting and fever. The child died during surgery performed two days after his admission to the emergency room. A short time before, his father had sent the child to a garage belonging to some friends of his as an apprentice.[3] These men, according to the child's own report, had, on several occasions, pumped air into his body through his rectum using the compressed air pump in the garage 'just to have a little fun.' The last of these episodes occurred 24 hours prior to the child's admission to the hospital. Neither the Doctors denounced the case, nor the parents took any legal procedure. The boy is dead and the murderers are still at large. (We frequently hear of similar cases but this one in particular, which occurred back in 1987, often returns painfully to my thoughts because I was helpless to do anything about it.)

The problems of the child labourer have many consequences. Child labour is related to basic needs not being met, a permanent state of subordination and family instability or a change in the child's status within the family. The very fact that the child is a wage earner and is removed from the family environment for many hours, days or even longer periods of time has a negative effect on the development of the child's personality. Premature assumption of the adult role and loss of play time due to long working hours are some of the factors which produce irreversible effects in the child's personality. In addition, as we

---

3   In 1970 the 'Apprentice Contract' was written out of Mexican Law. Such contracts had become regarded as a hold-over from the Middle Ages and an instrument by which, under the excuse of vocational education, the unsavory reality of a particular sort of work relationship was disguised.

have just noted, child workers are exposed to abuse and mistreatment in various forms in the street and at work. These jobs include house work in private homes, farm work and a long list of other 'invisible jobs',[4] that are carried out daily right under our noses and have become so natural, so much a part of every day affairs, that they fail to register in our minds as child labour.

Regarding the education of the child worker, the figures on grammar school education for Mexico give us some insight into the dimensions of the problem. In 1986 there were 17,295,000 children aged 6 to 14; 4,700,000 of these children, due to various reasons, did not attend school. Of them, 300,000 registered work as the main reason (INEGI 1986). These children not only missed a formal education but were frequently exposed to adult attitudes and behaviours (foul language, alcoholism, adult sexual situations, etc) which were far from favourable for their development. The working child's very life depends on his or her earnings. The formula is: if I don't work I don't have any money. If I don't have any money I don't survive. The desperate need for money often brings about antisocial behaviour. Theft, prostitution, drug addiction and pornography associated with child workers bring with them a high social cost. A study undertaken in a juvenile re-education centre in 1988 showed that 90 per cent of the residents of such centres had been child workers at one time or another and the main cause for their institutionalisation was theft.

THE CHILD'S SPEECH

In 1991 I collaborated in a research project in Mexico City (DFD 1992) involving children who worked and/or lived on the street. The study took in the 16 political units into which Mexico City is divided. In these areas, 513 'points of contact' were established using places which were known to be frequented by children. The census that was carried out in this way revealed a population of 11,172 girls and boys between 5 and 17 years of age. Of these, 1020 lived on the street and had no family connections at all and 10,152 worked on the street but lived with their families. Interviews were successfully carried out with children chosen from this population.

Of the population interviewed, 72 per cent had left school before finishing their secondary school education; 33.4 per cent indicated that they had left school for financial reasons (financial need was, therefore, the most important reason for dropping out of school – followed by others which included 'dislike' for school, as well as academic failure or expulsion and difficulties such as the school being too far from their home or lack of required documents, such as birth certificates and previous report cards) 75 per cent were illiterate and 10 per cent stated that 'they had never attended school in their lives'; 41.6 per cent

---

4   The existence of these jobs is widely known but they are hard to detect. Thus, they have not been taken into consideration by most programmes and studies.

claimed to eat one or two times a day while on the street (presumably such foods are inappropriate and inadequate, in addition to being prepared and consumed in unsanitary conditions, as the children are undernourished and disease-prone. The contaminated urban environment which they inhabit accounts for 96 per cent of the breathing, gastrointestinal, eye and skin diseases they suffer). Various types of abuse and mistreatment were reported by the children. The perpetrators included family members and other individuals (such as police). They also reported suffering accidents. In addition, 23 per cent of the children reported that they used marihuana, thinner[5] or pills.

More than half of the children interviewed said that they had decided to work on the streets because they needed money for food and clothings. Another 22 per cent simply responded that they liked to be on the streets and a further 20 per cent offered no response. Perhaps they, themselves, did not understand what they were doing on the streets. One-third of the children who lived and/or worked on the streets claimed that they thought that it was all right for them to be out there working. They offered no reasons to support this point of view but replied: 'it's OK for us to be working', 'it's a good idea' and 'it's all right'. Another third of the children said that work was part of a family or personal survival strategy. These children added: 'it's tough, but we've got to do it', 'it's OK, I wanna help my Mom out' and 'my Dad should look out after me, but since he doesn't, well...I've got to work'. A small group of these minors expressed the belief that work is a formative experience and one which aids the development of skills and helps them avoid a process of personal deterioration and delinquency, such as involvement with drug consumption or theft. Some of the responses of these children included: 'it's OK, it helps us to learn things', 'it's good for us so that we don't get into drugs' and 'it's good so that we don't get used to just sitting around'. Other responses included: 'well, I have my own money this way' and 'if I work I can buy the things I need and I can look out for myself'. The remainder of the children interviewed protested against their situation as child workers, saying: 'we can't enjoy our childhood' or 'kids should go to school and their parents should go to work'. Some of these children indicated that they were the subject of physical violence in connection with their role as workers: 'they beat me up if I don't go to out to work' or 'they want money from me'.

Although some children replied 'normal' and 'fun', 33.77 per cent replied that a day on the streets was difficult and boring. Almost a third of the children expected to be 'doing the same thing' or 'still working on the street' in three years time. One in five said that they would rather be in school than be working and others said that they would like to combine school with work or find some

---

5   A chemical solvent used in carpentry and in painting jobs. This substance is toxic and when inhaled produces a drug-like 'high'. In Mexico, thinner is readily available and is fairly inexpensive.

other type of job, but 15 per cent were not clear about what they would prefer to do – understandable under the circumstances. Perhaps for this reason, 18 per cent did not even bother answering that question.

Approximately half of the children answered that they did not know what they wanted to be when they grew up. Others said that they would like to go to college and become a teacher, an engineer, a doctor, an architect or a lawyer. Others told the interviewers that they would like to be a successful business person and run a business of their own. They also mentioned plans for their future personal life, such as 'getting married', 'having children' and 'having a wife'. Sixty per cent of the children interviewed had been working on the streets, about three years and were obviously raised on the ways of the streets, including its lack of organisation, instability in their life-style, poor personal hygiene and the absence of any type of guidance. The majority of them worked for more than six hours each day.[6]

THE HUMAN RIGHTS OF THE CHILD

Having reviewed the findings of one study on the problem of child labour in Mexico city, we now return to the question of the human rights of the child in this connection. The rights of the child are inalieable, definite and unrenounceable, yet some of the procedures currently used in dealing with child labourers undermine these rights. The following discussion addresses the assumptions that underlie the forms of management that threaten the rights of the child.

Some organisations that deal with children's work do not question such social exploitation and centre their approach on the paternal responsibilities. In this way, they accept this reality and try to solve it through 'apprenticeship' projects that become work centres where salaries and earnings are the main concern. We have to be careful when we analyse these 'helping' policies. They could easily become the fastest way to prepare passive, self-defeating individuals. They do not take into account that the child worker must almost inevitably deal with a double or triple workload if the child is to attend school and help his or her family in some way. No labour union would ever accept such workload for its adult members, yet this is expected from a working child. Under such an arrangement, no time is left for play, recreation or leisure – which certainly figure among the rights of the child.

The survival strategies which force the very early involvement of the child in the working world produce only limited benefits and only for a short period of time. The middle- and long-term social costs of child labour are high and, although research in this area is not abundant, the available evidence suggests that child labour has serious side effects. Frequently, child labour has a hidden

---

6   We found that children worked at 17 types of jobs, mainly in private business and the 'informal economy' sector.

social function because it covers an unpaid part of a worker's real wage. In this way, the child's labour helps sustain the production and perpetuation of the work-force on a daily and generational basis in the so-called third world countries. The working child replaces an unqualified adult worker, broadens the informal economic sector, keeps wages down, closes the poverty circle and reinforces the conditions of underdevelopment.

The exploitation of children belonging to the socially marginalised groups which have just been described is not simply a matter of the will to exploit on the part of a single employer, individual father or mother. It will not disappear because the income of the child is raised to a 'fair' sum or because the number of hours that the child works are reduced. This exploitation is firmly and cruelly rooted in our social structure. Their human rights are violated from the moment that children have to work as their *only* means of survival; means which lack any other alternative. Human rights are thus at the core of the social problem of the child worker and their defence is an aspect which must be recognised and promoted – as detailed in the Annex to this chapter, which provides a synopsis of the relevant parts of the UN Convention on the Rights of the Child.

SUMMARY

- No child should have to work to survive.

- No child should have to assume economic responsibility for his or her family.

- Establishing a code to govern child labour or to propose to ignore the minimum age is tacit acceptance of a deplorable practice.

- To ignore, as some people do, the potential role of laws that protect infancy, or to invoke the excuse of poverty and under-development to continue violating these universally-recognised principles, is to perpetuate this abuse.

- The child worker of today will be an unprepared, resentful worker in the future. What can we expect from an individual whose fundamental rights have been violated from an early age?

- It is a mistake to group abolition (child workers under 14 years of age) and regulation (workers 14 to 17 years old) within the same child protection policies or to deal with these problems using the same criteria. They are different situations. Alternatives and solutions will not be obtained while the importance of this distinction is ignored. Ambiguity leads to confusion, resulting in a lack of protection for both groups.

- Rights are not the privileges of minorities.

ENDING THE EXPLOITATION OF CHILDREN

To achieve the abolition of children's work and to protect working teenagers, to guarantee their survival, protection and development, and to ensure their rights and equality, we must bear in mind that any Programme will require many strategies with short- medium- and long-term goals. The efficiency of these programmes will depend on the commitment of national governments and non-governmental organisations – international, national and local – the private sector, productive, health and educational sectors and parents. Care must be taken to avoid duplication of programmes.

Countries with a large foreign debt will inevitably cut their public spending, thus worsening the social and economic circumstances of a sector of their population. In such countries the number of working children increases. Such an explanation, however, is not a justification. Working children exist in many spheres and take many forms. Strategies must be tailored to specific circumstances and based on scientific research. Most 'third world' countries already have adequate judicial frameworks, in particular those that have ratified the Convention on the Rights of the Child.

We recommend, therefore:

- Strict adherence to legal requirements laid down for ensuring the well-being of children.

- The ratification by all countries of the UN Convention and Agreement 138 regarding the minimum allowable working age and the ratification of the Recommendation 146 of the International Labour Office.

It is urgent to fight against the participation in the workforce of children in the following consecutive stages: First, adopt measures that guarantee the fundamental rights of the youngest working children and children involved in hazardous jobs (i.e. toxic substances, jobs involving heavy loads or long hours, jobs that take place in open urban spaces, etc.). At the same time, take direct steps (aimed at children) and indirect steps (aimed at their families).

With regard to such measures, efforts must be aimed to:

- Make governments implement social policies that link the private sector with unions and social groups to fight unjust conditions that adversely affect the developmental stages of the child.

- Improve the quality of the education system and involve teachers in attempts to end work-related school desertion.

- Insist on starting alternative income projects for the adult members of the working child's family.

- Create permanent public awareness programmes that educate people about the negative effects and dangers to the well-being of children who join the workforce early.

- Request technical co-operation from the ILO to help establish a diagnosis and to study possible solutions in each country with such a problem.

- Together with the ILO, develop programmes for low-income children that work to sustain their families and themselves.

ANNEX

The following is a synopsis of the first part of the Children's Rights Convention that describe every child's human rights.[7]

The preamble recalls the basic principles of the United Nations and the specific provisions of relevant human rights treaties and proclamations, reaffirms the fact that children, because of their vulnerability, need special care and protection, places special emphasis on the primary care-giver and the responsibility of the family and the need for legal and other protection of the mother and child before and after birth and stresses the importance of respecting the cultural values of the child's community and the vital role of international co-operation in achieving children's rights.

The articles of the Convention on Children's Rights are not isolated issues. One cannot violate one article without breaking others. We now refer to the major articles that can be violated when a child works out of necessity, although there are many others which touch on this.

Article 2. Non-discrimination: The principle that all rights apply to all children without exception, and the State's obligation to protect children from any form of discrimination. The State must not violate any right and must take positive action to promote them all.

Article 3. The best interests of the child: All actions concerning the child should take into full account his or her best interests. The State is to provide adequate care when parents or others fail to do so.

Article 6. The inherent right to adequate life conditions: The State's obligation to ensure the child's survival and development.

Article 18. Parental responsibilities: The principle that both parents have joint primary responsibility for bringing up their children and that the State should support them in this task.

Article 19. Protection from abuse and neglect: The State's obligation to protect children from all forms of maltreatment perpetrated by parents

---

7 The text is taken from *Convención de los derechos del niño. (Convention on the rights of the child).* Adopted by the General Assembly of the United Nations, 20 November 1989. Part I, official text and unofficial summary. Defence for Children International, Geneva, Switzerland, 1990.

or others responsible for their care and to undertake preventive and treatment programmes in this regard.

Article 24. Health and health services: The right to the highest level of health possible and access to health and medical services, with special emphasis on primary and preventive health care, public health education and the diminution of infant mortality. The State's obligation to work towards the abolition of harmful traditional practices. Emphasis is laid on the need for international co-operation to ensure this right.

Article 26. Social security: The right of children to benefit from social security.

Article 27. Standard of living: The right of children to benefit from an adequate standard of living. Providing it is the primary responsibility of parents and the State's duty is to ensure that this responsibility is first possible to fulfil and then fulfilled.

Article 28. Education: The child's right to education and the State's duty to ensure that at least elementary education is free and compulsory. Administration of school discipline is to reflect the child's human dignity. Emphasis is laid on the need for international co-operation to ensure this right.

Article 29. Aims of education: The State's recognition that education should be directed at developing the child's personality and talents, preparing the child for active life as an adult, fostering respect for basic human rights and developing respect for the child's own cultural and national values and those of others.

Article 31. Leisure, recreation and cultural activities: The right of children to leisure time, play and participation in cultural and artistic activities.

Article 32. Child labour:

1. States Parties[8] recognise the right of the child to be protected from economic exploitation and from performing any work that is likely to be hazardous, to interfere with the child's education, or to be harmful to the child's physical, mental or spiritual health or his/her social development.

2. States Parties shall take legislative, administrative, social and educational measures to ensure the implementation of this article. To this end, regarding the relevant provisions of other international instruments, States Parties shall in particular:

---

8 Governments that belong to the UN.

a) provide a general minimum age for admission to employment and provide minimum ages for hazardous jobs and schedules

b) provide appropriate regulation of the hours and conditions of employment

c) provide appropriate penalties or other sanctions to ensure the effective enforcement of this article.

Article 33. Drug abuse: The child's right to protection from the use of narcotic and psychotropic drugs and from being involved in their production or distribution.

Article 34. Sexual exploitation: The child's right to protection from sexual exploitation and abuse, including prostitution and involvement in pornography.

Article 35. Sale, trafficking and abduction: The State's obligation to make every effort to prevent the sale, trafficking and abduction of children.

Article 36. Other forms of exploitation: The child's right to protection from all other forms of exploitation not covered in articles 32, 33, 34 and 35.

Other international reference documents:

- *Convenio 138 y Recomendación 146 de la Organización Internacional del Trabajo (ILO),* 1973. (Agreement 138 and recommendation 146 of the International Labour Office (ILO), 1973, Geneva.)

- *Convención Suplementaria sobre la abolición de la esclavitud en su informe provisional de 11 de Julio de 1988.* (Supplementary convention on the abolition of slavery. Preliminary report. 11 July 1988, Geneva, ONU.)

- *Pacto Internacional sobre los Derechos Económicos, Sociales y Culturales,* Artículo 10(3). (International pact on economic, social and cultural rights. Article 10(3).)

- *Pacto Internacional sobre los Derechos Civiles y Políticos, Artículo 24(1).* (International pact on civil and political rights. Article 24(1).)

REFERENCES

Instituto Nacional de Estadística, Geografía e Informática (INEGI) (1986) *Agenda estadística 1990,* Instituto Nacional de Estadística, Geografía e Informática (INEGI) Mexico. (National Institute of Statistics, Geography and Informatics (INEGI). Statistical Diary 1986, Mexico. National Institute of Statistics, Geography and Informatics (INEGI)).

CHAPTER 6

A Safe Haven
Do International Standards and National Laws Protect Unaccompanied Refugee Children in the UK Today?[1]

Louise Williamson

First, just who is an unaccompanied refugee child? We will say that such a 'child' is anyone under the age of eighteen who has been forced to leave their country for their own safety and who has no adult with them who usually looks after them.

You may also ask: what circumstances lead to there being unaccompanied refugee children? The answer varies from case to case:

- In some countries, innocent children as well as adults may be arrested and tortured, and so may need to escape to safety.

- It is very easy during war for children to be separated from their parents by accident or because their parents die, with the result that they have no one to look after them.

- Some parents may send their children abroad to escape being forced to become soldiers or prostitutes for the army.

---

1   This chapter is based on a presentation of the same title made at the World Conference on Research and Practice in Children's Rights, Exeter University, 8–11 September 1992. The paper was written bearing in mind that young people at secondary school would be among the audience and the clear language of the original has been preserved with only slight revisions to indicate developments in the intervening period. For a more academic treatment of the same subject, see Williamson, L. (1995) A safe haven? The development of British policy concerning unaccompanied refugee children 1933–1993. *Immigrants & Minorities*, Vol 14/1, 47–66.

REFUGEES: THE WORLD SITUATION

In 1992 there were more than 17 million refugees the world over and the number is growing. This did not include the many millions of people who were forced to leave their homes but who stayed in their own countries. In 1995 UNHCR estimated the numbers to be 27 million refugees and almost the same number of displaced people (26 million).

Most of the world's refugees are women and children. Around three to five per cent of the total number are unaccompanied refugee children, which is actually a very large number of children. Thus, in one case, more than 3500 unaccompanied children were provided with special services in Thailand in 1980–2. Only a very few of the total number of refugees make their way to the UK.

UNACCOMPANIED REFUGEE CHILDREN IN THE UK

Unaccompanied refugee children have been resettled here through official or semi-official programmes at least since the 1940s. For example, nearly 10,000 almost exclusively Jewish children came with special 'children's transports' before the outbreak of World War II and at least 466 Hungarian children arrived in November and December 1956 following the Hungarian Revolt.

Since 1984, a small number of unaccompanied children, mostly from Vietnam, have come to the United Kingdom as 'programme' or 'quota' refugees. This means that they were given refugee status before they arrived, which the Home Office arranged, and the Department of Health then paid for their care after they arrived.

However, the exact number of unaccompanied refugee children now in this country, and where they come from, is unknown. Very few of the current arrivals of unaccompanied children have been planned and agreed on in advance by the Government – the arrival of most has not been known about beforehand. It was only in 1991 that immigration officers began to record the total number of unaccompanied refugee children whom they identified at the border – 82 in the period from December 1991 to May 1992. The children who appear in these official records are not the only ones entering the country. Some are not recognised as being unaccompanied at the border because they are travelling with an adult who appears to be their carer. They may then apply for asylum later, once they are in the country.

The Refugee Council Working Group on Unaccompanied Refugee Children and Adolescents has tried to estimate the number of unaccompanied refugee children who have entered the United Kingdom since the early 1980s. In addition to official records, they consult widely with refugee community groups who may know of children who were not recognised as being unaccompanied at the border. They have also developed good contacts with many of the social services departments in the London area who are looking after children referred to them. Apart from 1990, when about 170 children, mainly from Eritrea, entered the country in August and September alone, it seems likely that at least 200 children and young people come every year (a much more accurate estimate of the number of children has been made since the Panel of Advisers began to operate at the Refugee Council from April 1994). There may, of course, be other children who have never come to the attention of refugee groups or local authorities at all.

THE NEEDS OF UNACCOMPANIED REFUGEE CHILDREN

This chapter has been very factual so far. We will now look at the story of an unaccompanied refugee boy in order to consider what his needs are. I could have used a story about a girl but, in fact, more boys come than girls.

CASE STUDY

You are a twelve-year-old boy living in an African village frequently exposed to the gunfire of different groups of soldiers. Your parents are farmers, and have been saving up for a long time so that you can start going to school in the big town nearby. You are very happy and proud when you leave your parents, younger sisters and brother to go to school for the first time. You know that a good education means a chance to get on in the world. However, when you return home after a few weeks for a visit, you find that your village has been totally destroyed and your family and neighbours have disappeared.

The local mission takes you in. The nuns look for your family in the surrounding district but, after two months, they can find no trace. The mission is often visited by soldiers looking for 'traitors' who support their opponents. When they come, the nuns hide you, but eventually decide to send you to England for your own safety. They tell you that you will go to a good school, just as your parents always wanted you to.

A businessman known to the nuns agrees to look after you on the flight to London. However, the flight is delayed for many hours so, when you reach London, your travelling companion can only put you in the long queue at immigration before rushing off to catch his connecting flight. Your English is not very good but your travelling companion has told you to say 'I want political asylum' when you get to the desk. You don't know what it means but you trust him.

Try and put yourself in this boy's position. What will you need during your first few months in this country?

(At the Conference, at which this activity was used, lively discussion ensued at this point. In the feedback which followed, the needs identified of this imaginary unaccompanied refugee child included food, somewhere to live, warm clothes, someone who speaks his language, good legal advice, someone to care for him and help him to come to terms with the loss of his family and country, English language lessons, etc. It was recognised that he was likely to say that he had come here to go to school, which would not help his claim for asylum).

UNACCOMPANIED REFUGEE CHILDREN
AND INTERNATIONAL STANDARDS

The 1951 UN Convention Relating to the Status of Refugees and the 1967 Protocol refer to refugees regardless of their age. They set out the definition of a refugee. The UK is a party to both agreements. There are also provisions in the Guidelines on Refugee Children (adopted by the United Nations High Commissioner for Refugees in 1988) and the UN Convention on the Rights of the Child (which the UK Government signed and then ratified in December 1991) which relate specifically to refugee children. In addition, human rights treaties which the UK has signed recognise the right of a person to seek asylum, although, strangely enough, they do not also say that states have a duty to provide refuge. This undermines the right to seek asylum in practice.

UNACCOMPANIED REFUGEE CHILDREN'S NEEDS
AND BRITISH NATIONAL LEGISLATION

Unaccompanied refugee children who have entered this country come under our national laws. Three important areas of policy affecting refugee children concern immigration, child care and housing law:

Immigration law

The 1951 UN Convention Relating to the Status of Refugees and 1967 Protocol is part of our immigration law. This means that a person can apply for asylum here – that is, they can ask to enter the United Kingdom if they believe that they will be persecuted on grounds of their race, religion, nationality, membership of a particular social group or their political opinions in their home country. A child can apply for asylum in the same way as an adult. Unfortunately it can take up to two years or longer for a decision to be made – a long time for a child to wait. If the decision is negative, the person can appeal against the decision, but has to leave the country if they lose their appeal. Although the Home Office has rarely deported unaccompanied refugee children, it is, of course, not known how many children are prevented from getting here because of Government policies. For example, in 1991 the Foreign and Commonwealth Office instructed their staff in the Horn of Africa not to issue visas to children travelling alone. The Horn is an area from where millions of people, including many unaccompanied refugee children, have been forced to flee in order to save their lives. Visas are needed by people travelling from many countries. As well as being hard to get in a hurry, airlines have to pay heavy fines if their passengers do not have the right visa. That naturally means they make careful checks.

Another problem is that unaccompanied refugee children are rarely granted refugee status but are, instead, granted 'Exceptional Leave to Remain'. This does not give them the same rights as refugee status; for example, they have no right to apply for their family to join them for four years and they have to re-apply at intervals for permission to stay in Britain.

The Asylum Bill 1991 is just one example of the many ways in which the British Government appears to want to make things harder for asylum seekers in recent years. The Bill proposed changes in the law which would have made it very difficult to appeal against a decision to refuse asylum. Many organisations specialising in refugee and children's issues tried to make changes to the Bill before it became law. One suggested change of particular importance to unaccompanied refugee children involved the proposal that every unaccompanied refugee child should have his or her own 'care advocate' – someone with knowledge of the child's needs who would advise and speak for them when the asylum claim was dealt with. They would also make sure that arrangements were in place for the child to be looked after properly. However, before the Bill was passed, Parliament's business came to a halt when the General Election was announced. The new Asylum Bill promised in the Queen's Speech on May 6 1992 had not appeared at the time of the Exeter Conference. When it did appear in the following year, the Asylum and Immigration Appeals Act 1993 established a Panel of Advisers for unaccompanied refugee children on a voluntary basis; refugee and children's non-governmental organisations had campaigned for this to be statutory. The Panel is funded by the Home Office and has operated from the Refugee Council since April 1994, taking 700 referrals in its first 18 months of operation.

The Act also allowed the fingerprinting of asylum applicants without accepted forms of identification, as an attempt to reduce so-called 'multiple applications'. Campaigning to exempt children from this requirement was unsuccessful but provision was made that a child may not be fingerprinted except in the presence of an adult independent of the Home Office (Section 3(2)). Associated Immigration Rules, which came into force at the same time as the Act, included one specifically on child asylum-seekers (HC395), stressing that 'particular priority and care is to be given to the handling of their cases'.

Child care law

The Children Act 1989 covers family and child care law in Britain. It applies to all children in the country, regardless of their immigration status. Areas of particular importance to unaccompanied refugee children are: that the children's welfare must come first, that the wishes and feelings of the children are to be taken into account and that the children's religion, racial origin, culture and language must be considered when making plans for them. All local authorities have a general duty to provide accommodation for any children in their area who have no-one to care for them. They also have new powers to provide somewhere to live for young people between the ages of 16 and 21 if it promotes their welfare. If children are accommodated by social services and have no contact with their family, an independent visitor can be appointed to support them.

Housing Law

Under the Housing Act 1985, local authorities have a duty to provide housing to homeless people who are in 'priority need'. This includes those who are 'vulnerable', for example because of their age. It sounds as if this Act, together with the Children Act 1989, gives complete protection to unaccompanied refugee children and young people who need somewhere to live. However, the case of a homeless 17-year-old woman – an unaccompanied refugee not thought to be 'in need' by her social services department nor 'vulnerable' by her housing department – is currently going to court.

OBSTACLES TO FULL PROTECTION OF THE RIGHTS OF UNACCOMPANIED REFUGEE CHILDREN

One general obstacle is the racism of some people in this country and the Government's apparent suspicion of asylum-seekers and reluctance to grant them permission to stay here. Many articles appeared in newspapers in 1991 and 1992, sometimes written by or quoting government ministers, with stories about 'bogus refugees' who are said to come to this country in order to be better off financially. In reality, the majority of asylum seekers are professional people who can afford to flee to Britain and who had a very good standard of living in their own country.

A specific difficulty for social services departments accommodating refugee children is that of cost. Providing residential accommodation or foster care is very expensive and unaccompanied refugee children often have particular needs, for example staff and carers who speak their own language, additional help with English and so on. First, these costs are not covered by central government and, second, the costs are not evenly spread throughout the country because the majority of children live in London and in certain boroughs in particular. Unfortunately, some social services departments are extremely reluctant to take responsibility for unaccompanied refugee children referred to them. This is partly because of the expense at a time when the departments are having to cut back on their spending across the board. They try to argue that the children are the responsibility of some other authority where the children may have already stayed.

There are also very few authorities who successfully advertise and promote their services among refugee community groups who may be caring for unaccompanied refugee children in informal arrangements and who would appreciate some support. If you do not know about a service, you are not going to be able to use it. All local authority departments, not just social services, have financial problems. In some areas this has meant fewer support teachers for refugee children in schools and less English lessons in colleges. In spite of these difficulties, some local authorities have tried very hard to meet the needs of the refugees in their area and have made great efforts to look after unaccompanied refugee children in a culturally sensitive way, for example by recruiting refugee staff and foster carers.

Overall, it is true to say that there is a lack of knowledge about, and training for, working with refugees in general and unaccompanied refugee children in particular. Guidelines to meet this need have been drawn up by the Department of Health and they were to be published soon after the Children Act came into force in 1991. The guidelines, together with a detailed training pack, did not appear, however, until the Summer of 1995 (Department of Health Social Services Inspectorate 1995).

A similar delay occurred with a proposal first sent to the Department of Health in January 1990 by the Refugee Council Working Group on Unaccompanied Refugee Children and Adolescents, and supported by the Association of Directors of Social Services. The proposal was for a unit which could co-ordinate the services required to meet the needs of newly arrived unaccompanied refugee children. This was seen as potentially particularly useful for the local authorities who had not much experience with unaccompanied refugee children. The proposal was eventually rejected by the Department of Health.

CHAMPIONS OF THE RIGHTS OF UNACCOMPANIED REFUGEE CHILDREN

The work of the Children's Rights Development Unit (CRDU) to make the UN Convention on the Rights of the Child more a reality for all children was welcome. With regard to refugee children in particular, the CRDU, together with the Children's Legal Centre, campaigned for the Government to withdraw their reservation concerning immigration. This reservation could, for example, make it much harder for unaccompanied refugee children to be joined by their families here. The reservation, however, has not been withdrawn.

Another positive step is that the United Nations High Commissioner for Refugees established a new post of Co-ordinator for Refugee Children in Geneva. This person was to see how far the Guidelines on Refugee Children, drawn up in 1988, have been put into practice. The Guidelines have now been extensively revised to take account of the UN Convention on the Rights of the Child and were re-issued in 1994 (UNHCR 1994)

Other organisations in Britain have been keeping the needs of unaccompanied refugee children in people's minds. One good example has been the

Children's Legal Centre and their work towards getting care advocates for unaccompanied refugee children in connection with the Asylum Bill which was described earlier. Another example is the Refugee Council with its Working Group on Unaccompanied Refugee Children and Adolescents, which has made regular estimates of numbers of unaccompanied refugee children, has drawn attention to particular difficulties faced by certain children in specific local authorities and has continued to press the Home Office to provide training to its staff dealing with the asylum claims of children. A special 'Unaccompanied Children's Module' was eventually set up in the Immigration and Nationality Department in 1995 to deal with the claims of unaccompanied children. The officers in this section, and some immigration officers at ports of entry, had some initial training in working with children – a development which is to be welcomed.

CONCLUSION

At its best, Britain has offered refuge to a few of those in the world who have been forced to flee their homeland – some of whom are unaccompanied refugee children. Unaccompanied children are clearly among the most vulnerable of the increasing number of refugees in our world today. They need particular care and attention, for which the 'building blocks' are now in place in Britain: standards of international law, national laws, some good social work practice at local level and the commitment of some voluntary agencies and individuals.

More needs to be done to make sure that unaccompanied refugee children automatically get what they are legally entitled to receive in order that their needs are met. It is not right that a fuss sometimes has to be made for this to happen. Even though money is short, we must remember that many countries which are poorer than Britain look after many more refugees than are allowed to come here. The UK Government, on behalf of the whole nation, should accept financial responsibility for settling the refugees who come here, as it is unfair to expect relatively few local authorities to cope with the unplanned arrival of all refugees and to pay for this.

All of us, as individuals, can play a part too – in our homes, schools and places of work and recreation – as we speak up and make racism in Britain a thing of the past, and as we press our Government to stand by its commitment to the UN Convention Relating to the Status of Refugees, so that refugees of all ages can find a safe haven here.

(In the plenary session following this presentation, the Conference partici-pants unanimously voted that the Asylum Rights Campaign petition against the Asylum Bill should be signed on their behalf by Professor Mary John.)

REFERENCES AND FURTHER READING

Ayotte, W. and Lown, J. (1992) *Children or Refugees?: A Survey of West European Policies on Unaccompanied Refugee Children.* London: Children's Legal Centre.

Finlay, R. and Reynolds, J. (eds) (1987) *Children from Refugee Communities.* Derby: Refugee Action.

Goodwin-Gill, G.S. (1986) *The Refugee in International Law.* Oxford: Clarendon Press.

Department of Health and Social Services Inspectorate (1995) *Practice Guide on Unaccompanied Refugee Children.* London: HMSO.

Holmes, C. (1991) *A Tolerant Country? Immigrants, Refugees and Minorities in Europe.* London: Faber and Faber.

Jockenhövel-Schieke, H. (1990) *Unaccompanied Refugee Children in Europe: Experience with Protection, Placement and Education.* Frankfurt/Main: International Social Service German Branch.

Joly, D. (1992) *Refugees: Asylum in Europe?* London: Minority Rights Publications.

Parry-Crooke, G. (1991) *The Children Act and Youth Homelessness.* London: Young Homelessness Group.

Ressler, E.M., Boothby, N. and Steinbock, D.J. (1988) *Unaccompanied Children: Care and Protection in Wars, Natural Disasters, and Refugee Movements.* New York: OUP.

Thoolen, H. (1988) *A Selected and Annotated Bibliography on Refugee Children.* Geneva: Centre for Documentation on Refugees.

United Nations High Commissioner for Refugees (1988) *Guidelines on Refugee Children.* Geneva: UNHCR.

United Nations High Commissioner for Refugees (1994) *Refugee Children: Guidelines on Protection and Care.* Geneva: UNHCR.

White, R., Carr, P. and Lowe, N. (1990) *A Guide to the Children Act 1989.* London: Butterworths.

Books suitable for younger readers

Christians Aware (1992) *What Lies Ahead?: Listening to Refugees.* Leicester: Christians Aware.

Gershon, K. (1989) *We Came As Children.* London and Basingstoke: Papermac.

Molteno, M. (1992) *A Shield of Coolest Air.* London: Shola Books. [Novel]

Rutter, J. (1991) *We Left Because We Had To.* London: Refugee Council.

Warner, R. (ed) (1991) *Voices from Eritrea, Voices from Kurdistan, Voices from Somalia.* London: Minority Rights Group.

GLOSSARY

Editor's Note: At the Conference in 1992, each speaker was asked to provide a Glossary for the benefit of the younger participants. As an example of good practice at that event, the list provided by Louise Williamson is included here.

Advocate: someone who speaks on behalf of someone else, with their best interests at heart and on their instructions.

Asylum-seeker: someone who has left their own country and, on entering another country, asks for permission to live there on the grounds that they are a refugee.

Association of Directors of Social Services: each social services department in the country is led by a Director. All the Directors are members of this Association.

Bill: before Parliament decides whether to pass a law or not, they look at the law in draft form. This is called a bill.

Department of Health: the Government Department in Britain which is responsible for broad policy on children and child care, among many other things.

Home Office: the Government department in Britain which is responsible for immigration matters, among many other things. It is people in the Home Office who decide who is allowed to enter the country and for how long, and which asylum-seekers will be granted refugee status, which will be allowed to stay on humanitarian grounds and which will be deported.

Local Authority: Britain is divided up into local authorities where locally elected representatives are responsible for running local services, for example education, street cleaning, housing, etc.

Programme/quota refugee: a refugee who is accepted as such before they enter their country of asylum, often as part of a 'programme' or 'quota' of refugees from a particular group or country.

Prostitute: this is usually someone who receives money in return for giving sexual services. When girls are snatched in some countries in order to become prostitutes for the army, they are unlikely to receive any more than their food and lodging.

Refugee: the United Nations Convention Relating to the Status of Refugees (the 'Geneva Convention') defines a refugee as being someone who: 'owing to a well-founded fear of being persecuted for reasons of race, religion, nationality, membership of a particular social group or political opinion is outside the country of his nationality and is unable or, owing to such fear, is unwilling to avail himself of the protection of that country'. It is up to the countries who have signed the Convention to define what 'fear of persecution' means when they decide who is to be recognised as a refugee.

Social Services Department: department of the local authority responsible for providing social care services, for example homes for the elderly, day centres for those with learning disabilities, foster carers and children's homes, etc.

Unaccompanied refugee child: a child under the age of eighteen who has been forced to leave their country for their own safety, and who has no adult with them who usually looks after them. They may be an asylum-seeker, a recognised refugee or someone who can stay here on humanitarian grounds.

Visa: in order to travel to some countries, your passport is not enough. You have to apply for a 'visa', a piece of paper or official stamp which gives you permission to enter the country you are travelling to before you leave your own country.

CHAPTER 7

Marginality and Extermination in Brazil
From Uneasiness to Well-Being

Janina Gonçalves

INTRODUCTION
Extermination: the answer to a project

The issue of the extermination of children in Brazilian society is one way through which the marginalisation of the common citizen has been publicly demonstrated. There is, nevertheless, a fundamental aspect of this issue which we need to address: the way in which children come to symbolise popular causes and demands. Great importance is given to organised protests and demonstrations by different social classes, either those organised by the labour unions or by the political parties. It is also believed now that non-governmental organisations also serve to express popular social demands.

In this chapter, attention is drawn to the way demands are manifested, which is quite discriminatory but which, nevertheless, has a very strong impact – for instance, the repercussion of the present situation in the international press and the various European governments' censorship of the Brazilian government for having such hard-hearted responses to the social situation of extermination itself. This manifestation focuses on children, in their multiple exposure to pain, hunger, disease, prostitution, discouragement and death.

This being so, we would say, under such circumstances, that children cease to be the symbol of social disadvantage and become the living (or dying) evidence of social disadvantage itself. We demonstrate here that, whenever different ways of expressing demands become impossible, it is the very life of this layer of society that makes clear its desperate needs. This indeed has provided the strongest channel of participation that the popular layer found to express itself: revealing in all its crudeness their dire situations. Moreover, it is through this channel that the response encountered is the strongest: death and exclusion. Death in the streets, in the field, in the hospital, in the bordello, in the uterus.

We consider that these forms of death are today the clearest evidence that the Brazilian society has revealed itself. The response evidences the permanent militarisation of this society, a response armed with wooden sticks, scalpels and the most modern weapons. The answer is NO, you do not have the right to citizenship, you may not exist, to you the way is closed. The answer is death.

CONCEPTUAL – OPERATIONAL OVERVIEW

The various dimensions of the problem

The issue of social exclusion was analysed in *The Social Policy for Children and Adolescents* (Gonçalves 1991a), from the standpoint of the various strata of society considered marginal to the structure of economic productivity. Such an analysis of the concept of marginality, combined with an analysis of the consequences of the internationalisation of financial capital, led to a recognition that these strata in the productive structure can no longer serve traditional views about a reserve of industrial labour, which, in its classical form, it has been argued, gave rise to deviations which were considered essential elements in the theory of marginality (Nunn 1977). Such an approach can be seen as one which is a Parsonian version of the so-called 'integrationist perspective' on what refers to popular conceptions of social stratification which have guided social policy from redistributive mechanisms right through to the specifics of care and support.

The examination of the theme of social exclusion, centred on the industrial legion of reserve seen within the frame of foreign aid and the internationalisation of capital, leads to other considerations which not only affect theoretical perspectives or the social layers affected by social policy but practical divisions of a budgetary and programmatic nature in relation to these self-same politics. The significance of such an approach, in terms of capital internationalisation, was helpfully drawn together by the concept of 'channels' (Gonçalves 1991b), where we identified a new form of political expression which is relevant and emerging in the present economic context.

It is important to emphasise such a form, which we made concrete in the way in which we identified channels of political participation – such participation being multi-varied and multi-faceted and manifesting itself socially as projects. Such a modality presented itself to our analysis in the form of the executive aspects of Latin American politics which, whilst implicit, has consolidated itself throughout the years by means of what exists most specifically in Brazilian society in terms of the creation, distribution and consolidation of power, what we call a 'colonialist' model. It is a reductive, pulverising and totally defeating way of exercising power (as it permeates the State and the civil society) which affects the creation of benefits for both sides. This is where we feel there emerges a good possibility of interpreting the social issue and it was from this standpoint that we looked at the problem of extermination.

Other than the emotional and political aspects of the extermination of children, already largely diffused and denounced by the press and by organisations of defence of rights, we were interested in examining this in terms of the (perverse) 'logic' of the capitalist system within the context of the internationalisation of capital. We wished to do this because, beyond the intention of the agents involved in these activities, what needs to be thoroughly examined is the logic behind the productive system which, in the present economic and political culture, can argue that such interventions are 'natural'.

However, the path we followed to establish our analysis was mediated by indirect relations which have made the implications of extermination real in perspectives that were not revealed until now by the entities which denounce them. Basically, three facets were approached by us:

- extermination and land conflicts
- extermination in health
- extermination's historical background.

This work is the result of advisors participating in the Marginality Project, an investigation conducted by us within the scope of the Brazilian Centre for Childhood and Adolescence (CBIA's Division of Studies). This investigation deserves merit not only for the structural analysis of extermination in fields previously not examined, but mainly for revealing links with infra-structure issues which might help us further understand the logic in this model.

However, the historical background of extermination, produced by Rosilene Alvim (1991), tells us of a movement constituting the political *object* of extermination rather than the social action itself. This is further illuminated when two other works suggest the links of this gruesome frame to aspects of the infra-structure we consider important: the conflict in the field and in the health area.

It was through that route, contradictory as it may seem, that we reached the issues of the protection of well-being. We dare to suggest that child extermination, being part of the logic of the ruling capitalist model, arises from the lack of concern about the well-being, happiness and prosperity of the individual and community, that is it is a state of disequilibrium and disharmony. Such uneasiness, characterised by the situation of extermination, relates to the lack of concern with welfare and what has been most appalling is the death due to adverse living conditions. It is in this sense that the well-being denied and evidenced by the situation of extermination makes clear the need for social benefits which might improve such living conditions.

In view of such a situation, what is the problem?

We would like to propose an expansion of the concept of welfare together with the notion of benefit to open here a discussion on welfare related to one on development. Such a bond generates a definite impact on welfare policy: welfare provision should go beyond the offer of benefits to include actions which affect the infra-structural conditions for development, such as agrarian reform and income distribution, as well as public health – which altogether indicates a course of development aimed at improving the living conditions of the lower social strata.

Welfare, in terms of social policy for children and adolescents, was analysed by the Marginality Project by means of advice offered by UNICAMP (Universidade Estadual de Campinas), an opportunity in which the linkage between state and society was designed as proposed actions to be developed by NGO's. These works, later published in *Cadernos CBIA (no. 1)* discuss an important aspect of the modern Brazilian society: the role that the private sector plays, not only in the offering of support services and assistance but, most of all, in relation to the ability to express and respond to demands originating in different social sectors and merge with the State in order to satisfy such demands.

In the specific case of the Policy for the Child and the Adolescent (a policy constituted by programmes and projects according to the law that established it), it is important to observe that the advice offered by UNICAMP clarified and analysed the constituents of the system of child assistance. As this policy is being structured, there still needs to be some clarification about the way in which welfare assistance will be offered, especially, and most importantly, in relation to the meaning of action that acknowledges the rights of the child and adolescent. The change that was underlined by the proclamation and dissemination of the Child and the Adolescent Statute is important insofar as it represents a milestone in the transformation of a policy that operated on the basis of relatively oppressive procedures into one that struggles for the recognition of individual rights.

The Marginality Project, however, proposes that the agencies which represent the Brazilian Centre for Childhood and Adolescence work on the effective promotion of welfare. Such promotion involves the concession of concrete benefits to the population, through their associations and representative entities, as well as the active representation in the legislative and economic spheres (in the infra-structural sense) for the structuring of the development that leads to welfare.

FROM UNEASINESS TO WELL-BEING

The trajectory of a social policy for children and adolescents in Brazil

The issue of children and adolescents' extermination in the country has been dealt with in an emotional and political way. We would like to point to the different dimensions of this issue, with the objective of making clearer the phenomena which, in our view, permeate it. Approaching the matter of extermination through land conflicts reveals the first structural link in the system which, amazingly, has not yet been covered by the press in Brazil in their general denunciation of the situation. The violence implicated in the Brazilian agrarian issue has a perspective which is both symbolic and concrete.

The symbolic is the expropriation of peasants from their relationship with production, represented by a piece of land, and so rendering them landless. The concrete result of this has been the death of those peasants. Berno (1991) reveals this in its multiple manifestations, from its geographical circumscription to the most diverse ways of imposing pain and death. What is even more astonishing in this situation is the unbelievable ignorance of the society in general, and of national and international political groups, on the subject as it relates to the child and adolescent issue.

One starts to consider the meaning of this. Why the preservation of the concern with street-children when death in labour, especially in rural work, is proportionately greater? The damage that this distortion causes to possible reformulations in child and adolescent policy in the country is enormous. Any linkage of this policy to the structural situation must take the agrarian issue into consideration. The very modalities of violence and extermination of children and adolescents point to a characterisation of what is the agrarian issue seen from the standpoint of violence having both symbolic and concrete dimensions: slave labour in agrarian and rural projects, in the reforestation companies (Berno 1991) or the 'tea slaves' (juvenile prostitution in the mining industry, white slavery and traffic of underaged young people) as well as clandestine graveyards. The specificity of deaths is also a geographic indicator, such as the murders and deaths of children and young people caused by agro-toxic products, drought and hunger. The cause of death and the degree of violence demonstrated – lynching, hiding of the corpse, death in labourers' transportation, kidnapping, illegal arrests – add to the argument. Witnesses to these illegal acts suggest a violence that is even worse – such violence generally occurs at home, in front of the young person's parents or during work.

It is by thoroughly studying extermination that we will be able to understand why this rural violence is ignored. Extermination is a social phenomenon generated in the city, a kind of 'object' of intervention produced in agreement with the press and international organisations and with the intense participation of NGO's (Alvim 1991). The contribution given by Alvim to the Marginality Project leads us to recognise the role of these main actors in constituting this object of extermination mainly based on the street-children issue. Through this study one can see the influence of established alliances between these actors in defining a priority for the child/adolescent policy, the structural aspects of it being left aside.

The schedule of actions and investigation of the extermination issue, elaborated by Alvim, indicates that in 1983 a special commission of the Secretariat of the Civil Police was created in Rio de Janeiro to investigate crimes committed by extermination groups, which were denounced by the Justice and Peace Commission, in the suburb of Nova Iguancu. Since then, a number of movements have been set up to denounce such crimes and request concrete action from the government. Even Amnesty International concerned itself about the subject and requested support from the CBIA. Nevertheless, demographic data about the country in 1993 revealed a very different situation: violence and extermination by collective death not only proliferates but becomes intensified under the economic depression in which we are living.

This is the second structural linkage of extermination: its linkage to the living conditions of the low-income population, or what is conventionally thought of as 'suffering and hardship'. In this sense, mortality as a result of health conditions (Minayo 1991) reveals a further sordid side to the question. Many Brazilian children are not killed in the streets but perish earlier, before birth or in infancy, due to hunger and living in unhealthy and disease-ridden conditions.

This being so, we consider that extermination has worked more as an 'ideological' banner for the focus of certain forces, which we would like to analyse here. We have already mentioned that the historical background of extermination reveals a collusion between the press, NGO's and international organisations in presenting this issue. We should, therefore, analyse the participation of these actors in the setting of the Brazilian policy for children and adolescents so that we are able to understand not only the State's and society's distance from the structural dimensions of the problem but also the way in which this has come about and how this situation can be modified.

WELFARE ACTIONS

A new institutionalisation of the concealment of the problem?

Child and adolescent's policy has recently been characterised as a new form of institutionalisation, where, starting from the change in legislation (The Child and Adolescents' Statute), certain actors have played a special role in the formulation and implementation of this policy. A new paradigm is foreseen (Castanhar 1991), in which rules will establish new rights for those formerly called under-aged and now recognised as a child or an adolescent. A few specific groups (especially certain sectors of the population) identify negative aspects in this new code, which aims to regulate the relationships between the emergent and the marginal societies in Brazil. Such groups refer particularly to situations in which the population feels menaced by delinquents and the police are not able to help.

In the favourable context in which the new law has been received, and the somewhat euphoric reception of the political advance it represented, the extermination of children is forgotten. We seem to be living in a new Brazil (a term much used during President Collor's government). Even the mission of the part of the Brazilian government structure responsible for the standardisation of the Brazilian policy for children and adolescents was defined by its President Gomes da Costa[1] as the guarantee of rights (also defined in the law which created the Brazilian Centre for Childhood and Adolescence, which replaced FUNABEM).

This is how we observe a complete misinterpretation of the reason for a national institution to exist: being responsible for the standardisation of a policy, it abandons the macro-level of action to the control of others and acts as a simple auditing agency. In order to understand this situation, we chose to examine what we call 'welfare' – the interaction of these new actors, who are considered key elements in this new instituationality.

The NGOs and their role in social assistance

A report produced by UNICAMP (Berno 1991; Vianna 1991) begins with the following phrase: 'recently, hope augmented on the role that non-governmental organizations – NGOs could play in the field of social policy...'. The report approaches the question of establishing a new concept of social policy as needing a prior and indispensable condition regarding the choice of the most adequate instruments to facilitate the increased participation of NGO's, not only during its execution, but also, and most importantly, during the crucial stage of the formulation of such a policy. It examines very thoroughly the existing literature and available published information with the aim of knowing better the multi-faceted nature of those organisations, as well as the views of the most important scholars in the field on what are the relevant factors in its implementation.

In a general sense, the work carried out by UNICAMP points to a change in the relationship between civil society and political society through the work of NGOs. The concept of channel (Gonçalves 1991b) takes account of this change. However, this concept calls attention to a typically Brazilian way of political participation given by the 'colonialist' way of social action, where benefit is an essential part of the relationship. As distinct from the explanations that want to consider NGOs as suppliers of the state power, the concept of channel considers them as 'arms' of that state, interlocutors as they are of the public powers close to the population insofar as the distribution of benefits are concerned.

We have now to identify ways in which such organisations relate to international organisations. Such an analysis cannot be made without fully

---

1 A. C. Gomas da Costa has been an expressive person in the field of politics for children and adolescents in Brazil. He has been a consultant to UNICEF and was nominated for the presidency of the Brazilian Centre for Childhood and Adolescence (CBIA) in 1992. During the period in which he presided over the institution, CBIA became an institution that operated as a regulator of the implementation of norms. It did not play the role of policy formulator as expected by the 'Marginality Project' or other projects that were already under way.

understanding the changes in the economy, or what is called 'of trans-nation-alisation' and even 'inter-nationalisation' of the economy (Salama 1978; Santos 1979).

Other authors point to changes in the financing of the social services with the emergence of the NGOs. Such changes are followed by a change in the very structure of social services, since the NGOs have had to organise themselves administratively to receive financial resources and this fact has had repercus-sions in its business form.

This being so, the role played by NGOs cannot be considered in an isolated way as an exclusively political phenomenon, in the sense of the decentralisation of power. It is part of a new and more important infrastructure change, namely that of the relationship between the social and economic structure. However, in order to analyse this theme we have to focus right down to the changes at the work level. This is, in fact, the big issue behind all the changes which are said to be changes in 'paradigm'. These are changes in the structure of the demand for assistance as the country's socio-economic conditions deteriorate.

A 'lost decade' is spoken of when the 1980s are referred to by economists dedicated to studying poverty. This situation existed even before then as development decelerated since 1970. This situation of depression has been discussed by the theorists of poverty, trying to explain its possible linkage to growth (Bonelli and Ramos 1992). Besides the traditional discussions about the relationship between education and poverty, or even race and poverty, such discussions have shown that growth is not simply a concomitant of the elimination of the financial depression. Nevertheless, we are still left with the questions surrounding the changes in the structure of the demand for social services, given the impact caused by the changes in the relations of work (Sabóia 1992).

Attention needs, therefore, to be focused on the political approach made to the issue of extermination, and the one made by Minayo (1991) – in which health conditions are linked to the massive death rates of children and adolescents – or that made by Berno (1991), in which work relations in the field are identified as determinants of the massacre of peasants and their children. In the specific case of the policy for children and adolescents, this issue was seen in super-structural terms, since the proclamation of the Child and Adolescent's Statute displaces the planned pressure for change in the economic organisation by that of the guarantee of rights. This occurs under the New Republic, where the organised political manifestations of non-governmen-tal entities, and organisations for the defence of human rights assume the leadership in this struggle. It is within this context that Castanhar (1991) names the new situation created by the approval of the Statute a 'change of paradigm'.

New actors emerge on the scene and an institutional re-ordering in the new entity that substituted FUNABEM (National Foundation for the Welfare of Children and Adolescents) must take place now, as suggested by the results of our Marginality Project. However, this institutional re-ordering does not follow the matrix of interelations proposed by Castanhar (1991) or the Strategic Planning defined by CBIA after the intervention made by Vianna (1991). There is a continuity, shown by the Institutional Mission arbitrarily designed by A. Gomes da Costa in 1992, of the longings and political objectives defended by what was called 'Movement for the Child and Adolescent's Statute'. The contradictions stun even the most incautious or naïve.

Although CBIA have hired experts and specialists to research these issues, the institutional discourse remains the same. It seems as if CBIA was governed at a distance by remote control, even by international organisations. And this is how we see the reports of all funded projects (including those on extermination requested by the President himself) put into drawers, the division responsible for them demolished and the ongoing projects interrupted. CBIA staggers alongside infrastructural issues, getting rid of them as if they were simply papers to be filed or thrown away.

Reality, however, is untameable and other organisations are there to reveal the truth which has generated so much activity to keep it hidden. IBGE's statistics demonstrate, supermarket sackings scream, IBASE's data about street children alarm: there is something behind the granting of human rights, there is a crucial point that has to be touched, even if it hurts, even if it is unpleasant – the denying of rights is social inequality. This indeed is the beginning of a real sense of social service.

The Marginality Project was co-ordinated by me from 1991 to 1993, having the present chapter as one of its outcomes. The project was developed upon the methodology of settings, which presupposes the hiring of advisors with specific training in the fields which the investigation aimed to approach. The issue of 'uneasiness' was therefore approached from the standpoint of the extermination of children in land conflicts, in unhealthy living conditions and hunger and through the background of extermination, pointing out the main actors who took part in this issue. As for the well-being (welfare) issue, it was explored by means of three different advisories provided by UNICAMP (Universidade de Campinas) and Neppi (Núcleo de Estudos de Políticas Públicas), directed by Professor Sonia Draibe, who investigated the role played by NGO's in child policy within the new institutionalisation created by the proclamation of the Child and Adolescent Statute of Brazil. The third advice was in the field of strategy planning for the definition of a new course for child policy in Brazil provided by Dr Marco Aurélio Vianna and Dr Júlio Mourào. The last advice was provided by Fundaçâo Getúlio Vargasm, more specifically by Professor J. C. Castanhar and Professor Silvia Vergara, to map a matrix of the main interrelationships between the institutions that were responsible for or linked to the issue of child policy in Brazil – also delineating a new course for it. The Marginality Project was a project conducted and co-ordinated by me and aimed at analysing the marginality issue, focusing on the child and adolescent policy.

That being so, I decided to break down the marginality issue into two different aspects: the aspect of 'uneasiness', which I characterised through extermination, and the aspect of 'well-being', that would relate to what is denominated new institutionalisation of the policy for children and adolescents, which I covered under three different perspectives: strategy planning, the role of NGOs and the matrix of interrelationships. It is a unique project, since it did not involve apprentices or assistants. It received collaboration from Dr Ireneu Corrêa who played the role of researcher and these advisors had the role of investigating the aspects defined as priority by the research project. It is important to emphasise that the hired consultants had their research objects formulated by me as co-ordinator of the project.

REFERENCES

Alvim, R. (1991) *O Histórico do Extermínio.* CBIA, Rio de Janeiro, RJ.

Amadeo, J.E. and Camargo, J.M. (August 1992) *The Mirror's Image – The Labour Market Response to the Cruzado and Collor Plans.* IPEA/International Seminar on Labour Market Roots of Poverty and Inequality in Brazil, August 1992, Rio de Janeiro, RJ.

Berno (1991) *Extermínio no campo* UNICAMP, NEPPI, CBIA, Rio de Janeiro, RJ.

Bonelli, R. and Ramos, L. (1992) *Income Distribution in Brazil: Long Trends and Changes in Inequality Since the Late 1970s.* IPEA/International Seminar on Labour Market Roots of Poverty and Inequality in Brazil, August 1992, Rio de Janeiro, RJ.

Castanhar, J.C. (1991) *Relatório de consultoria técnica prestada ao Centro Brasileiro para a Infância e Adolescência por consultores da Escola Brasileira de Administração Pública.* Fundação Getúlio Vargas, Rio de Janeiro, RJ.

Gonçalves, J.M.F. (1991a) *The Social Policy for Children and Adolescents.* CBIA, Rio de Janeiro, RJ.

Gonçalves, J.M.F. (1991b) *Channels as a Mechanism of Policy Formation.* Unpublished Ph.D. Thesis, University of Swansea, UK.

Minayo (1991) *O Extermínio pela Saúde.* CBIA, Rio de Janeiro, RJ.

Nunn, J. (1977) *Super Población Relativa. Ejército Industrial de Reserva. Masa Marginal.* Revista Latinoamericana de Sociologia. Vol. V – n.2.

Sabóia, J. (1992) *Intervenção Governamental e a Participação dos Agentes na Definição da Política Salarial no Brasil: Efeitos sobre a Pobreza e a Distribuição de Renda.* IPEA/International Seminar on Labour Market Roots of Poverty and Inequality in Brazil, August 1992, Rio de Janeiro, RJ.

Salama, P. (1978) *Specificité de l'internationalization du capital en Amérique Latine.* Tiers Monde, Tome XIX.

Santos, W.G. (1979) *Cidadania e Justiça: a politica social na ordem brasileira.* Editora Campus, Rio de Janeiro, RJ.

Silva, Nelson do Valle (1992) *Racial Discrimination in Income.* IPEA/International Seminar on Labour Market Roots of Poverty and Inequality in Brazil, August 1992, Rio de Janeiro, RJ.

Vianna (1991) *Extermínio no campo.* UNICAMP, NEPPI, CBIA, Rio de Janeiro, RJ.

CHAPTER 8

Teenage Sexuality World-Wide

David Treharne and Wendy Thomas

This chapter is not an attempt to make a definitive statement about teenage sexuality, if indeed that were possible, but to examine some of the issues that we consider to be important in moving forward towards producing a more coherent and positive educative climate and structures and to inform further discussion and research into some important, but easily overlooked, areas of concern which need to be addressed as a matter of some urgency.

A STATISTICAL OVERVIEW

There are, according to the United Nations (1993), one billion teenagers in the World. Of these, 165 million live in the 'developed' world, a figure that represents about 17 per cent of the total. There are an estimated 905 million who live in the less-developed world. It would be tempting to assume that the issues that confront each of these groups are discreet and different. We believe that the situation is a complex one in which there are both issues that are common to both groups and, at the same time, different issues which concern both. Such a situation makes the implementation of a common educative programme even more difficult to deliver. A common strand that unites both groups is repression, although manifestation of this may differ according to nationality or grouping.

Let us look further at some statistics (IPPF 1995; PAI 1994; UN 1993; UNFPA 1995) which are helpful in focusing on the context and the size of the challenges that adolescent sexuality presents. Of course, there are inevitably questions as to how representative such statistics are, the conditions under which they were collected, the assumptions influencing the choice of sample chosen and the questions asked, etc. Even with these caveats in mind, the picture presented is provocative.

Adolescents (10–19 years)

- 1995 – 18 per cent of the world's population is made up of teenagers. By the year 2000 this figure will be 18.7 per cent.
- In the developed world, 14 per cent of the population is made up of teenagers. These teenagers constitute only 3 per cent of the world's population and make up only 16.2 per cent of the world's teenagers.
- About half of all HIV infections have occurred in people younger than 25 years.
- In many developing countries more than 60 per cent of new HIV infections are amongst 15–24-year-olds.
- About one in five adolescents use some form of contraception.
- In Ghana, only 17.5 per cent of sexually active unmarried teenagers use any method – only 0.9 per cent use a modern method. In Kenya, the figure for any method is 13.8 per cent; in El Salvador, 4.32 per cent; in Jamaica, 40.9 per cent. In contrast, in France, Sweden and the Netherlands contraceptive use rates vary between 80 and 90 per cent.

There is hardly any difference in age at first sexual contact between developed and developing countries: in both of them boys and girls tend to start during their teenage years. However, pregnancy rates are 5–20 times higher in developing countries because sexual and contraceptive education and services are usually absent.

DEFINING SEXUALITY

Sexuality is clearly a very difficult term to define. We are particularly concerned about the differentiation between 'sexual health' and 'reproductive health', the importance of which is not immediately clear to anyone outside this professional field. In our view, an undue concentration on reproductive health has meant that many important issues in sexuality, which are not necessarily procreation-associated or oriented, have not been dealt with. In thinking about sexual health, we have been very much influenced by the work undertaken by Kabir, Homans and Newman (1996). This work provides a useful starting point for further discussions. When thinking about programmes of intervention (particularly around population control matters) which have been initiated by a variety of agencies around the world in reproductive health, they usefully draw attention to the following issues:

1. When we are talking about 'sexuality', whose sexuality are we referring to?

2. What are the differences between sexual and reproductive health?

   i. Are these terms used interchangeably with justification?

    ii. Has the professional split that exists between reproductive health and sexuality affected the way that programmes of intervention are organised?

    iii. Is it possible to start to include sexuality in reproductive health programmes and expect that such issues as sexual violence, harassment, abuse and rape will be taken into account by such a programme?

3. Is reproductive health, by definition, oriented towards heterosexuality, and, if so, is it possible and right to posit sexuality as a reproductive health issue? If it does, however, belong in this area, why has it not been addressed in so many international and aid programmes?

They also go on to raise questions as to whether sexuality is addressed in HIV/AIDS work and whether sexuality issues are different to those which are the focus of work on population control. Our attention is drawn, by their questioning, to considering that, historically, there has been an implicit moral agenda within the family planning movement which has led to the idea that some sex is acceptable (and therefore a variety of services should be available to facilitate it) and some sex is not. They question whether we have managed to move beyond these assumptions in any way and whether indeed the 'international community' is ahead of or behind programme realities when terms like reproductive health are used. This is particularly important when we are considering teenage sexuality where pleasure rather than reproduction provides the motivation.

The issue of 'reproductive health' is difficult to isolate as one discreet topic, since it embraces topics and issues as diverse as family planning, sexual health before and after child bearing, sexually transmitted diseases and the scope and nature of sex education. However, we believe that, particularly in reproductive health, education remains the major key. By education here we mean not only to help overcome and eradicate illiteracy and its effects but also to change the ways in which information is, or could be, disseminated. During a trip to Ethiopia to visit projects being part-funded by Population Concern, for example, it was noticeable that the nature and value of much of the work being attempted in education was being held back by a failure to target some potential clients. The result was that these people did not come forward as they remained unaware of programmes that were on offer or available. The need to seek alternative methods of dissemination to the distribution of literature is obvious and urgently necessary. In some cases it may be possible to use other media, and in other cases to extend the use of workers in specific geographical locations.

It is undoubtedly true that highly publicised World Conferences, such as the World Population Association Conference in Cairo and the United Nation's World Conference on Women in Beijing in 1995, serve to raise consciousness about such needs at Governmental and Non-Governmental Organisation level, but this new awareness is very slow in being translated into day-to-day insight and action where the pressures are greatest, that is in the field.

Even where there have been attempts to educate an indigenous population about the nature of the services offered, the scope and value of what is provided can often be limited by insensitive practices. For example, Population Concern has noted that, in some African countries, information about sexual and reproductive health is primarily delivered by males, who often bring to the work a different set of assumptions than the women who constitute the main client group. The International Planned Parenthood Federation in Pakistan, for example, has been much more effective and successful. There the service is delivered predominantly by women. It is also notable that schemes which appear to be successful are those where the educators act as local agents working with the people in their own home areas or villages, rather than trying to encourage groups themselves to travel away from their homes or home areas.

Even so, it is evident that, even with the scale and scope of these projects, family planning alone is not a solution to issues of population control and sexual health. It needs to be put in place together with empowerment and practical help, as well as education, if it is to achieve the desired effect with the groups that appear to be most at risk.

RISKS TO REPRODUCTIVE AND SEXUAL HEALTH

According to figures produced by the World Health Organisation (1995), the scope of the problem to be faced is enormous:

Pregnancy and childbirth

- 15 million women aged 15–19 are two to three times more likely to die in childbirth than women aged 20–24. Girls aged less than fifteen years are five times more likely. There is a high risk of maternal and infant morbidity due to obstructed labour – often resulting in becoming a social outcast – and premature babies, low birth-weight babies and sudden infant death are more common.

- Over a third of women in Latin America have had their first child before the age of 20 years. In many African countries, over half of women have had their first child by 20 years. In the USA this is 20 per cent.

- World-wide birth rates for women under 20 years are dropping but the total number of births to adolescent women is increasing.

- In Botswana and Liberia, pre-marital proof of fertility is culturally acceptable.

- In Cameroon, Nigeria and Cote d'Ivoire, approximately one in five women aged 20–24 had conceived pre-maritally and given birth before the age of 20 years.

Half a million women a year die in pregnancy-related fatalities, and of these, 150,000 die as the result of illegal abortions. WHO identifies that, within these figures, females in the 15–19 age range are two to three times more likely to die in childbirth compared to other groups and that there are 15 million births each year within this age range, a figure which, in 1995–96, formed 11 per cent of the total global figure (WHO 1995). Disturbingly, these figures appear to have remained constant throughout the World for the past 20 years.

Unwanted births

- Abortions amongst young women aged 15–19 years are estimated at 5 million – one in ten of all the abortions world-wide. Most of these are unsafe abortions. These young women are more likely than older women to seek later-term, more risky abortions, or attempt abortion themselves, and will leave it until later to visit the hospital emergency facilities.

- In some countries, 60 per cent of all women hospitalised for abortion complications are adolescents.

- A significant proportion of the 67,000–100,000 deaths from unsafe abortion are of adolescent women. There is also the associated risk of infertility and chronic infection, ruining many women's chances of marriage and fulfilling their reproductive desires.

Sexually transmitted disease

Every year, one out of every twenty teenagers contracts a sexually transmitted disease. The highest rates of incidence of such diseases are in the 20–24 years age group followed by the 15–19 age group.

EDUCATIONAL APPROACHES

The World Health Organisation (1995) has stated that there is no evidence to show that sex education increases sexual activity and lowers the age of first intercourse. We indicated earlier that there are estimated to be one billion teenagers in the World, of which 165 million live in the 'developed' world, a figure representing about 17 per cent of the total. There are an estimated 905 million who live in the less-developed world. We have earlier questioned whether it is possible to think of these young people having commonalities as well as differences. In trying to deliver a common educative programme for this group of young people, the differences cannot be ignored and the common experiences may have differences of meaning according to the cultural context.

There are clearly identifiable strands of behaviour and attitudes that make coherent and common educative programmes difficult to co-ordinate. Amongst these are commonly-held, and often unchallenged, attitudes which reinforce ideas like the notion of 'woman as victim' and which perpetuate such ideas as 'men cannot do anything to control their urges'. There is also the problem that, for both groups from the developed and developing world, training in 'reproductive health' is inadequate, though not always for the same reasons.

EDUCATIONAL AND TRAINING NEEDS

There are unanswered questions which confuse activities and thinking, leading to a clouded view of the nature of the training that is needed. Work undertaken by Population Concern suggests there is, in particular, a woeful inadequacy of training for projects which involve the delivery of programmes to young people by their peer group. One of the major differences in provision between the developed and less developed world is that, although there has been, for example, much research undertaken in Europe about the role that young people would wish to adopt in taking an active part in training, there appears to have been little coherent research done in less-developed parts of the world.

One of the obstacles to the introduction of meaningful and coherent programmes are uncertainties and questions about the value and validity of substantial amounts of the research that has been undertaken in countries, and particularly African Countries, on which existing programmes are often based.

We believe that, although it is important to undertake research in order that programmes can be developed and targeted most effectively, the existing research is often over-generalised, lacking in sufficient detail and consequently misleading. For example, the figures for first intercourse puts the age at 15.6 years in Uganda, 16.4 years in Nigeria and 17.2 in Tanzania (WHO 1995). There is, however, little evidence of the *social status* of the group sampled, which may well be a highly influential factor in relation to the age at which young people become sexually active. Nor is their any indication of the standard or *level of education* reached by the group. These are important facts to take into account in countries where there is likely, in any case, to be a gender imbalance in education provision. For example, in several African countries, such as Ghana, there is a tendency for males to have a longer secondary education than females – a pattern that is also apparent in several areas in the Indian sub-continent, particularly Bangladesh. Such figures suggest that the social and educative status of the female response group might be that in which sexual activity is commenced later than the majority population of that region. We suggest that the use of such statistics, which may have been collected from the more privileged and articulate young members of the population, deflects attention and, indeed, the planning of services away from younger sexually active groups, groups which would benefit most from a structured programme of education in relation, particularly, to sexual health and well-being. In fact, the statistics, as presented, engender a misplaced confidence in what is happening and make the development of appropriate services less urgent than it should be.

The crucial nature of such information is also highlighted by research in Latin America and the Caribbean which seems to indicate that young women usually have their first sexual encounter with a man who is three to five years older. In such cases it may well be that, although the sexual education may usually be targeted at females who are, or are about to become, sexually active, the group best empowered to adopt responsibility for contraception and sexual health are the male partners, who often are not encouraged by present campaigns to take such responsibilities.

We believe that many of the programmes that are being delivered and developed tend to ignore the importance of the educative function of the peer group. Much of what is delivered, even when it is delivered from within the peer group, seems motivated by agendas driven by either health considerations or safe-sex functions rather than the presentation of a balanced set of views based on, or sharing, personal experiences. There is a widespread assumption, that is often drawn from these figures, that *any* sex education must be beneficial. We believe that it is only really effective when it is combined with the development of services that complement such programmes. Population Concern noted in Mexico that many sexually active teenage females had received sex education but that this was not supported by services which would have allowed them to resolve the underlying tensions brought about by finding that sexual activity was both enjoyable and gratifying. It was also noted that in South Africa many of the issues of health and contraception that arise as the result of the high incidence of rape, particularly in the former 'homelands', could have been more sympathetically dealt with by the provision of services delivered closer to the homelands and which was undertaken by females.

In general, we also note that, in many observed cases, there is a high correlation between sexual activity and alcohol abuse, and again there seems to be a crucial case to be made for education to include health-related advice which encompasses the likely effect of alcoholic intake on reckless and irresponsible sexual activity.

It is crucial, in our opinion, to assess, wherever possible, needs in all relevant health-related areas so that the whole process of the development of educational strategies can be planned comprehensively and coherently to include all these aspects.

We are also aware of the apparent contradiction in stressing the need for the delivery of information in many less-developed countries to be undertaken *in situ* by female workers, whereas in countries like the United Kingdom there is a need to reappraise the role of men in relation to the whole issue of sexual and reproductive health. We note that, in many ways, males have tended to be sidelined in this function, and consider that future policies in the developed world should reappraise this and policy making, particularly in the developed world, might be better if the role of males were reappraised.

THE ROLE OF NON-GOVERNMENTAL ORGANISATIONS

Non-governmental agencies have an important role to play in developing educational programmes. Given the post of one of the authors, this may seem like special pleading. We fervently believe that NGOs are often able to assume, encourage and develop an overview that would be more difficult, given the special allegiances of the more directly government-funded agencies or those bodies which have morally-based or religiously-motivated missions. In particular, it is often easier for non-governmental organisations to address some of the most crucial issues that we consider central to widening the scope of any educational programme, for example seeking to redefine traditional male/female roles and examining the nature of the qualifications or expertise needed in the delivery of programmes. Non-governmental organisations are also better placed to determine the most propitious delivery point for any ongoing programmes.

We would include here the development of programmes which address issues related to cultural mores regarding adolescent sexuality. Included here would be matters associated with cultures in which very early marriage is accepted or encouraged as a norm. Non-governmental organisations are also better placed to deal with other cultural issues, such as the question of sex segregation, particularly in its consequences for educational equality and opportunity and religious doctrines or teaching which are part of a climate in which the encouragement of moral restraint in sexual relationships is favoured. Often, NGOs are well placed to be able sensitively to contribute to changing such a cultural climate and to replace negative or censorious approaches with attitudes which promote a positive approach to sexuality and programmes of education in this domain.

We would also suggest that non-governmental organisations are often better placed for work with parents in developing positive and supportive attitudes in the parental role.

THE PARENTAL ROLE

In many ways, programmes which work with parents may be at the heart of making significant and lasting changes to problems that, as we noted earlier, have not significantly changed during the last twenty years. Parental attitudes may well be a major influence on the use, or otherwise, of contraception by teenagers. Parental attitude is probably a major factor in determining the level and availability of adequate sexual- reproductive- and health-related educational information. In particular, there is evidence that parents can develop a high degree of personalised preventative motivation in their children and provide, or direct them towards, balanced and rational information. It is also true that often a parent or parents are best able to help develop the self-confidence and communication skills which may help teenagers or adolescents to feel able make positive choices and decisions related to their own sexuality. Here again we would emphasise that, in the case of Britain and, possibly, some other European countries, we would wish to see further involvement of fathers, male siblings and relatives and other males in this. Finally, though not exclusively, we also consider that parents are often best placed to encourage and develop easy access to acceptable services for young people.

In stressing the important role education has to play, a word of caution is in order. In enlisting parents as part of the process of the education of young people about sexuality and reproductive health, there can be an implicit reinforcement of a belief that parents have an ownership of young people, so such an approach can, unwittingly, imply views about parental control and young people's dependency. A reappraisal of the young person's role, and a gradual devolvement of responsibility for health to the young people themselves, should be part of an educational process that is truly empowering.

CONCLUSION

Any educational programme that is put in place cannot stand alone. Such provision needs to seen as part of a coherent and ongoing programme which includes needs assessment, as well as action. That the problems associated with teenage sexuality have appeared to remain constant over the last twenty years ought to act as a spur to encourage and promote further education on a broad front, rather than to see a steady state and containment as a sign of success.

Addressing some of the foregoing issues is the central key in work that needs to be developed and undertaken to unlock significant ways to start to change what, at present, seems to be an unyielding issue.

REFERENCES

International Planned Parenthood Federation (IPPF) (1995) *Planned Parenthood Challenges*. London: IPPF.

Kabir, S., Homans, H. and Newman, K. (1996) 'Where's the sexuality in reproductive health?' Private paper circulated for discussion – for further details contact Mrs Sandra Kabir, Population Concern, 178–202 Great Portland Street, London W1N 5TB. Tel. 0171 631 1546 (direct)/0171 637 9582 (switchboard).

Population Action International (PAI) (1994) *Youth at Risk*. Washington DC: PAI.

Population Concern (1995) *Annual Report 1995*. London: Population Concern.

Population Concern (1996) *Annual Report 1996*. London: Population Concern.

United Nations (UN) (1993) *Sex and Age Distribution of the World Populations*. New York: UN.

United Nations Family Planning Association (UNFPA) (1995) *Youth and Adolescent Health*. New York: UNFPA.

CHAPTER 9

School Exclusion in the UK
An Entitlement at Risk?

Vanessa Parffrey

INTRODUCTION

This chapter argues that some children – particularly certain adolescents – are rendered vulnerable as a result of political and systemic failure and reinforces some of the anxieties expressed by Judy Cashmore in Chapter Three. Such children become scapegoats for that failure and, by being excluded, have their rights to education and proper attention to their emotional and behavioural needs, at best, compromised, at worst, violated. Recent figures showing steeply increasing exclusion rates in the United Kingdom are used to illustrate the point, together with pupils' own perceptions of being excluded. A systemic conceptualisation of the problem is offered and its implications for policy and practice discussed.

POLITICAL AND LEGISLATIVE BACKGROUND

The 1981 Education Act in Britain offered special education a new spirit and a new vision. It was one that promoted inclusiveness, a new entitlement for all children to have their intellectual, physical, emotional and behavioural needs met, wherever possible, within the mainstream classroom. Difference was to be celebrated and embraced; schools worked co-operatively to meet these needs; a sense of shared responsibility for all children predominated. Integration was the key word.

During the 1980s, this positive spirit towards children who were different, and even difficult, grew and flourished. The 1986 Education Act and the Elton Report (1989) focused particularly on the problems of discipline in schools. Both reiterated the spirit of integration and common responsibility and both promoted the need for positive, preventive approaches and clear behavioural policies in order to reduce the disruption in our schools. There were children, of course, who were still not responding to this clarity and were unable to keep within the boundaries of acceptable behaviour as defined by the behaviour policy. For these children, a procedure resulting in their permanent exclusion from the school, or, in some cases, for a fixed term of 4 days, was applicable. For those permanently excluded, alternative schooling had to be found and this was provided either by home tuition or by attendance at a small unit for excluded children. In both cases, once a pupil was excluded from school, it was the local area authority that was responsible for meeting the pupil's educational needs, but was only obliged in law to provide five hours a week of teaching to these children. (This was then reduced to 3 hours in 1993.)

In 1988, the Education Reform Act was passed in the UK. This established a National Curriculum consisting of core subjects with additional cross-curricular input of themes such as citizenship, health education and other broader issues including personal and social education and a consideration of values, attitudes, social skills and moral behaviour. Its main purpose was to provide a common entitlement in education for all children to receive opportunities to promote their spiritual, moral, cultural, social, physical and mental development. However, along with this apparently egalitarian ideology was a series of measures to raise quality and standards in British schools, which thrust schools into an educational market-place. Overnight, the spirit of co-operation and shared responsibility between schools was replaced by competition over the recruitment of pupils. Schools' academic performance results were published for public scrutiny and comparison in league tables and schools suddenly became judged and compared on criteria that, hitherto, had been perceived to be only one of their tasks. Academic attainment alone became the sole indicator of their success. A school's effectiveness in the many other areas deemed relevant and part of a child's education (including those parts referred to in the National Curriculum documents quoted earlier) was, in one swoop, ignored and, consequently, devalued. Thus, because the sole indicator of success was academic attainment, comparison between schools became both public and stressful. Schools became more exclusively interested in only those pupils who could academically perform. One could argue, therefore, that the scene became threatening for the welfare of pupils who, for one reason or another, could not or would not achieve academically. Thus, political, legislative and ideological changes within education meant that the pastoral care and teaching of children with difficulties and differences – particularly behavioural and emotional difficulties – was one of these curricular casualties.

Schools were given charge of their own budgets, which immediately thrust them into matters of choice and ethics. They had to choose how they spent their money – whether, for instance, on books and resources or whether on painting the front of the school or planting a rose garden. Schools became preoccupied with their 'image' and whether that image – of buildings and pupils – would attract consumers. Furthermore, this phenomenon of budget devolution and increased competition for a common, but ever-decreasing, pot of money was also affecting health and social service provision in the UK. Again, whereas previously the three main services impinging on children would collaborate in policy and practice to provide for the needs of difficult or displaced children, now the three services were in competition with each other for money, staff and provision. 'Passing the buck' – abdicating responsibility to another agency – became commonplace.

It could be argued that certain children, therefore, were rendered vulnerable by these legislative changes, both within education and across the entire welfare system. Indeed, one could suggest that the very ethos of the new Act being based, as it was, on market-place economics, created 'human unsaleable goods'. Hence the paradox: the very Act proposed to protect the right and entitlement of all children to a broad and balanced education was, by its very nature and ideological underpinnings, fatally flawed to be able to deliver this promise of protection and entitlement.

The new anxieties over image and performance, I suggest, caused schools to revert to a pre-1981 state of intolerance and impatience towards difference and difficulty; of education for the 'norm', of selection criteria, of segregation, of a narrow definition of the purposes of education. Moreover, with the emphasis on parental choice, this meant greater power to those parents who knew how to choose and felt empowered to make that choice. Some children had such a well co-ordinated parental lobby – the dyslexic, the physically disabled, those with partial sight, for instance – but some did not.

The parents of difficult children are themselves often disruptive or difficult and are often unco-ordinated and ineffective. Typically, many of them are not *au fait* with procedures and bureaucracy. Frequently, they themselves are disempowered, do not like to make a fuss, or to appeal; they often feel guilty or are blamed for their children's behaviour. They often feel bewildered or belligerent at the way their children are being treated. None of these feelings are a good basis on which to build a successful parental lobby. Moreover, the professionals in the system often feel helpless over these children. They, too, are pressed for time with a multitude of demands from a wide range of children and family needs. They, too, often find these children difficult and demanding and solutions slow to find. So, even from the natural advocates within the system from which a special child might reasonably expect support, it might well not be forthcoming.

Children who are not able to conform to the school rules or, for one reason or another, consistently misbehave in classrooms are already a vulnerable group within our schools – already hampered by a variety of emotional and behavioural difficulties. The recent political developments seem to have rendered this already vulnerable group even more vulnerable – vulnerable to exclusion, vulnerable to under-resourced alternatives, vulnerable to having their rights to education, in its fullest sense, violated.

So, we have a socio-political climate which actually fails to protect vulnerable children and, indeed, exacerbates their difficulties. Special needs children within a market economy came to be seen as bad news. One cannot make a profit out of children with difficulties – especially if these are behavioural difficulties.

These developments in the UK – the devaluing of the whole child while overplaying the significance of academic achievement, the insidious beginnings of marginalising a vulnerable, educationally excluded group – were at odds with global concerns with Children's Rights. At this time, momentum was gathering around the drafting of the UN Convention on Children's Rights, resulting in the 1991 ratification including Articles 28 and 29 which stated every child's right to a comprehensive and inclusive education.

The examination of both quantitative and qualitative data collected by the author between 1990 and 1995 is instructive in that it indicates quite clearly some of the consequences of the 1988 Act for disruptive children in our schools.

The figures, combined with what the children themselves have to say about the experience of being excluded from school, demonstrate that recent legislative and ideological developments within the UK clearly compromise their rights under Articles 28 and 29 of the UN Convention and also Articles 12 and 13 regarding children's rights to be heard and have their opinions taken into account in decisions affecting their lives.

EXCLUSION FIGURES

Below are presented the exclusion figures for one area within one rural local authority in Britain in the period 1991–1995. The graphs represent permanent exclusions from a range of schools: city comprehensives, rural comprehensives, primary and special schools. The figures represented as percentages of the total population, when plotted over time, show quite clearly the ever upward trend in the number of exclusions. When plotted in terms of percentage of a school's population, the high excluding schools are reaching two per cent of their total population. Over time, these figures show quite clearly the ever upward trend in the number of exclusions.

The general conclusion from these figures is clear – an ever-increasing tendency for schools to seek exclusion as a solution to the problem of disruptive pupils. The dip during the spring term of 1991 followed by the sharp increase represented in the summer term figures reflect the phenomenon of 'capitation'. This is a day in the school year when total numbers of students are counted and returns made to the local administrative authority. Schools are then allocated their budgets on the basis of how many children they have on roll at that time. Obviously, the more pupils a school has, the more money it receives. Therefore, it is financially advantageous to have as many pupils as possible at this point of census, as each child represents £x. However, after this time, the school can exclude any undesirables with alacrity – they do not lose the money but rid themselves of further trouble and difficulty.

These figures together with those contained in Paffrey (1994) demonstrate that some schools 'hold on' to their pupils better than others – some are less exclusive than others. Is this because they have less disruptive children than other schools, a different catchment area and intake, or is it because of a different set of attitudes, a different policy towards disruption? For instance, the figures show that one particular rural comprehensive excludes proportionately more pupils than any of its inner-city counterparts and even more than a similarly placed school that happens to be one of the largest comprehensives in the country. Also, there is an increase over time of the number of primary schools excluding children, even small, rural ones – hitherto an unknown occurrence. On the contrary, such schools, historically, would often have held on and worked with even the most difficult children as part of a caring, inclusive community. We also see the appearance of the county special schools beginning to exclude children (Paffrey 1994).

It would seem, then, that the entire education system, even those parts designed to cater for children with emotional and behavioural difficulties, is becoming increasingly intolerant and exclusive.

Imich (1994) cites evidence that some schools' rates have trebled in three years. The Government department responsible for education's estimate 1993 figures were double those of 1991 – and they are still rising.

Indeed, there is little dispute as to the reality of the rising exclusion rate. The recent report by the National Association of Headteachers (NAHT 1995) in the UK admits that exclusions have trebled since the right to exclude pupils indefinitely was removed in 1994. Rising numbers of children out of school, then, is indisputable. It is the reason attributed to this rise which is in contention.

Inspection and comparison of these general trends – see Figures 9.1, 9.2, 9.3 and 9.4 – also indicates that:

- Schools that in 1991 were NOT excluding pupils, are now, apparently, less tolerant, for example schools E and F.

- Others are excluding less than previous years, for example schools C and L.

- Schools with a common catchment area, that is schools E, F, G, H, I, reveal quite different exclusion patterns.

It would seem then that the differences between schools cannot be simply accounted for by variance in children's behaviour and/or the catchment area. As other researchers conclude from their evidence: 'Two schools with comparably affluent catchments, similar proportions of pupils with reading difficulties or attendance problems, had suspension rates differing by a multiple of eighteen.' (McManus 1987). Imich (1994) also concludes that differences in

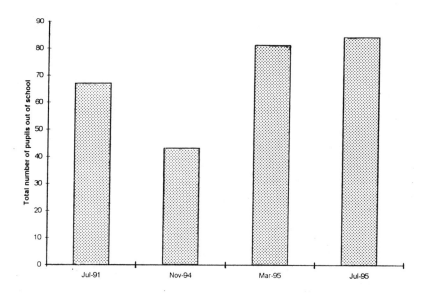

Figure 9.1 Number of exclusions in one area of one LEA, UK

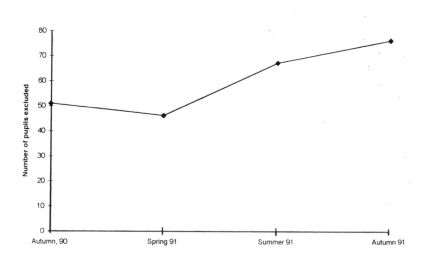

Figure 9.2 Patterns of exclusion over a short-term period

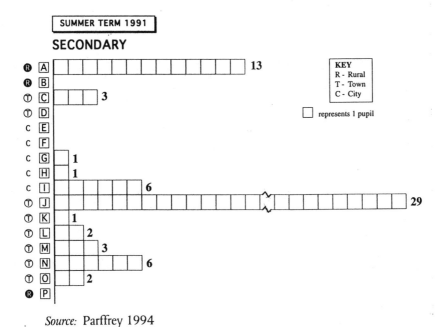

Source: Parffrey 1994

Figure 9.3 Number of exclusions: one area of a local administrative area: UK

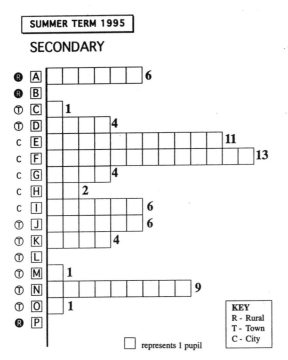

Figure 9.4 Number of exclusions: one area of a local administrative area: UK

exclusions 'cannot be accounted for solely in terms of the socio-economic status of the catchment area.'

It would actually seem as though, rather than trying to explain the rise in exclusions by claiming the deterioration in pupil behaviour, it is in fact, *school* behaviour that is far more likely to account for the variance in the figures.

These figures have also to be understood alongside the nature of the provision for these pupils once excluded from schools. What we find is that provision is often patchy, part-time (minimum three hours, maximum three days) under-funded, under-supported by support services and inadequate to meet the range of needs of excluded children. The staff involved with these children are often on poor contracts and paid less than other teachers working with difficult children. Children also often have to travel large geographical distances to reach any provision, thus being moved away from their natural, local peer group. As an example of the quality of provision for these children, Figure 9.5 represents the children at a joint-funded social service/education resource. This is a unit for children who are both in the care of the local authority and also excluded from school.

Twenty-five per cent of the children in this establishment came from schools for pupils with emotional and behavioural difficulties (EBD schools) and 30 per cent of the other pupils came from just three secondary schools.

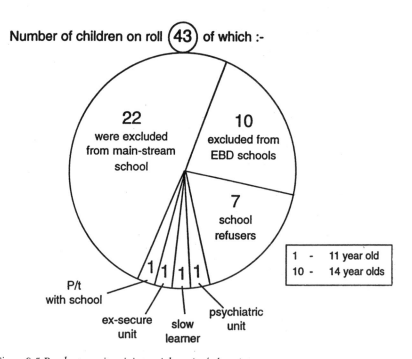

Figure 9.5 Barchester unit: a joint social service/education resource

In addition to these pupils, and those who had been excluded from school (50%), there were also seven children who refused to go to school, one slow learner, one child due to go to the psychiatric unit, one from a secure unit and one pupil on a part-time contract with a local school. The majority were 14 and 15-year-olds but one boy was just 11. One boy was here although he had no social worker involvement – he simply was too young for the exclusion unit that only took 15/16-year-olds.

Issues arising from this and associated data can be summarised as follows:

- Exclusion figures in some schools reach two per cent of that school's population.

- Variability amongst schools despite common catchment areas.

- Increasing numbers of primary schools and special schools for children with emotional and behaviour difficulties excluding children.

- Disempowered parental lobby.

- Schools able to exclude after a certain date and yet still keep the capitation money (this practice was stopped in April 1995).

- Patchy, part-time units having to meet a wide range of pupil needs.

- Political and legislative changes within education, health and social services.

THE PHENOMENOLOGICAL EXPERIENCE

The following represents a summary of interviews undertaken with six adolescents in an exclusion unit and in a social service unit with educational provision on the premises.

Figure 9.6 represents the feelings of the children interviewed. Scrutiny of the original transcripts reveal both these feelings and a number of other phenomena:

1. The general disillusionment, powerlessness and anger amongst the pupils with social services, in particular, and puzzlement at their educational treatment:

   'I'm really angry at the moment – feel like kicking hell out of them all. Well you just wait. At 16, I'm gonna say F...you, arse-holes – thank you and up yours.'

   'I dunno why I'm here'

   'No point being angry – can't do anything about it.'

   'Social workers are pillocks. Think they know how you feel. But they don't, not really.' 'Yeah – they're arse-holes.'

   'They're always mucking me about – foster families and school.'

2. That these children, at best, had 'double the trouble' – experiencing disruption at the hands of both social services and the education authority. Apparently, two systems were failing them and together created yet another net through which they could fall.

> 'Ever asked about all these changes?' 'No – mum had to keep going to meetings. I just got told.'

> 'First time I was ever asked what I wanted to do – first time was last year – first time in 13 years who I want to live with.'

3. Psychological help or counselling was not made available to the pupils despite obvious personal difficulties and even, in some cases, requests to see a psychologist.

> 'Ever see a counsellor/psychologist?' 'Well my mum did ask 'cos a few years ago my brother was killed in a car accident. But I never did – although my mum kept asking...Oh yeah – I did – once – for one hour just before my last exclusion...she gave me tests – maths and reading.'

4. An educational psychologist was seldom seen prior to exclusion and in the one case where s/he was, gave a Maths and English test, arguably totally inappropriate to a child with behavioural problems.

5. Parents were seen but not heard.

6. Many excluded children did value education and did want to do well at school.

> 'I quite like the work – and I can do it. But I like a bit of a laugh as well though... But it's no good, I'm thick now – been out of school four months. Want to do my GCSEs – but I can't here – no facilities, no books...dunno what I'm doing...dunno where I'm gonna end up.'

7. One young person spoke of his 'bored record' – that he was getting into trouble with the police – drugs and petty theft – due to being so bored (it is worth remembering here that obligatory provision is only three hours per week home tuition). At the time of writing, this has now been increased to five hours per week. Others spoke of 'never going out' in case they got into trouble, for example with drugs, at the local arcades, or described a quality of life inappropriate for a young person.

> 'I got kicked out for punching a teacher. I was out of school for six months. That's when I got my criminal record – my "bored record" – couldn't go and get work, nothing...'

EXCLUDED CHILDREN FEEL …

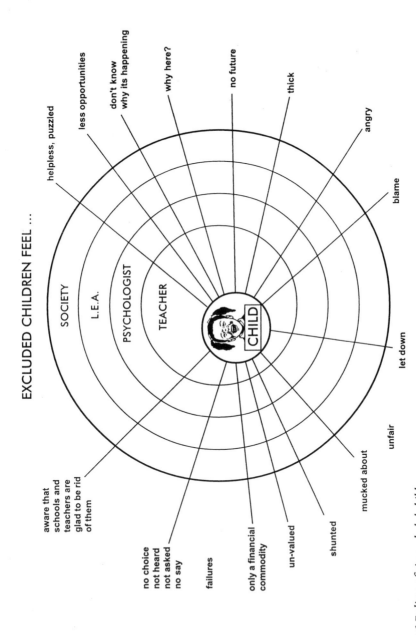

Figure 9.6 Feelings of six excluded children

'I've been in trouble ten times in the last three weeks – mugging a postman, shoplifting...'

'I'm addicted to arcades. They're swarming with drugs... Yeah...but I don't touch anything now – so don't go down the arcades.'

'I haven't got a home tutor. I never go out – just sit at home with my Mum and Dad. Dad's just had his leg amputated – so I just sit there with him.'

8. There is also some evidence that these young people are picked on by police as potential trouble-makers.

> 'The other day I got done for trespassing – I was just taking a short cut through the College – it's open like, often do. Everyone does. And suddenly the police were there, saying I was trespassing.'

9. A hostile reaction to re-instatement by some schools – 'I'm going to make sure you don't stay here for long'. 'I'm going to do all I can to get rid of you' – and a general insensitivity in practice, for example returning an excluded pupil to the tutor from whom he had had previous difficulty.

> 'The Head didn't really want me back. The Deputy said to me when I came back: 'I'm going to do everything I can to get you out.'...Then I got sent to the same tutor. He didn't like me either. He sent letters to the Head about me – about all the things I was doing wrong. So they sent me here'.

10. The pupils were excluded for reasons such as 'running out of class', 'messing about in class', 'having a laugh', 'truancy', as well as more serious misdemeanors such as 'hitting a teacher' but, invariably after 'being teased' or 'humiliated in front of class by a teacher', PE/showers were over-represented in reasons given for this behaviour. It is questionable whether such behaviour, *per se*, would be reason for exclusion in other, inner-city, LEAs for example.

> 'I kicked the Head on the shins 'cos he was chasing me to make me do PE... I was 11 – I used to get beaten up but I'd get my own back.' (This boy was overweight, undersized and hopeless at PE.)

> 'At school, I had a brand new pair of £80 trainers. The PE teacher ripped them off my feet and threw them on the ground.'

11. Excessive moving from one school to another, staying in any one for only a short time.

MARK: 'I've been to four primary schools, two secondary and one EBD school. Now I'm here'.

PHIL: 'Well, I'm 14 now – been to five primary schools and three secondaries.'

12. Evidence that, even when in school, disruptive pupils might be isolated from their peers for long periods of time.

'I had to work alone through all lessons...I wasn't allowed with my friends. Even at break and dinner I was alone... This went on for 4 weeks... Then they threw me out'.

13. Living in one place, school in another and job in another.

'Well, I'm here two and a half days, half a day at my Mum's (15 miles away) and two days of work experience (25 miles away).'

Figure 9.7 represents the views of 12 staff interviewed in the Exclusion Units.

In both sets of interviews, staff and pupils' esteem and hopes were higher when provision was full-time, a broad curriculum was followed, pupils' emotional and behavioural needs were systematically addressed and staff were appointed with equivalent conditions of employment to staff in other establishments. Even here, however, it was pointed out that, with social service provision closure, the type of child coming to the unit was of a much more disturbed nature than was originally intended and, again, a mix of children's needs was having to be catered for out of a budget, and with a staff, originally appointed to cater for other sorts of needs. In particular, the theory, criteria and provision distinguishing EBD, disaffected and psychiatrically disturbed young people, was unclear.

It is noteworthy also in 'What staff feel –' that they mention the trouble they have with referring schools – little or no co-operation during the pupils' stay at the unit and none at all regarding taking them back. Most schools, it would seem, 'just don't want to know':

'We do find it difficult with schools. They're not really interested in putting themselves out. Some schools will not even have them (excluded pupils) back to let them take the exams.'

'I think the system is simply playing with these children.'

The similarity between what excluded pupils and the staff that work with them are saying, is particularly striking. We have, it would seem, almost a ghetto of exclusion – of individuals feeling disempowered, helpless, hopeless, angry, depressed, failed, undervalued, confused and unconsulted. They feel guilty and are liable to blame those whom they consider fail them. Interviews with parents are yet to take place but some preliminary research attempting to obtain the parents' perspective on the issues of exclusion has proved abortive. Very few

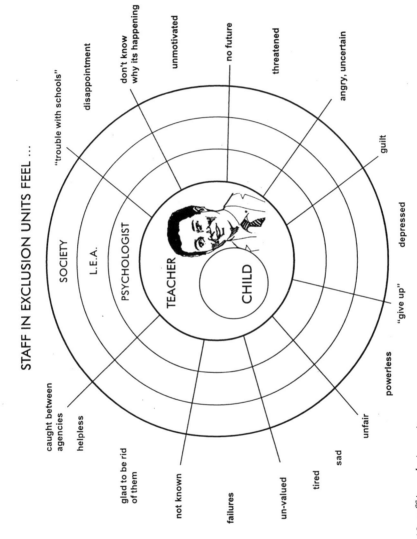

Figure 9.7 *Views of 12 staff in exclusion units*

parents replied to the initial request for information. Might this be that they, too, feel disempowered, hopeless and guilty?

When we listen to these children, we have to ask: whither resilience and independence? whither self-respect? whither the strengthening of the human spirit and the building up of personal reliance and resources?

For these children, it would seem (for their teachers and their parents also, perhaps), there is only powerlessness, hopelessness and a broken spirit.

SUMMARY

I have outlined evidence, both quantitative and qualitative, which reflects on the validity of original hypotheses about the phenomenon of exclusion and its threat to entitlement.

Numbers

The number of children out of school has increased dramatically. Some schools are excluding up to two per cent of their population and none of these pupils have the protection of a Statement (a Statement of Educational Need is a statutory contract in the UK whereby the local administrative authority agrees to make provision for pupils with significant special educational needs). Out of 80 children, 20 had been out of school for over a year. There is still considerable over-representation in units from some schools who are hostile to taking on behaviourally difficult children. Some schools are, apparently, better at holding onto the children than others, while other schools are more obviously image conscious and less tolerant.

Provision

Funding changes to education, health and social services has significantly disrupted local educational provision. One LEA interviewed had no places left at its local EBD school for local children since a neighbouring LEA had bought up all the places. Similarly, one area of a county may buy places in another area, rendering that one bereft of places to place their local children. This creates a situation where children are having to travel large distances away from their community and family base in order to avail themselves of an educational opportunity. This dislocation of lifestyle disrupts opportunities to belong and be known by any particular community.

Provision remains undifferentiated with a potentially unhealthy mix of pupils with different needs lumped together, for example excluded, school refusers, excluded and in care, awaiting EBD place and no proper provision for younger adolescents (11–14) or primary aged children. Provision in at least some local administrative areas is still part-time (three days per week). Children are being placed in provision that is designed as short-term, but then staying, in some cases, for up to two years.

Agencies

Professional support by certain agents in the system, such as school psychologists, is hard to come by. Some argue that psychologists could be natural advocates for Children's Rights in education, but education funding and legislative changes has meant school psychologists' time is predominantly taken up in mainstream schools with pupils with learning difficulties. Excluded and EBD children have low priority in the allocation of time, either as individuals or to their schools and units. Furthermore, psychologists are not obliged to be involved in the pre-exclusion procedure (Association of Educational Psychologists guidelines on Exclusion 1988).

Health service funding arrangements make psychiatric support for EBD schools and units very difficult to finance, despite the fact that all units (and EBD schools) note the increasing level of complexity, difficulty and disturbance of their pupils. Some inter-agency co-operation is evident but that work, at the time of writing, is very much in the planning and rhetoric stage. Key practitioners (and researchers) are not members of appropriate working parties.

Values

Education officers are very aware that schools are paying for LEA services and that they 'must not upset them'. This allows Heads, who so wish, to be obstreperous, demanding and/or refusing children's entry. In the educational (and moral?) market-place, Heads are the dictators, officers the servants and children the losers. Furthermore, some Heads deny that they exclude children – despite clear figures indicating that they do. Others claim their right to 'get rid of children and clear them out...for after all, we are trying to run a business here, you know'.

Bureaucracy

Paperwork demands are lengthy and often not completed in time for key decision-making days for the placement of excluded (or EBD) pupils. This makes the amount of time children are out of school much longer before alternative provision is found.

Pupil experience

The experience of exclusion is negative both for pupils and for staff that teach them.

Parents

There is emerging evidence that parents have little say in the process of exclusion, either by their children being taken into the care of the local authority, or, when they do request help, it is ignored.

One might ask what happens to these children once they have been excluded from their main reference group (the school). A recent report on the exclusion of primary school children concludes: 'The prospect of what these children might become, and what might happen to them, without appropriate provision, is frightening.' (Parsons *et al.* 1994). The children interviewed have talked of their disaffection, anger, the development of their criminal behaviour and isolation from drug-taking peers and family. Other research suggests also that exclusion from school renders children vulnerable to drug abuse (Palin 1996), delinquency (Wragg 1992), homelessness and even, appallingly, extermination (Gonçalves 1996). School exclusion leads, it would seem, not only to social exclusion but to frightening possibilities of vulnerability and potential abuse.

CONCLUSION

It is difficult not to be depressed. The statistical picture is even worse than in 1991 and the political and economic backcloth arguably more likely to increase the vulnerability of some of our children through the creation of an exclusion ethic – an ethic which not only renders children educationally excluded but also puts them socially at risk.

We have a situation which is clearly in direct contravention of Articles 28 and 29 of the the UN Charter on the Rights of the Child. Children are being denied access to an inclusive, broad and balanced education suitably differentiated to meet their particular needs. These children – by definition children whose particular needs are to develop social skills, moral and ethical awareness and a vocational identity and purpose – are denied access to the very opportunities that could meet those requirments. The very areas of the curriculum that could promote independent thinking, positive values and attitudes, team-work, social and spiritual awareness, citizenship and personal skills are 'out of bounds' for excluded children. In three hours a week, a teacher cannot but help concentrate on the basics of reading, writing and subject knowledge, rather than venturing into the unknowns of personal wholeness and empowerment. Moreover, what we also find is that current practice also contravenes Articles 12 and 13 of the UN Charter. Children are not being consulted over major life decisions – they do not have a voice; they are not heard; they do not matter.

In a paper concerned with the social exclusion of vulnerable children, Holman (1993) calls for the 'need for a corporate will and clarity of purpose and priorities...the need for material and social resources to be made available' and 'a spirit of fraternity...and co-operation' if we are to find ways forward out of this apparent impasse.

But, corporateness and fraternity will need to be interpreted far more broadly than simply a couple of agents in the system working alongside one another. It will need schools, units, education officers, social services, school psychologists, teachers and parents, AS WELL AS THE YOUNG PEOPLE THEMSELVES, to be involved in finding creative solutions if all children in our educational system are to have access to the entitlement which is their right.

How might we go about this? First, we need to listen to young people and give them a forum in which to tell their stories. This, in itself, could be empowering. The children interviewed in this chapter were very keen to be heard – it was, they said, the first time they had ever been asked about their experiences or their wishes and they wanted their stories to be told to as wide an audience as possible. Maybe one way forward would be to develop this notion to enable young people to help each other tell one another's stories and to begin to develop solutions for themselves. As Don Cupitt (1991) suggests, through retelling our own stories from the past, so may we create the stories of our futures.

Second, as professionals, we could have greater involvement with difficult children before exclusion – to provide opportunities for reflection, self-awareness and positive self-esteem – so that they are protected by their own personal resources and resilience.

Third, by creating more continuous experiences within any one community or school, so that opportunities to belong, be valued and to contribute may be experienced. Thus might they be motivated and energized by the strength of their own human spirit in community with others.

Such a view presents a challenge to us all. As researchers, how do we ensure our methods empower and enable participation? As school managers, social workers or school psychologists, how do we challenge the attitudes, the denial, the lack of planning, the mutual blame – the downright lack of care about excluded children? How do we ensure prevention and consistency in these children's lives? How do we empower, protect and enable? In short, we need nothing less than a revolution in attitudes about our children; we need a change of heart. But heart-changing can only ever start with ourselves in whatever capacity we might find ourselves: 'The starting point for what's worth fighting for (in schools) is not change in the system or in others...but *change in ourselves.*' (Fullan 1992)

REFERENCES

Association of Educational Psychologists (1988) *Working Party Report on Exclusions from School and the role of the Educational Psychologist*. Durham: AEP.

Cupitt, D. (1991) *What is Story?* London: SCM Press.

Fox, M., Pratt, G. and Roberts, S. (1990) 'Developing the Educational Psychologists' Work in Schools'. *Educational Psychology in Practice 6, 3.*

Fullan, M. (1992) *What's Worth Fighting for in Headship?* Buckingham: Open Univesity Press.

Gonçalves, J. (1996) Chapter 7 in the present volume.

Holman, R. (1993) *Class, Politics and Vulnerability.* Unpublished keynote address at British Psychological Society, Division of Educational and Child Psychologists Annual Conference, Torquay, January.

Imich, A. (1994) 'Exclusions from School: current trends and issues.' *Educational Research 36*, 1.

McManus, M. (1987) 'Suspension and exclusion from High School – the association with catchment and school variables.' *School Organization 7*, 3.

NAHT (1995) *On Pupil Behaviour, Discipline and Parental Responsibilities.* Haywards Heath: National Association of Headteachers.

Palin, W. (1996) Chapter 15 in this volume.

Parffrey, V. (1994) 'Failed children or systems failure?' *School Organisation 14*, 1.

Parsons, C., Benns, L., Hailes, J. and Howlett, K. (1994) *Excluding Primary School Children.* London: Family Policy Studies Centre.

Wragg, E. (1992) 'Seeds of destruction being sown in a three-class system'. *Observer*, May 17th.

CHAPTER 10

Children as Witnesses
in the Crown Court

Etta Mitchell

INTRODUCTION

In the highly acclaimed film *Witness* an 8-year-old boy sees an horrific murder
in the men's room at a train station in Philadelphia. The film goes on to follow
the boy and his mother in their flight from the murderers, protected and helped
by a dashing detective (played by Harrison Ford). The story is, of course,
fictitious but the sad truth is that children sometimes witness violent crimes in
real life. In fiction, a 'happy ending' might involve bringing the culprits to court
and eventually sending them to prison. However, in the real world it is an
unfortunate fact that the legal process, which is supposed to resolve the problem,
can sometimes be almost as traumatic and painful as the original events. Imagine
that this crime happened in England. By taking this imaginary case-study, we
can describe some of the kinds of concern that might face a child witness.

The earliest stages of the investigation would typically involve police
interviews to establish the circumstances and facts of the crime, and to obtain
a statement from the child. This would usually have been done in the presence
of a parent or guardian at the police station. However, if the parent was also a
witness to the crime, or involved in some other way, the child would probably
have been interviewed in the presence of complete strangers. The interview
would be conducted in an interview room within the police station by the
officer in charge of the case. This would normally be someone who has special
knowledge and experience of dealing with children. In the course of the
proceedings the child might often be required to make an identification of the
suspect. If the identity of the suspect was known, this would involve an identity
parade. If the suspect's identity was not known, the child would be asked to
try and make an identification from photographs.

Until 1991, the case would have been sent to the Magistrates' Court where
the child would be called to give evidence. These trials at the Magistrates Court,

known as 'old-style committals' were often used to test a witnesses' evidence and were extremely intimidating for adults and children alike.

PROBLEMS FACING CHILD WITNESS CIRCA 1985

The average time between an accused person being arrested and the trial date is about 9–12 months. Even for adult witnesses this wait is harrowing. Most people would like to 'get on with it and get it out of the way'. The trial and its outcome play a major part in the recovery of victims. The period spent waiting for the trial can, therefore, cause great anxiety. Witnesses know that it is the final hurdle before starting back on the road to recovery. The delay can be particularly difficult for young children because their sense of time is quite different from adults. For example, for a five-year-old, one year is 20 per cent of their whole life! Abstract concepts like time, weight and height are very difficult for them to cope with.

During this period, the child may not be allowed any form of therapy or counselling. The reason for this is the concern that the therapy process may result in suggestions being put to the child about events and emotions surrounding the crime. The problem for the criminal procedure is that it may be these suggestions, rather than the true facts of the case, that could come out in the hearing. In order to protect the defendant's right to a fair trial, it is considered important to avoid such contamination of evidence. The result, however, is that the child's therapy needs may be left unaddressed until after the trial. Occasionally, a different approach is employed. This is a procedure which permits counselling and support, provided that all sessions are video-taped and made available to the Judge so that he or she can ascertain that there has been no contamination of crucial evidence.

FEAR OF CONFRONTING ACCUSED

In very serious cases, the suspects may be kept in custody prior to the trial, and there would be no contact between defendant and witnesses over this interval. However, the witness would often have to confront the defendant in the Court itself. This could be a traumatic event. Handled badly, this confrontation might have taken place in a pre-trial waiting room. In such a situation, defendants, and their supporters, sometimes behaved in a threatening manner towards witnesses. Even when this did not happen the witness may go through the trial in fear of some kind of confrontation or reprisal.

WAITING

Most witnesses have to spend an extraordinary amount of time just waiting within the Court building. They will have been warned to attend Court on the trial date, usually for 10 o'clock on the morning of the first day of the trial.

What they may not have taken into consideration is the fact that various additional procedures have to be dealt with. These include: swearing in the jury, taking the defendant's plea (guilty or not guilty) and the lawyers' opening remarks. All of this takes time. Most Courts cannot function without taking into account all the minor pleas, bail applications, etc., that are most easily handled before full trials commence. This is a necessary part of the Court business but witnesses are frequently left in ignorance of what is happening and this can increase their level of anxiety and concern. For young children there is the very real difficulty of keeping them not only calm but also distracted.

Sometimes witnesses, children and adults, will wait for a trial to begin, only to be sent away without being called to give evidence. This might happen because the Judge has ruled that evidence, or some of it, is inadmissible. This is particularly stressful for victims and witnesses because they tend to think that not enough account has been taken of their feelings and what has happened to them.

UNFAMILIARITY WITH COURT PROCEDURES

Courts, by their very nature, are intimidating. All Court proceedings are highly formal. Dress is designed to set the legal professions apart. The Jury are seated together, the Judge sits high 'on the Bench', the defendant in the dock. Even the ushers and clerks of the court are wigged and robed. In addition to all these procedural considerations, the Court language is unfamiliar. There will be frequent reference to 'mitigation', 'adjournments', 'learned friends', etc. It is not surprising, therefore, that victims find the proceedings daunting and forbidding.

The defence counsel's primary responsibility is to represent the interests of the defendant. Occasionally, the most effective way of defending the case may be to cast doubt on the evidence of the prosecution witnesses. This might involve close and aggressive questioning and this can be threatening and unpleasant for the witness. In the case of a child witness, this aspect of the proceedings can be particularly distressing. Barristers' questions are rarely age-appropriate and often repetitive. This may be particularly upsetting to a child, since repeating a question in different ways may make them feel that the answers they are giving are wrong.

WHAT HAS CHANGED SINCE 1985

In February 1988, Home Office guidelines were sent to Police and Crown Prosecution Service to ensure 'speedy progress' for child abuse cases. These guidelines stated: 'that the damage done by child abusers to their victims must not be added to by avoidable delay in bringing criminal proceedings.'

The Criminal Justice Act 1991 included provisions designed to reduce the stress on young children giving evidence in criminal proceedings. The three main recommendations were:

1. That child abuse cases should be given priority and go straight to the Crown Court without the need for a trial at the Magistrates in which the child would often be called to give evidence (Criminal Justice Act 1991).

2. That, although the child would still have to attend in order to be cross-examined, this part of the proceedings could be conducted by using the live video-link (Criminal Justice Act 1988) in conjunction with the video-taped statements and interviews (Criminal Justice Act 1988, s.32A).

3. That children should not have to swear the oath but should instead be tested for their ability to understand and also tell the truth (Criminal Justice Act 1988).

Of these changes, perhaps the most valuable is the use of video facilities. If it is thought that a TV link would be useful, the prosecution can make an application to the Judge, within 28 days of committal, and it will be on his or her direction as to whether or not it is granted. This is beneficial to the child inasmuch as they will not have to appear in open Court in order to give evidence. However, it should be a priority that the child, in a pre-trial visit, has not only been introduced to the usher who will accompany him into the video-link room but has also seen the video in operation. Measures designed to reduce stress and anxiety can only work if all steps are taken to introduce them to the child. Without doing this, the child's anxiety level will be just the same.

Another innovation has been the use of screens. These were first applied for at the Old Bailey in 1988. The use of screens ensures that, although the child may be in the court-room giving evidence, she is screened from the defendant so that they cannot see one another. It is for prosecuting counsel to apply for screens and it is the Judge's decision as to whether or not they are granted. It is, though, rare for a Judge not to allow the use of screens following such an application.

WITNESS SUPPORT GENERALLY

The above measures in the Criminal Justice Act 1991 were designed to reduce the stress on children who give evidence. These reforms are likely to benefit children most where practical support is made available to prepare them for the experience of going to Court. Over the last few years this has been provided by a number of different agencies such as NSPCC and Victim Support. It was felt that children would feel more confident and better equipped to appear at Court if they understood the legal process and their role within it.

The aim of charities such as the NSPCC and Victim Support is to provide trained volunteers who will help prepare the child for Court, both practically and emotionally. This has been greatly facilitated by the NSPCC provision of a Child Witness Pack. This contains, amongst other things books, activities, a pop-up model of a court and explanations of Court language. A child's confidence can be built up through explaining the roles of the various people and the situations they are likely to encounter. The Child Witness Support volunteers make efforts to encourage the child to reveal fears and misapprehensions about being a witness which, in turn, will allow these concerns to be addressed and reassurance given.

The Crown Court Witness Service was a Victim Support initiative. Following consultation with the Home Office and Lord Chancellors Department in 1990, pilot projects opened in seven Crown Courts in England. It was their success in showing the need for witnesses to have support at Crown Court that led to the Home Office providing funding for a Witness Service in every Crown Court by the end of 1995. The Witness Service aims and objectives are to provide emotional support and practical help for witnesses when they attend Crown Court. For most witnesses this is a terrifying ordeal. For many it will be the one and only time that they have this experience.

FAST-TRACK

Another useful development has been the so called 'Fast-track' system whereby child abuse cases receive special attention and every effort is made to ensure trial at the earliest possible date. This involves all the criminal justice agencies. The aim of Fast-track is to get the case heard within 122 days of the defendant first appearing in the Magistrates' Court. This is a great improvement on the current 9–12 months. It enables full counselling to take place as soon as possible, without the suggestion by the Defence that the child has been rehearsed or had her evidence contaminated.

It is important to note that Fast-track has only been implemented in a few courts to date. In Plymouth, the combination of Fast-track and the Child Witness Support team has greatly improved the situation for young witnesses.

PROBLEMS THAT REMAIN UNADDRESSED

The use of video-taped statements and the video-link are still used at the judge's discretion and an application to the trial judge to use these facilities runs the risk of not being approved if it is thought inappropriate.

It must be borne in mind that most of the above provisions are in place to protect the child victims of abuse. Many other children are victims and witnesses to other crimes. They are treated in the same way as adult witnesses and frequently not even recognised as juveniles. In fact, their worries and fears are just the same as the abuse victims. All cases involving children should be subject to the same rules.

WHAT FURTHER IMPROVEMENTS MIGHT BE MADE IN THE FUTURE?

One of the recommendations made by the 1989 Advisory Group on Video Evidence, the Pigot Committee, (Plotnikoff and Woolfson 1995) was that a child should not have to attend court at all but be examined and cross-examined at an out-of-Court hearing – the results of which could be shown at the trial, together with the original video-recorded interview. The Government did not act on this recommendation because it was felt that there would always be the possibility that a child would have to be called to give evidence again if problems arose, and this would entail two lots of questioning. These recommendations, however, if adopted, would greatly reduce the anxiety for most child witnesses. The hearing would 'appear' to be much more informal without the use of wigs and gowns and it would not have the added dimension of the court room itself.

Given that we are unlikely, in the near future, to adopt the Pigot recommendations, we need to make sure that the impact of the Court appearance on a child is as slight as possible. This could be done by implementing the Fast-Track system in all Courts, thus ensuring that children do not have to spend an unnecessary amount of time waiting for the case to come to trial.

It should also be possible for child witnesses to spend as little time as necessary waiting at the Court. In some areas, for example Newcastle, children can wait at home until telephoned to attend Court. Newcastle Crown Court Witness Service volunteers are allocated to a child. The volunteer will make a home visit in order to prepare the child for their day in court and accompany them when they attend. The child waits at home or at school, with a telephone or pager and, when called to give evidence, will come at short notice. She will enter the Court a short while before giving evidence and leave immediately after, often by a separate entrance.

While the use of screens has undoubtedly been very helpful, it would be in the best interests of the child if the outcome of the application for this facility was known before the trial date. Again, it is the fear of not knowing what is going to happen that is the most difficult for witnesses to deal with. Witnesses of any age would benefit from knowing whether screens will be in place for the hearing.

One major problem with the overall provision for the needs of child witnesses is the lack of consistency in the way they are dealt with. No national good practice guidelines are in operation. Fast-track still remains to be implemented in a number of Courts. The use of these procedures across all of the national courts would itself deal with some of the delays in the system by allowing child abuse cases to be flagged and dealt with within the prescribed time limit. In a study by Plotnikoff and Woolfson (1995), it was concluded that, out of 200 study cases, only 51 were marked as child abuse by the Crown Prosecution Service. Applications for the use of the video-link should be made, by the Crown Prosecution Service, within the 28 day rule. The study shows that almost half were made out of time, on average 76 days after committal. It also found that only five Crown Prosecution Service files conformed to the full endorsement procedures required for expediting the hearing. Finally, examination of case notes revealed little sense of urgency on the part of Judges or listing officers in dealing with the cases, even though the Victims Charter and the Criminal Justice Act 1991 had given unequivocal directions that child abuse cases should be given priority. Clearly, it would be beneficial if the agreed Fast-track procedures were implemented more effectively across the country.

As an additional measure, it would be helpful if listing officers were able to schedule cases involving children in such a way that they begin at a time when they could be reasonably certain that the child would not have to wait unnecessarily. In some Courts, cases involving children are listed to begin 'not before 2.00 pm' (or something similar). This has the advantage that the business of starting the trial, swearing in the jury, hearing the plea, etc., takes place in the afternoon and the child is asked not to attend until the morning of the second day.

CONCLUSIONS

It would appear that several essentials are now in place for the protection of children within the criminal justice system: the provisions of the Children's Act, fast-tracking, video-link, screens and support systems. However, without effective overall, national, monitored guidelines pulling everything together, child victims and witnesses will continue to be marginalised. Their treatment within the criminal justice system is haphazard. We know what we should be doing and we have a fair idea of how it should be done but sometimes it seems that little has changed since 1985.

They deserve better.

REFERENCES

Plotnikoff, J. and Woolfson, R. (1995) *Prosecuting Child Abuse*. London: Blackstone Press.

PART FOUR

Family – A Safe Haven?

CHAPTER 11

Domestic Violence
and Child Contact Arrangements
Children's Right to Safety

Marianne Hester and Chris Pearson

INTRODUCTION

This chapter examines the problems and issues concerning the safety of children which arise from living in a context of domestic violence – where mothers are being assaulted and abused by their male partners. Domestic violence provides a context where not only mothers but also children are likely to be abused and, in such circumstances, contact with the abusive father after the parents separate may not be in the best interests of the child. Contact provides a situation where abuse by violent men of both women and children can continue. The chapter draws on the findings from research, carried out by the authors, into the negotiation and arrangement of contact between children and parents after parents separate.[1] The research focused exclusively on situations where there had been a history of domestic violence.

According to the UN Convention on the Child, children have the right to know and maintain meaningful contact with both parents, should the parents,

---

1   The main findings from the research are published in Hester and Radford (1996). The chapter draws on this and other published material from the research (see Hester and Radford 1992; Hester *et al.* 1994; Hester and Radford 1995; Hester and Radford 1996a). The research was carried out by Marianne Hester and Lorraine Radford with Maja Fogh, Julie Humphries, Anne Mette Kruse, Chris Pearson, Khalida Qaiser and Kandy-Sue Woodfield. It consisted of an ethnographic study of negotiations and arrangements of child contact by 53 women in England and 26 women in Denmark, plus associated professionals and advisors – 77 in England and 22 in Denmark, including court welfare officers, voluntary sector mediators, refuge workers and solicitors.

for example, separate or divorce.[2] This 'right to know' both parents is echoed
by the British Children Act 1989.[3] Guidance on the Act presents contact with
parents as a right of the child and it is generally seen to be in a child's best
interests to know both parents and maintain a relationship appropriate to their
needs and specific circumstances.

Enshrined in the UN Convention regarding children's 'right to know' both
parents is the proviso that it may, however, not always be in a child's best
interests to maintain contact with one or both of the parents if this goes against
the child's welfare.[4] The British Children Act may be seen to contain a similar
proviso. There is a 'welfare checklist' outlined in the Act which gives professionals and courts a guide to ascertaining how a child's best interests are served,
and which includes reference to the wishes and feelings of the child, welfare
of the child and the ability of parents to parent.

However, one of the major shifts in practice which has arisen since the
Children Act came into force in 1991 is a commitment to the idea that contact
should take place at all costs. This was a trend that was already apparent before
the Children Act but has been taken further since then (Smart 1989).[5] The
courts, and many of the professionals associated with the negotiation and
arrangements of child contact, are interpreting the Children Act such that the
'*best interests of the child*' are always equated with *contact* with the absent parent
(Hester *et al.* 1994). This 'paramountcy principle' regarding contact has been
compounded by case law.[6] As a consequence, it has become more difficult to
take issues of safety into consideration in family proceedings. Even formal
evidence of child abuse may not detract from the contact 'paramountcy
principle'. It is even more difficult to have the detrimental impact on the
children of domestic violence taken into account.

---

2 'States' Parties shall respect the right of the child who is separated from one or both parents
   to maintain personal relations and direct contact with both parents on a regular basis, except
   if it is contrary to the child's best interests' (Convention on Rights of the Child 1989, Article
   9).

3 The Children Act 1989 (as well as legislating about child protection and child care services)
   changed the notions of 'custody of' and 'access to' children post-separation/divorce of the
   parents, to 'parental responsibility' and 'contact' – reflecting a change in emphasis from the
   'ownership' of children to 'responsibility' for children. Married parents automatically have
   parental responsibility for their children. Lone mothers automatically have parental
   responsibility and unmarried fathers can apply to have parental responsibility. The
   non-resident parent can apply for contact with the children (Hester and Radford 1996a;
   Eekelaar and Dingwall 1990).

4 '...except if it is contrary to the child's best interests' (Convention on Rights of the Child
   1989, Article 9).

5 Prior to the Children Act there was a shift in judicial decisions from sole custody to joint
   custody of children when parents separated.

6 See Re P (A MINOR) (CONTACT) (1994) 2 FLR 374; and Re F (A MINOR) (CONTACT)
   (1993) 2 FLR 762.

WHAT IS DOMESTIC VIOLENCE?

By domestic violence we mean violence and abusive behaviour used to control and dominate, which, in the vast majority of cases, tends to be violence from men to women (Dobash and Dobash 1992; NCH 1994).[7] The House of Commons Home Affairs Committee suggests that domestic violence involves 'any form of physical, sexual or emotional abuse which takes place within the context of a close relationship. In most cases, the relationship will be between partners (married, cohabiting, or otherwise) or ex-partners.' (1993, p.vi).

Domestic violence is not limited to any particular class, or ethnic or social group, but occurs across the social spectrum – even if it may be experienced differently by women from different contexts (Mama 1989; Kelly 1994; Hester and Radford 1996).

The term 'domestic violence' is clearly problematic. The word 'domestic' appears to limit the context for the violence to those who live together, whereas violence from male partners often continues after women leave (Evason 1982; Binney, Harkell and Nixon 1981; Hester and Radford 1996). The word 'violence' may indicate exclusively physical abuse, whereas women experience a range of different forms of abuse from their violent partners – including physical assault, sexual abuse, rape, threats and intimidation, humiliating and controlling behaviour, deprivation, isolation, belittling and criticising. Frequently the abuse will involve a mixture of these, with the emotional abuse, constant criticism, undermining, humiliation and living in fear having equally detrimental consequences upon the health of victims – as has the physical and sexual violence (Kirkwood 1993; Hester and Radford 1992). As Barron *et al.* (1992) point out, domestic violence may 'include a range of abusive behaviours, not all of which are, in themselves, inherently "violent"'. Moreover, 'domestic violence' masks the issue of gender: the fact that perpetrators are overwhelmingly men and their victims women.

In this chapter the term domestic violence is taken to include all violence and abusive acts against women by male partners, both during and after a relationship, which serve to control and dominate. We favour an approach that takes women's experiences of domestic violence, and the impact of such violence, as the starting point for definition and analysis.[8]

In Britain, the 1990s have brought a growing awareness of domestic violence as a serious and depressingly common crime. Twenty-five per cent of the assaults recorded by the police are cases of domestic violence (British Crime

---

7   NCH Action for Children, in their study on domestic violence and children, suggest that 90–97 per cent of domestic violence is from men to women (1994, p.6).

8   We would argue against the more mechanistic use of 'types' of violence, divorced from individual impact, as such 'types' give an erroneous picture of what domestic violence involves – as exemplified by the Conflict Tactics Scale (see Straus, Gelles and Steinmetz 1980; Johnston 1992).

Survey 1989; Dobash and Dobash 1980). In England and Wales, 45 per cent of female homicide victims – two women per week – are killed by their present or former partners (Criminal Statistics 1992). Domestic violence is widespread in marital relationships (Kelly 1988; Mooney 1994; Mirrlees-Black 1995). The 1992 British Crime Survey data indicates that 11 per cent of women who lived with a male partner had experienced some degree of physical violence within their relationships, although the survey excluded both sexual and emotional violence (Mirrlees-Black 1995). It has been estimated that as many as one in three of all divorces are the result of domestic violence (Borkowski, Murch and Walker 1983). Domestic violence can have a devastating impact upon the health and welfare of both the adults and children concerned.

Domestic violence is unlikely to cease on the separation of the spouses or partners. Violent male partners will continue to abuse and harass their ex-partners and will use any situation where both are present, or in contact with one another, to do so (Hester and Radford 1992; Hester *et al.* 1994). We have found that child contact is often the major flashpoint for the post-separation violence (Hester and Radford 1996; and see Johnston 1992).

DOMESTIC VIOLENCE AND CHILDREN

Domestic violence affects children in many ways, both directly and indirectly. Men who are violent to their wives and partners may be directly physically or sexually abusive to the children. That is perhaps not surprising, as abuse of the children may also be a part of the attempt by some men to control members of 'their' families (Hester and Radford 1992). They may also use the children to further the violence and abuse against wives/partners and children may be assaulted in their attempt to protect their mothers from abuse. Perpetrators of domestic violence probably abuse children physically in 40–60 per cent of cases (Mullender and Morley 1994; Hester and Radford 1996; Bridge Child Care Consultancy Service 1991). Sexual abuse is an issue in perhaps up to 30 per cent of cases of domestic violence, although incidence is difficult to determine from the research which has been carried out so far (Casey 1987; Hanmer 1989). In our research, twenty-one of the fifty-three women interviewed in England reported that children had been physically and/or sexually abused by fathers, five specifically mentioning sexual abuse. Witnessing violence to their mothers can also be emotionally abusive to children (Saunders *et al.* 1995; NCH Action for Children 1994; Christensen 1988). In our study, the majority of children were reported to be adversely affected by witnessing violence to their mothers (Hester and Radford 1996):

> '...she had nightmares and everything after [witnessing violent assault on mother]... My eldest daughter is affected very, very badly and I mean, she's tried to settle into senior school this year and her teacher's been really worried because of the effect this is having on her.' (*Laura*)

'...he saw a lot of violence and his speech is very delayed.' (*Davina*)

The added impact of racism on black children also needs to be recognised. Umme Farvah Imam (1994), in one example, describes how the children's experience of racism in a refuge created greater pressures on their mother to return to her violent husband. Despite the fact that the children 'were frightened of our father and hated what he was doing to Mum', they found the racism from other children and mothers in the refuge was worse.

What stands out from the way children deal with domestic violence are the various and often complex strategies for survival which children of all ages adopt in order to reduce the violence to themselves and/or their mothers. In our study, these strategies included direct attempts to protect the mother or taking on of responsibility for reducing the violence in other ways, including staying with the violent father after the mother's separation (Hester and Radford 1996; see also Imam 1994; Christensen 1988).

Children of all ages were reported in the study we carried out to have taken on responsibility for protecting their mothers. Two young children tried to stop the repeated violence to their mother by screaming and threatening to hit the father. Another, a six-year-old boy, would deliberately come into the room where his father was being violent to his mother because he knew that the father would not continue hitting and shouting at his mother if he was present. Other children were said to have intervened by screaming at their fathers to stop hitting the mothers or to stop threatening them with knives or other weapons:

> 'On one occasion I'd gone out and when I came back I found her standing by the back gate with a big stick ready to defend me if he attacked me.' (*Rowena*)

In some instances the children had become implicated in the violence through being forced to further the father's abuse. One father, for instance, made a seven-year-old boy kick and punch his mother, despite the child's protestations and crying:

> 'He made them kick and punch me and they did because they were so frightened of him. [boy] kicked me, he punched me in the face. But, when he had done it his father told him he hadn't done it hard enough, and he was to go and put his shoes on and do it harder...' (*Hilary*)

Some of the men had used the children to force the women to stay within the relationship. One father ensured he always had one of the children with him so that the mother could not leave the relationship, as he knew she would not leave without them. Another dangled his nine-year-old daughter over a balcony threatening to drop her if the mother left. (By the end of the research this child lived with the father).

Overall, domestic violence provides a context where abuse of children is likely, but this link tends rarely to be taken into account by the professionals involved in establishing arrangements for children. The professionals and advisors whom we interviewed – in particular, court welfare officers, mediators and, to a lesser extent, solicitors – seemed largely unaware of the implications for children of living in circumstances of domestic violence and the possibility that such violence and abuse would continue after separation of the parents. They tended to separate what they saw as the welfare of children from the context of violence to mothers. For instance, only a minority of the court welfare officers we interviewed felt that cases of child abuse commonly coincided with violence to mothers. The rest felt that there was little overlap, although witnessing violence might sometimes be seen as having an effect upon the children. Even those who focused on domestic violence in their practice felt it was unlikely that domestic violence and the parenting needs of children coincided (Hester and Radford 1996).

There has been increasing recognition in recent years of the problems women face when separating from violent men and that domestic violence should be taken into consideration in cases of divorce and separation. In circumstances of domestic violence it should not be expected – indeed is likely to be dangerous – for ex-partners to negotiate directly with one another about the outcomes for children (or other matters). The government's Home Affairs Committee Report on domestic violence (1993), the report on domestic violence by the voluntary sector organisation 'Victim Support' (1992) and, more recently, the National Standards issued to court welfare officers, express concern about this issue.

However, a number of problems remain. On the one hand, this apparent increase in awareness of domestic violence as an issue in family proceedings also needs to be implemented in the actual practice of the courts and related staff. It remains difficult for situations involving domestic violence to be recognised, largely due to problems of definition and identification. Currently, both court welfare staff and mediators tend to rely on women themselves or women's solicitors to bring up the issue, despite the difficulties women generally have of disclosing violence they have experienced. Systematic screening of all cases for domestic violence is only rarely used (Hester and Pearson 1993; 1996). Moreover, making the link between domestic violence and the need to ensure safe outcomes for children also requires that staff question their adherence to the 'contact paramountcy' presumption. This needs a considerable change in emphasis by family proceedings staff, and by judges in particular.

CHILDREN AND CONTACT

In debates about the reform of child care law leading up to the Children Act, concerns were expressed about the effects upon the welfare of children when contact with fathers breaks down (Law Commission 1986). Although there has been no conclusive research showing that fathers who wanted access to their children post-separation were denied this (Hooper 1994), lobbying by fathers' rights organisations, among others, led to a greater emphasis on fathers' involvement with children post-separation (Smart 1989; Harne and Radford 1994). The 'contact paramountcy' principle since the Children Act came into force can be seen as a direct outcome of this.

Solicitors, mediators and welfare officers interviewed in our study reported an immediate and sustained increase in the rate of applications for contact after the Children Act came into force. The initial increase was caused by absent fathers and grandparents attracted by the publicity which accompanied the legislation.[9] There is a general view amongst the professionals concerned that publicity surrounding the Children Act has given absent fathers the impression that they now have automatic or increased 'rights' to their children – although the Act does not talk about such 'rights' but about 'parental responsibility'. In practice, fathers are, therefore, claiming these perceived 'rights'.

The Children Act gives a bigger role to *both* parents and, in this sense, has increased the focus on *men* as parents to a greater extent than was previously the case. The notion of continued parental responsibility and the emphasis on contact at all costs thus ensures fathers' relationships and responsibilities to care for the child(ren), but without focus on their parenting skills and capacity to care. Professionals in the study often appeared over-optimistic about the parenting skills, prospective care and motives of abusive fathers. In relation to domestic violence, we need to ask whether fathers are actually wanting to pursue contact with their children in order to act out a parenting role or whether they are merely using parental responsibility and contact as a means of continuing their violence towards, and control over, their ex-partner. Our research has come across many cases of the latter. Some of the fathers unable to get access to mothers in our study eventually voluntarily stopped their child-contact visits. This would indicate that, in domestic violence cases, some men have used contact to maintain ties with their ex-partner rather than with their children. When they realise that reconciliation is not possible, contact eventually stops.

CHILDREN, CONTACT AND DOMESTIC VIOLENCE

Our study has confirmed fears that children of women who experience domestic violence are highly at risk from abuse during contact visits (see Brophy 1989; Johnston 1992). Where men continued to be violent to their wives/partners post-separation, that is, in the majority of instances in our study, the possibility

---

9   The Children Act widened the range of individuals who can apply for parental responsibility or contact to include, for instance, step-parents, grandparents and co-parents.

of further violence to children remained. Failure to address the risks or to make provisions for safety meant that, for a substantial proportion of children in our study, contact with fathers had an adverse effect upon their welfare. Instances of child abuse and neglect resulting from contact with fathers included:

- threats to kill the children
- physical abuse – punching, slapping, kicking
- sexual abuse – three of the five instances of sexual abuse from fathers to children, which women mentioned, had taken place during contact
- child snatching and keeping the children against their will
- failure to treat a sick child (this lead to the death of a four-year-old boy who was taken overseas)
- pumping children for information on the mother's whereabouts or activities
- using children to convey threats and abusive messages to women
- involving the children in plans to kill the mother
- neglect and an inability to care for children resulting from alcohol or drug abuse dangerous driving which, in one case, resulted in a whiplash injury to a child
- witnessing violence to mothers – the majority of children were said to have witnessed the abuse of their mothers by fathers on contact visits.

One of the children we interviewed described the following incident taking place during contact:

> '...he (father) was in a really bad mood...and he just grabbed me and started throwing me around and that...he'd hit me before but not like that, 'cos he got me and threw me into the door...' (*Anne, aged 13*)

She was also concerned that her father, at times, used his contact to try and persuade her to let him into the refuge where she and her mother were staying. This she found particularly worrying in view of the father's repeated threats to kill the mother:

> '...sometimes, because my dad like threatened to kill her...when I'd go over there and see him, he would be like, you've got to let me in the refuge...' (*Anne, aged 13*)

For the women involved in our study, it was very difficult to stop contact when problems developed for the children. It was argued that any risk to the child had to be very clearly demonstrated:

> '...the child has to be in obvious, definite danger then they'll, you know, they ask for things proved and double-proved almost.' (*refuge worker*)

But this need for 'proof' is very problematic in terms of emotional, sexual and psychological abuse as there is often no visible supporting evidence, or none that can be tied in firmly with the father's actions. Emotional abuse is particularly likely to be overlooked or minimised. Only few of the professionals appeared to consider the long-term emotional and psychological problems which can be associated with children having lived through domestic violence. However, even where there was proven physical or sexual abuse, there was a worrying tendency to encourage the father's contact and dismiss concerns about the children's reluctance – thereby seemingly legitimising further abuse of the children:

> 'Even where the child has been abused by the father, there's still the question of whether it's better for the child to have some sort of supervised contact with this man and keep this demon under control or just to have this whole area of fear.' (*Solicitor*)

The father in this instance had recently been released from a six-year term of imprisonment for sexually abusing his step-children. Within a week of his release, the father had renewed supervised contact with the children.

Eleven women in the study had actually had contact with social services about some form of child abuse, but that did not necessarily place constraints on, or stop, contact. Women who brought up fears about possible abuse to children reported that they were often seen as obstructive by court welfare staff (Hester and Radford 1996).

It is particularly worrying that some of the children in our study ended up residing with their father, or wishing to reside with him, as a result of the latter's abusive behaviour. This happened in at least five instances. (A total of seven children, including three teenagers, finally ended up residing with the father). In a couple of instances, fathers had threatened suicide in front of the children in order to make women stay and the children wanted to reside with the father to 'protect' him. In two other cases, fathers had sexually abused their children and the children were drawn in by the 'specialness' of the relationship (Hester and Radford 1996).

There is no doubt that children may still have positive feelings for their fathers despite the violence they have witnessed, and possibly experienced directly. But there is also a need to focus on the safety of outcomes for children. We found that where children expressed a wish to stay with or to see fathers, the professionals concerned accepted this quite willingly. In some of the instances where there was prior documented proof of child abuse, supervised contact was used. But where mothers expressed concern about the safety of any contact between children and abusive fathers, this tended merely to be seen as obstructive and hostile. Where children expressed a wish to stay with mothers rather than with fathers, there was a greater focus by professionals on the parenting skills of the mothers concerned than was the case with regard to fathers.

Women in our study whose children remained with the violent man or who returned to live with him after the relationship ended expressed grave concerns about the children's welfare. In one case, the mother suffered a period of clinical depression after her teenage daughter, with the support of the court, returned to live with the ex-husband, who was not the girl's father. The mother's distress arose over the girl's ability to make a rational decision because of the effects upon her of living with violence. Women recognised the effects which abuse designed to dominate and control had upon themselves and feared that their children remained under the control of their ex-partners. Women felt that any possible impact of the father's violent behaviour to themselves or the children, including the impact on children's opinions, tended not to be taken into account (Hester and Radford 1996). In our study, contact only 'worked' in seven out of fifty-three cases, that is there was no further abuse or harassment of the women or children involved.

TAKING CHILDREN'S VIEWS INTO ACCOUNT

The UN Convention on the Child places a focus on children's own views and wishes when parents separate or divorce. This was also introduced as a new and welcome addition to the British Children Act 1989. The Welfare Checklist in the Act indicates that the ascertainable wishes and feelings of the child should be taken into account with regard to contact with parents. Those who tend to see children are court welfare officers, in their role of compiling welfare reports for the courts. It is expected that the wishes of children aged eleven and over are ascertained by talking to the children concerned. Children under this age may also be talked with and/ or observed.

We have found, however, that, far from an increase in attempts to ascertain the wishes of children directly, there appears, in family proceedings, to have been a move away from seeing children since the Children Act. The reason is that court welfare staff – who would be most likely to see and talk to children about contact – are seeing a change in their practice: away from investigation towards reporting. Previously, they would attempt to see children (of all ages) separately from their parents and to make observations of the children in the parents' homes. Increasingly, they merely report the parents' wishes about the outcome for their children and any arrangements that have been agreed through meetings with the parents. We found only a few instances where court welfare officers had attempted directly to ascertain children's views with regard to contact with the absent parent. These amounted to only eight instances out of a total of fifty-three cases (Hester and Radford 1996).

Where professionals do talk with or observe children, there are great variations in the way this information is interpreted or the extent to which it is incorporated in decisions about contact. For instance, professionals may feel that the parents are best able to articulate the views of the children and that what children say cannot be taken at face value. Children are not always listened to as separate individuals and professionals' own value judgments and beliefs may take precedence.

Welfare officers compiling welfare reports may see the children only once or twice before making a report, but those professionals involved in trying to ascertain children's wishes regarding contact may need to do so over a period of time. It might take some children quite a long time to be able to trust another adult enough to be open about what has been happening and what they want. One refuge worker had experienced this with some children in the refuge:

> '…when the welfare officer went to speak to them they wouldn't say anything, so access was granted…and then little by little it started coming out and eventually they stopped the access.' (*refuge worker*)

Even if a child does not have the verbal skills to express her/his wishes directly, there could be many non-verbal indications – which would only be picked up through close observation and investigation. For instance, in one example we were given, a four-year-old girl was seen by refuge workers to be adversely affected by contact with her father:

> '…she may not have been old enough to actually say what was going on, but she was old enough to, like show signs of real depression and withdrawal in a normally bright and bubbly child…' (*refuge worker*)

Many children, despite violence to their mothers or themselves, wish to see their fathers, but some children do not. It is often difficult, however, for children to say that they do *not* want contact with their father – on the one hand because the dynamics of parent-child relationships are such that this might be a very difficult thing for children to do, and on the other hand because professionals may dismiss or ignore children's views. We have found that mediators, and in particular solicitors and court welfare officers, often dismiss children's claims that they do not want to see their fathers in the belief that children are unduly influenced by their mothers. As a result, contact might be established even when children do not want it or when it is not in the best interests of the child.

Where listening to children is concerned, our research in Denmark has produced some interesting findings. In Denmark, when parents do not agree about arrangements for contact after separation, they are expected to attend mediation. This is free, funded by the state and carried out by child-related professionals 'on loan' to the state from child psychology, child psychiatry, child guidance or child social work (see Hester and Radford 1992 for further details of the Danish legislation and discussion of practice). Some of the mediators have also developed a practice of seeing the children separately over a period of time, especially if it becomes apparent that there has been a history of domestic violence and/or child abuse. These mediators feel that seeing the children in this way serves two important purposes: first, the children can talk about their experiences of living in abusive situations and their experience acknowledged and taken seriously and second, the mediators have time to ascertain from the children what contact arrangements they would prefer and to discuss what options are actually possible. Especially interesting is our finding that the more these professionals focus on the children, seeing them separately and discussing their experiences, the greater the likelihood that restrictions on contact (or no contact) is recommended (Hester *et al.* 1994).

In Britain, some women's refuges now have children's workers whose work includes some of the tasks outlined in the Danish example. Workers may talk with children about their experiences of living with domestic violence and help them to deal with the issues involved in leaving violent fathers. The specific needs of black children are also incorporated in some instances (see Higgins 1994). But there is a chronic lack of funding for children's workers. Some workers are funded via the local authorities through the provision of the Children Act Section 17(10) – which requires authorities to fund work with 'children in need'. But, as Thangam Debbonaire (1994) points out: 'With few exceptions, local authorities in England still do not specifically fund the work done in refuges with children, despite the fact that it clearly comes under this definition' (p.159).

CONCLUSION

This chapter has highlighted the links between violence to women from male partners and the abuse of their children, and the importance of taking into consideration children's safety and welfare in relation to such violence. There is a need for professionals involved in the negotiations of arrangements for children post-separation of the parents to focus on the possibility of domestic violence and its impact on both women and children's safety in the long term. Contact with violent fathers should not be presumed to be in the best interest of the child. There is also a need to acknowledge children's experiences of living with domestic violence through the development of direct work with the children themselves.

ACKNOWLEDGMENT

The research was funded by grants from the Nuffield and Joseph Rowntree Foundations. It does not necessarily express the views of these organisations.

REFERENCES

Barron, J. (1990) *Not Worth the Paper: the Effectiveness of Legal Protection for Women and Children Experiencing Domestic Violence.* Bristol: Women's Aid Federation England.

Binney, V., Harkell, G. and Nixon, J. (1981) *Leaving Violent Men: a Study of Refuges and Housing for Battered Women*. Leeds: Women's Aid Federation England.

Borkowski, M., Murch, M. and Walker, V. (1983) *Marital Violence: the Community Response*. London: Tavistock.

Bridge Child Care Consultancy Service (1991) *Sukina: an Evaluation of the Circumstances Leading to Her Death*. London: Bridge Child Care Consultancy Service.

British Crime Survey (1989). London: Home Office.

Brophy, J. (1989) 'Custody law, childcare and inequality in Britain.' In C. Smart and S. Sevenhuijsen (eds) *Child Custody and the Politics of Gender*. London: Routledge.

Casey, M. (1987) *Domestic Violence: the Women's Perspective*. Dublin: Women's Aid.

Christensen, E. (1988) 'Children's living conditions: an investigation into disregard of care in relation to children and teenagers in families of wife maltreatment.' *Nordisk Psychologi 42*, Monograph No. 31.

Debonnaire, T. (1994) 'Work with children in Women's Aid refuges and after.' In A. Mullender and R. Morley *Children Living with Domestic Violence*. London: Whiting and Birch.

Dobash, R.E. and Dobash, R.P. (1980) *Violence against Wives*. Shepton Mallet, Somerset: Open Books.

Dobash, R.E. and Dobash, R.P. (1992) *Women, Violence and Social Change*. London: Routledge.

Eekelaar, J. and Dingwall, R. (1990) *The Reform of Child Care Law: A Practical Guide to the Children Act 1989*. London: Routledge.

Evason, E. (1982) *Hidden Violence: Battered Women in Northern Ireland*. Belfast: Farset Co-operative Press.

Hanmer, J. (1989) 'Women and policing in Britain.' In J. Hanmer, J. Radford and E.A. Stanko (eds) *Women, Policing and Male Violence*. London: Routledge.

Harne, L. and Radford, J. (1994) 'The politics of the family and the new legislation.' In A. Mullender and R. Morley (eds) *Children Living With Domestic Violence*. London: Whiting and Birch.

Hester, M. and Radford, L. (1992) 'Domestic Violence and Access Arrangements for Children in Denmark and Britain.' *The Journal of Social Welfare and Family Law 1*.

Hester, M. and Pearson, C. (1993) 'Domestic violence and mediation: some recent research findings.' *Family Mediation*, Summer.

Hester, M. and Pearson, C. (1996) *Domestic Violence and Mediation – Issues and Problems*. Paper presented to the Socio-Legal Studies Association Annual Conference, Southampton University, April 1996.

Hester, M., Humphries, J., Pearson, C., Qaiser, K., Radford, L. and Woodfield, K.S. (1994) 'Domestic violence and child contact.' In A. Mullender and R. Morley (eds) *Children Living With Domestic Violence*. London: Whiting and Birch.

Hester, M. and Radford, L. (1995) 'Safety matters! domestic violence and child contact, towards an inter-disciplinary response.' *Representing Children 8*, 4.

Hester, M. and Radford, L. (1996) *Domestic Violence and Child Contact in England and Denmark*. Bristol: Policy Press.

Hester, M. and Radford, L. (1996a) 'Contradictions and Compromises: the impact of the Children Act on women and children's safety.' In M. Hester, L. Kelly and J. Radford (eds) *Women, Violence and Male Power*. Buckingham: Open University Press.

Higgins, G. (1994) 'Hammersmith Women's Aid childhood development project'. In A. Mullender and R. Morley *Children Living with Domestic Violence*. London: Whiting and Birch.

HMSO (1992) *Criminal Statistics*. London: HMSO.

Home Affairs Committee (1993) *Third Report: Domestic Violence. Vol II*. London: HMSO

Hooper, C.A. (1994) 'Do families need fathers? The impact of divorce on children.' In A. Mullender and R. Morley (eds) *Children Living With Domestic Violence*. London: Whiting and Birch.

Imam, U.F. (1994) 'Asian children and domestic violence.' In A. Mullender and R. Morley (eds) *Children Living With Domestic Violence*. London: Whiting and Birch.

Johnston, J. (1992) *High Conflict and Violent Divorcing Families: Findings on Children's Adjustment and Proposed Guidelines for the Resolution of Disputed Custody and Visitation: Report of the Project*. California: Centre for the Family in Transition.

Kelly, L. (1988) *Surviving Sexual Violence*. Cambridge: Polity Press.

Kelly, L. (1994) 'The interconnectedness of domestic violence and child abuse: challenges for research, policy and practice.' In A. Mullender and R. Morley (eds) *Children Living With Domestic Violence*. London: Whiting and Birch.

Kirkwood, C. (1993) *Leaving Abusive Partners*. London: Sage.

Law Commission (1986) *Review of Child Law: Custody*. Working Paper No. 96. London: HMSO

Lobel, K. (1986) *Naming the Violence, Speaking out About Lesbian Battering*. Seattle, Washington: The Seal Press.

Mama, A. (1989) *The Hidden Struggle, Statutory and Voluntary Sector Responses to Violence Against Black Women in the Home*. London: London Race and Housing Research Unit.

Mirrlees-Black, C. (1995) 'Estimating the extent of domestic violence: findings from the 1992 British Crime Survey.' *Home Office Research Bulletin 37*.

Mooney, J. (1994) *The Hidden Figure: Domestic Violence in North London*. London: Islington Police and Crime Prevention Unit.

Morley, R. and Mullender, A. (1994) 'Domestic violence and children.: what do we know from the research?' In A. Mullender and R. Morley (eds) *Children Living With Domestic Violence*. London: Whiting and Birch.

Mullender, A. and Morley, R. (1994) *Children Living with Domestic Violence*. London: Whiting and Birch.

NCH Action for Children (1994) *The Hidden Victims – Children and Domestic Violence*. London: NCH Action for Children.

Saunders, A. *et al.* (1995) *It Hurts Me Too: Children's Experiences of Domestic Violence and Refuge Life*. Childline/ National Institute for Social Work/ Women's Aids Federation England.

Smart, C. (1989) 'Power and the politics of child custody.' In C. Smart and S. Sevenhuijsen (eds) *Child Custody and the Politics of Gender*. London: Routledge.

Straus, M.A., Gelles, R. and Steinmetz, S.K. (1980) *Behind Closed Doors: Violence in the American Family*. California: Sage.

Victim Support (1992) Domestic Violence; Report of a National Inter-Agency Working Party. London: Victim Support.

CHAPTER 12

Working With Children
Who Have Been Abused

Ann Catchpole

Thankfully, it is recognised nowadays that children and young people are able to talk as truthfully about events that have happened to them as any adult. Indeed, in many cases, their very youth may be what gives their stories that smack of truth. However, when their voices are heard and their tales believed, there still remains the perplexing problem of what to do. In Britain, the responsibility for investigating such allegations of abuse lies jointly with social services (or the NSPCC) and the police and, from their investigations, either criminal or civil prosecutions may follow. Abusers may be removed from home by force of the criminal law or by the decision of the non-abusing partner, or children may be removed from home as a result of care proceedings or by agreement with a parent who has parental responsibility under the Children Act. More often than not, the child, through lack of proof, may have to stay at home and continue to live under the same roof as the abuser. Whether or not this is the case, it will still be important that the experiences of the child are treated seriously and therapeutic help is offered. This chapter will attempt to explore some of the ways in which this help may be offered, the timing of such help and its impact upon those who offer it. It will do this in the light of the writer's own personal experience of eleven years as a practising social worker and five years of working with the Joint Agencies Child Abuse Team in Exeter.

A PERSONAL PERSPECTIVE

Whatever the work we do, we all bring to that work a particular perspective which is influenced in part by our training and in part by our life experiences. When working with children who have been abused it is important to recognise these influences, so that we can identify their effect upon us, which will, in turn, affect the way we interact with the children. Those influential life experiences which I am able to identify are:

1. A personal experience of 'minor' extra-familial abuse as a child and adolescent, which has made me able to identify with others who have suffered in a similar way and to understand at first hand some of the effects of such abuse.

2. The upheaval of a last-minute evacuation, as a toddler, from Malaya, leaving my father behind to be taken prisoner-of-war, which deprived me of his presence during the early formative years of my life and left me particularly vulnerable to other losses, both small and large, which occurred later, and has made it easier to identify with children who have 'lost' fathers in other ways and for other reasons.

3. The separation for nearly six months from our first-born child while she received specialised treatment for a medical condition which required her hospital admission far from home, which has given me some understanding of the suffering of parents when a child has to be removed from home.

All these experiences obviously affect the way I am with the children and parents with whom I work. The way in which I work with children, and with parents, is also influenced by the way in which I was trained and by other work experience. Fifteen years as a Samaritan in another part of the country gave me a profound sense of the therapeutic nature of listening and of just 'being there' for a person. I still believe that the best chance we have of helping people change both themselves and their circumstances is by giving them hope and by having belief and confidence in them, demonstrated by how we are with them rather than by what we say. In my work as a field social worker, which I do part-time in tandem with my work at the Joint Agency Child Abuse Team, I have seen situations in families radically altered simply because they were, for the first time, listened to properly and their potential for change recognised and acted upon.

I am social work trained and follow no particular 'ism' when I work with children. Much of such expertise as I have has been learned from listening to, and observing, colleagues from other disciplines at work. These colleagues make up the Joint Agencies Child Abuse Team.

THE JOINT AGENCIES CHILD ABUSE TEAM

This team, known by its acronym JACAT, was set up some years ago through the inspiration of the then medical chair of the Child Abuse Team in East Devon, Dr Juliet Gardner. She was concerned by what she perceived to be a gap in the system, whereby many children who had been abused were discussed at such meetings and their names placed on the Register. In some cases, these children were removed from home but were not, in most cases, offered any therapeutic help. This seemed to be partly because such services were not easily obtainable and partly because the need for them was often unrecognised – this was especially the case where sexual abuse was suspected or known about. Although her own background was medical, Dr Gardner saw the importance of a holistic approach to a problem which itself was so all-embracing in its possible consequences. JACAT was, therefore, set up as an agency jointly funded by social services and health. It was given a wide brief, which entailed offering support to all professionals working with children in the field of abuse – whatever its nature – heightening the awareness among other professionals of the nature of abuse – its symptoms, consequences and possible treatment – and working therapeutically both jointly with other agencies and alone with children who have been abused – using individual therapy, family therapy, family work and group work. The members of JACAT come from a variety of backgrounds in the social services and health and their training varies considerably. It has members who are trained as health visitors, occupational therapists, social workers and educational and clinical psychologists. All work part-time for JACAT and part-time in their chosen profession. This emphasis on part-time work is a deliberate policy aimed at keeping its members with their feet firmly set in the real world and enabling them to maintain credibility with the professionals who come for help. The variety of training and background also means that problems can be viewed from a wide angle and the person with the most expertise with a certain age-group or type of abuse made available for the work required. There is no hierarchical structure within JACAT, members support and supervise each other, as appropriate, under the leadership of the co-ordinator, until recently, Dr Gardner herself.

WHY INTERVENE AT ALL?

Therapeutic work with children who have been physically, emotionally or sexually abused is still in its infancy. Thirteen years ago, when I began my training as a social worker, the emphasis lay on changing the home circumstances of the child, with little thought being given to the lasting psychological and emotional effects on the child and still less how these might be ameliorated. Nowadays there is a recognition among at least some professionals that an attempt to work with such children should be made. However, among many parents, schoolteachers and others in day-to-day contact with children and young people there are understandable fears that any attempt at intervention will only make matters worse, as it will keep the memory of that abusive experience alive in the young person's mind. Such fears are not without basis. The forcing of a young person to tell and re-tell his or her story as part of an information gathering exercise or within court procedures can be almost as damaging as the original experience of abuse itself, especially if handled insensitively. On the other hand, I have worked in several cases where teenagers have demanded that they be given the chance to tell their story to the police so that there may be a chance of their abuser being brought to court. In such cases, the re-telling of the story can be therapeutic in itself, as it emphasises that adults believe the child and take his or her allegations seriously. I have also known colleagues who have had a similar experience with a child even as young as five. In working with such children and young people, the emphasis is never on re-telling the history of abuse but rather on activities which increase the sense of self-worth as well as improving the ability of the child to protect himself or herself in the future.

Experience tells us, and research supports this view, that children who have been abused, particularly sexually but in other ways as well, are vulnerable to further abuse, not only in childhood and adolescence (Peters 1988) but within relationships which they make as adults with their partners (Briere and Runtz 1988). In my experience, this link between childhood experience of abuse and adult vitimization is often present where physical abuse or emotional abuse are concerned as well. Many of the women we have worked with at JACAT, because their children have been abused by their partners, turn out themselves to have been both abused as children and to be trapped in an adult partnership which is abusive to them. Attempts to break this chain of abuse, which sometimes goes back generations, is surely one of the best possible reasons for intervening therapeutically where abused children are concerned. If further reasons were needed, they may be found in the often long-lasting effects of abuse in childhood upon the mental health of adults. Research shows that a high percentage of adults in our mental institutions are able to recall profoundly abusive experiences in their childhood which have scarred them emotionally and psychologically. 'Women in the contact abuse group were significantly more likely than women who experienced no abuse...to have experienced at least one major depressive episode since the age of 18' (Peters 1988, p.108). The long-term effects of physical abuse will not be seen only in the area of the physical scars or permanent physical damage, but in the emotional scars suffered by the victim. As a social worker I have observed the effects of this abuse on the profoundly depressed adult, whose needs are so great that it is difficult to meet the needs of the children in the family and whose self-esteem is often so low that he or she chooses a partner who abuses either or both the adult partner and the children. Such parents have a deep-seated desire to protect their children but are often prevented from doing so by their own low energy levels, preoccupation with their own unhappiness or a tremendous sense of guilt that makes it impossible to acknowledge the abuse to which their children have been exposed. In such cases, only therapeutic intervention with both adults and children, together with the necessary changes in the home situation, can hope to have any lasting effect. A small boy with whom I worked expressed to me most succinctly the way in which he saw untreated abuse working: 'Take my lunch-box', he said, 'and put an apple in it. If you leave the apple there in the unopened box it will eventually go bad and send anything else you put into the box bad as well.' Out of the mouths of babes and sucklings...and he was only eight at the time.

WHEN SHOULD ONE INTERVENE?

If therapeutic intervention is to have some hope of success, it needs to be well timed as well as well executed. Work can only be successfully undertaken when the child or young person sees the need and is ready for it, or when the symptoms he or she shows are such as to demonstrate a pressing need for intervention. The 'cry for help' syndrome is well recognised in Samaritan circles and in the field of mental health when suicide attempts are made or other examples of self-harm take place, but in children, the cry for help is often made in other less easily recognisable ways. Schoolteachers are particularly likely to come across these as they observe their pupils: children whose attention span is very poor, who seem to have little sense of their own self-worth, who are quiet and introverted or unusually active and destructive in their play, children who seem to have little consideration for their own safety or the safety of others, children who are afraid to go home and linger in the playground, children who frequently bring notes excusing them from swimming or games which would require them to remove their outside clothing, children who find sitting down or movement painful and who duck all questions about home life or children who behave in an inappropriately sexualised way with other children or adults. All these may be signs of possible abuse of one kind or another and cries for help, but they are often missed. I was once visiting a school when I was told, with some amusement by a male teacher, that a nine-year-old girl pupil had asked him if he'd 'like to have it off with her' behind the bicycle shed. He did not recognise this as a possible indication that the girl might have been sexualised at an early age in a way that was abusive.

Having said that timing is all important, it may be necessary to offer an opportunity for therapy, if circumstances dictate it, even when the child is not necessarily asking for it or recognising the need for it. This is particularly the case with young children where, again, understanding of both what has happened to them and of its potential effects is likely to be non-existent or very limited.

In such cases, time and a therapeutic play setting can be offered and much can be achieved, even at this seemingly low level of intervention. I once worked week-by-week with a small girl, just six at the time, simply chatting with her while we made a model replica of her house, which she had chosen to do. Abuse was not mentioned and the child gave me no leads into what I knew had happened to her. Imagine my astonishment when, at the end of the first term I had spent with her, the school commented on the immense change I had brought about in her behaviour and her demeanour. Subsequently she acted out for me the details of her abuse and we were able to tackle it more straightforwardly. This time, as so often in the past, I found Khadj Rouf's book *Mousie* (1989) most helpful in opening up the topic of abuse and in airing the feelings it arouses. Mousie, despite his name, is a teddy bear, and I keep a timid looking teddy who bears a strong resemblance to Mousie in my repertoire of toys.

HOW FAST SHOULD ONE GO?

The above case illustrates how important the pace at which one tackles work with children is. It must be conducted at a pace which is comfortable for the child, rather than at a pace dictated by the worker or, worse still, by others who have an interest in moving the child on or making his or her behaviour more acceptable in a particular environment. Much harm can be done to a child by attempts to force the pace, although scarce resources, a desire for quick results, and boredom on the part of the worker can all dictate otherwise. One of the serious effects of child abuse brought about by the imbalance of power between abuser and abused is the sense of lack of control over his or her own life which the child experiences. Children who have experienced abuse of any kind may find it difficult to make their own wishes known. Sexually abused children are significantly more likely than non-abused children to be 'overly compliant, too anxious to please, or overly affectionate'. (Conte and Schuerman 1988, pp.157–170). In my experience, this over-compliance has been shown more often by girls. Boys often react with anger and aggression first when attempts are made to help them. If this lack of control spills over into the therapeutic session, then the child must feel helpless indeed. As adults we need to remember, too, how hard it is to trust others sufficiently to confide in them or how difficult it is to explain to our doctor things of an intimate nature, so that we do not expect children to do things which we would be unwilling or unable to do ourselves or try to force them to speak before there has been time to build up a relationship of trust. Children are usually too polite to say 'why should I tell you?' when asked about their feelings, but they often have good cause to do so. I have found various tools that are useful in building up confidence in a child. In each case, they provide a way of saying to the child or young person: 'this is the sort of person I am'. Sharing the poetry of Roger McGough, the Irish Liverpudlian poet – which covers such subjects as burps, bottoms and noses – shows that I am not easily shocked. A thirteen-year-old boy, who does not find reading easy, fell upon McGough's poem about the sack which hides under the bed to escape its owner's smelly feet, and learnt it off by heart. He recites it from time to time with glee. With older children, made-up collections of cards with unintrusive questions on them, which we take in turns to answer, enable us to learn about each other without threat.

HOW FAR SHOULD ONE GO?

As well as thinking carefully about the pace of our work, I believe that we should also recognise that the amount we can cover must be limited by the capacity of the child or young person and governed by his or her willingness to go on. It has been my experience, and that of my colleagues, that it is sometimes necessary to work with children again and again as they enter different stages of their development. This seems to be partly because different questions, or more sophisticated questions, occur to them as they get older or because events in their lives, such as the onset of menstruation or their first serious relationship, throw up difficulties for them or trigger memories long buried. This pattern may continue into adulthood, with the arrival of the first child often arousing uncomfortable emotions. For some women, the guidance of the child may be all important. I have known several cases where mothers have parented a female child very successfully but were unable to cope with a male child who, by his maleness, reminded them of their male abuser. Just recently, I was asked by a young person of fifteen to work through some of her life experiences with her because she had forgotten much of the work we did together when she was eight or it was no longer sufficient to satisfy her. Fortunately, wearing my social work hat, I had remained in contact with her over the years, so she was able to ask me to help her make sense of the questions that were nagging away at her mind to the detriment of her school work – questions which were making her feel unhappy and guilty. I am quite sure that she is now ready to look at things in a much more realistic light than she was when she was younger. At the age of eight she had presented a very idealistic picture of her life at home, which I knew through first-hand experience to be false but to which she needed to cling in order to survive.

IN WHAT WAY SHOULD WE INTERVENE?

Since we have all received different training and have different life and work experience, the tools which we bring to our work are different, but each of us, I am sure, tries to adapt our methods to suit each individual child or young person. There are numerous toys available on the market today which can help a child express what he or she is feeling or demonstrate how the world is perceived. Along with these go books – ordinary books from ordinary book shops, inexpensive and colourful books, with such intriguing titles as *Its Your Turn, Roger* (Gretz 1985), a book for younger children which illustrates the variety of eating habits present in families, or, for the older child, *Goodnight Mr. Tom* (Magorian 1983), the story of a boy aged eight who is evacuated during the War and finds himself billeted with a gruff sixty-year-old single man who ends up adopting him when the full extent of the physical and emotional abuse the boy has suffered at home is finally revealed. Another book which evokes strong feelings in its readers is *Can't You Sleep Little Bear* (Waddell 1990). I shall never forget the silent tears which slid down the face of a six-year-old girl to whom I was reading it, giving the first indication of how strongly she felt the absence of a father figure in her life. Many children find it easier to explore the world of feelings if they are allowed to distance themselves somewhat by the use of such things as puppets through which conversations can take place. These puppets often become very special to the children concerned and I make a gift of them at the end of our work together, a reminder of what we have been through together and a source of comfort when the going gets rough. Similarly, the use of drawings and paintings can be helpful in demonstrating feelings or clarifying situations.

For young children, play is the natural medium for exploration and communication and offers the adult a way of 'looking in' on the world of the child in a way which is not threatening. I always carry around in my large work bag, a source of great amusement to my fellow workers, an assortment of items which I feel may be useful in my everyday contacts with children in their houses, away from the more formalised meetings in the therapeutic setting. These include: coloured pens, pencils, crayons, paper and cardboard, glue, scissors, wooden pegs (excellent stand-ins for toy figures) and a selection of books. However, one of my favourite tools is just too heavy to carry around with me: a box of assorted pebbles – some large, some small, some plain, some wonderfully coloured – each capable of representing anything I or the child or young person wants it to represent. Usually I use these pebbles in an early session, as an ice-breaker. Their symbolism never needs to be explained to a child. I remember the glee with which a twelve-year-old girl selected the smallest, dirtiest pebble of all to represent her father who had behaved like a tyrant towards her and whose power she had always feared. Now, for once, she had him at her mercy and could control him at will. When I used these same stones to ask a girl who lived in her house with her, she chose, quite spontaneously, to put them in groups which illustrated their relationship to her. I was able to observe how she had placed all four adult members of her family in one group and placed all the children, including herself, in another group. The imbalance in power and lack of protection and security in that home was there to see at a glance.

I believe that rituals and symbols are both hugely significant in the life of children. They feel comfortable and cared for in pleasurable situations which are repeated week after week. With one child, whom I see in the lunch-hour, I share a picnic meal partly supplied by each of us and she chooses the book that we read while the meal is progressing. Children are generous in their wish to share their love, making cards and pictures which contain affectionate messages and appreciating, in their turn, the recognition of a birthday or Christmas.

I have become increasingly aware of the importance of endings when working with young people and, therefore, of the giving of a small gift as a symbol of continuing care. These are often quite inexpensive but are carefully chosen so that their meaning is clear to the child. Sometimes it is a copy of a book whose sharing has been important and sometimes it is a poem, illustrated by hand and framed, which carries a message of hope for the future. One of my favourites is *Poppies on the Rubbish Heap* by Madge Bray (1991) which she uses at the beginning of her book on working with abused children. It is a poem which is rich in symbolism and which reflects the hope that healing will occur even in the most inauspicious circumstances.

Working with children and young people who have been abused is, at times, rewarding and, at times, frustrating but always it requires a great deal of devotion, as well as carrying with it a heavy sense of responsibility. Sometimes it is the content of what we hear that is burdensome – illiciting in us strong feelings of anger, pity or despair and sometimes it is the frustration of knowing both that a child must continue to live in abusive circumstances because lack of proof prevents any change being possible and also that the therapeutic intervention we would like to offer can, at best, be only a palliative and, at worst, be even counter-productive. Sometimes, at JACAT, we attract the anger of other professionals because we turn down a request to work therapeutically with a child because his or her current circumstances make this work impossible. It can be dangerous to awaken in a child a deeper understanding of what has happened to him or her and to encourage the expression of appropriate emotions when that child will be at greater risk if these emotions are expressed in the presence of his or her abusers.

I have found the use of video to be most helpful here, as it enables more experienced colleagues to view my work rather than merely having my account of what is going on. This was particularly helpful in the work that I undertook with a profoundly deaf teenager, where the fact that I was working with an interpreter brought with it an extra dimension of difficulty. I was constantly struggling with the fact that what I observed was out of synchronisation with what I was hearing, as the emotions expressed by the girl were always a step ahead of the translation. It was an exhausting experience, trying to concentrate on both, and the recording of each session on video enabled me to keep my colleague in touch with events without the need for wearisome repetition. It also allowed me to go back over some of the more important sections to check on my own responses and to see what I had missed or if I should seek further elaboration in later sessions. There was an extra bonus in the symbolic passing on of the burden when I delivered the video to my colleague's pigeon-hole and knew that the burden of its content was no longer mine alone to bear. Work with disabled children is particularly demanding, both in terms of the additional skills of communication and assessment which may be required and also the draining of the worker's emotions. The abuse of any child is abhorrent, but that of a disabled child promotes an extra sense of outrage. Unfortunately, such children seem to be particularly vulnerable to all forms of abuse so such work is vital.[1] As Geoffrey Watson (1989) observes, the connection between disability and vulnerability to abuse is not confined to the field of sexual abuse alone. It applies equally to that of emotional and physical abuse as well: 'Families with handicapped children can have immense frustrations… They may suffer social isolation and cannot see the end to the care. And the child may appear to be totally unresponsive. It is not surprising that carers may develop antagonistic reactions to the child and a negative perception of the child's behavioural difficulties' (pp.113–118). Since disability itself, rather than being a bar to abuse, actually seems to be a possible precondition for it, it follows that those children whose disability makes them ultra dependent and necessitates intimate personal care are likely to be particularly vulnerable. There is an excellent training pack available for those who work in the field of the protection of disabled children.[2] Moreover, it is important to remember that disability of many kinds can make it more difficult for a child to complain, to be understood, to be believed and to give evidence concerning the abuse.

I hope this chapter will have thrown a little light on the experience of working with children and young people who have been abused. There are many men and women up and down the country doing similar work and many others who would do it if only they had the confidence. If I have succeeded in stripping away some of the mystique that surrounds this work, then I shall be satisfied.

REFERENCES

Bray, M. (1991) *Sexual Abuse: The Child's View.* Edinburgh: Canongate.

Briere, J. and Runtz, M. (1988) 'Post sexual abuse trauma.' In G.E. Wyatt and G.J. Powell (eds) *Lasting Effects of Child Abuse.* London: Sage.

Conte, J.R. and Schuerman, J.R. (1988) 'The effects of sexual abuse on children.' In G.E. Wyatt and G.J. Powell (eds) *Lasting Effects of Child Abuse.* London: Sage.

Finkelhor, D. (1984) *Child Sexual Abuse: New Theory and Research.* New York: MacMillan.

Gretz, S. (1985) *It's Your Turn, Roger.* London: Collins.

Magorian, M. (1983) *Goodnight Mister Tom.* London: Puffin.

Peters, S.D. (1988) 'Child abuse and later psychological problems.' In G.E. Wyatt and G.J. Powell (eds) *Lasting Effects of Child Abuse.* London: Sage.

1   On the connection between the child's make-up and his or her vulnerability to abuse, see Finkelhor (1984). Finkelhor's theory is developed in Senn (1989) who looks at the way in which failures which make normal children vulnerable and notes that there are additional factors at work only indirectly related to their intellectual ability.

2   The ABCD Pack: Training and Resource Pack for trainers in Child Protection and Disability. Funded by the Department of Health and produced, in collaboration, by The National Deaf Children's Society, the NSPCC, Way Ahead Disability Consultancy and Chailey Heritage.

Rouf, K. (1989) *Mousie.* London: Children's Society.

Senn, C.Y. (1989) *Vulnerable. Sexual Abuse and People with an Intellectual Handicap.* Downsview, Ontario: G Allan Roeher Institute.

Waddell, M. (1990) *Can't You Sleep Little Bear.* London: Walker.

Watson, G. (1989) 'The abuse of disabled children and young people.' In W.S. Rogers, D. Hevey and E. Ash (eds) *Child Abuse and Neglect.* London: Batsford.

CHAPTER 13

Protecting Children
or Policing Innocence?
The Role of the Mother After Disclosure
of Child Abuse in the UK

Sheila Townsend

THE NATURE OF THE SERVICE

One of the functions of the statutory Family and Child Service provided by the Health Authority in the UK is a therapy group for children who have been sexually abused. Within the service, children are offered group counselling in weekly sessions over a period of about one year. The groups are established in response to the client base to ensure that the child participants are of similar age and experience. Group therapy with abused children is now a common practice among health and social workers within the UK and internationally. It could be said, however, that work with mothers is still emerging as a recognised and valued part of the rehabilitation process.

This chapter will attempt to identify how and why the mothers' group evolved into an organised and professional part of the service to children. The chapter also includes a case study that demonstrates many of the difficulties faced in ensuring the best interests of the child – as defined in Article 3 of the UN convention – are served after disclosure by the child of sexual abuse and the value of professional support to mothers throughout this process. This is, therefore, approaching the issue of the child's right to protection from the perspective of the mothers.

THE EMERGENCE OF THE INITIAL MOTHERS' GROUP

Mothers as the prime carers – identified under The Children Act 1989 – accompanied their children to the therapy sessions and spent the hour-and-a-half session time in a communal waiting room whilst their child was in therapy.

It was observed that as the weeks progressed the mothers were forming themselves into an *ad hoc* support group, sharing their feelings, experiences and problems. In response, the Health Authority decided to offer them a more private room where they could have their own refreshments and a therapist to facilitate the group.

Once established, the value of work with mothers was quickly recognised. It was clear that the work with mothers not only improved their understanding and ability to respond to the process in which they were involved but that this work had a direct impact on the effectiveness of the children's therapy group. The mothers' group became a standard part of the service offered and, through developmental analysis, a systematic approach to work with mothers as part of the child's rehabilitation process was developed. Over time, participation in both groups has become a requirement as work with children has been so greatly enhanced by the mothers' group – obviously children who have no one single primary carer to substitute the mother's role have different needs and are offered an alternative service.

FUNCTIONS OF THE GROUP

The parallel mother and child groups are each confidential. However, the therapists of the two groups work as a team sharing concerns and the direction of the groups and of individuals to inform areas of support and discussion for both the mothers' and children's groups. The group makes mothers feel part of their children's rehabilitation process, rather than distrusted and excluded. It also gives the mothers the skills and understanding to respond appropriately to their children continuously in the time outside the weekly therapy sessions. The group provides a chance for mothers to off-load their views about how difficult it is coping with their children after the disclosure and to be reassured about their child's behaviour and their own role. After disclosure of abuse, mothers feel such intense guilt that they find it hard to judge an appropriate response to their children. When the children are badly behaved, this leads to intense frustration, guilt and anger. The group provides a safe opportunity for mothers to get all those feelings out of their system. It also helps mothers understand the importance of allowing their children to be childish – many people, including mothers, see an abused child as one who has lost their innocence, their 'childhood'. It is important that mothers are able to allow their children to be children, which sometimes results in a regression of their behaviour.

A CASE STUDY

Here we can begin to investigate the pressures on mothers after one or more of their children disclose that they have been a victim of sexual abuse and how, in practice, the mothers' group was able to support one mother and, in turn, her family.

Jenny, aged 11 years, was referred to the child and family service following her disclosure of sexual abuse by her stepfather. After two assessment sessions with a clinical psychologist, it was decided that Jenny would benefit from inclusion in a therapy group for girls aged 10–12 years who had been the victims of sexual abuse. Her mother, Sue, was offered the opportunity to attend a parallel group for the mothers of the girls. Jenny had a three-year-old half-sister, Chloe, who was offered a place in the clinic's créche for the time that Jenny and Sue would be attending their respective groups. The therapy groups were of one-and-a-half hours duration, with an intended run of 16 sessions. There were two therapists, one male and one female, for the girls and one female therapist for the mothers' group.

The background to Jenny's abuse was that her stepfather, Tom, had sexually abused her over a period of some months. At the time, he was having numerous problems – his small business was collapsing and he had begun to drink excessively. Sue had taken on an evening job to help out financially, exacerbating Tom's sense of failure. The relationship between Tom and Sue deteriorated to such an extent that Tom eventually left the family home. However, Sue maintained in regular contact with Tom for his daughter Chloe's benefit. Jenny had little contact with her natural father and Sue did not want Chloe to have the same experience. Time apart gave Sue and Tom the opportunity to re-evaluate their relationship and they began to discuss the possibility of a reconciliation.

Two days before Tom was due to return to the family home, Jenny disclosed to her mother that before Tom had left he had been sexually abusing her. The abuse occurred while Sue was at work. Initially, Tom had watched pornographic videos in Jenny's presence but the abuse had escalated to attempted penetration. Jenny had not disclosed previously because the abuse had stopped when Tom had left, she now feared his return and had found the courage to tell her mother.

Although shocked and devastated by Jenny's disclosure, Sue informed the police. Tom confessed to the allegations and, some months later, was sentenced to 30 months imprisonment. Both Chloe and Jenny were placed immediately on the 'At Risk' register. Sue, in common with the majority of those who have attended groups, felt that this was in part a punishment for her inability to protect her children.

Sue felt powerless in the process of responding to professional agencies and attending case conferences and formal proceedings. Sue's low self-esteem following Jenny's disclosure was compounded by her perception that, unless she complied with all the suggestions and beliefs of the professional agencies, she would 'lose' her children. Whether real or perceived, mothers of sexually abused children commonly feel that their right to be part of defining the best interests of their children has been denied them by professionals. Responding to this concern has been a significant feature in the role of the mothers' group. The response has been at both a personal and practical level. The process and objectives of the professionals is carefully explained to ensure that these are accessible and understandable to mothers and, simultaneously in this process, to rebuild mothers' self-esteem and self-confidence, thus enabling them to voice their concerns and opinions. An example of these feelings can be seen in Sue's case, where she felt under pressure to divorce Tom in order to demonstrate that her children were her primary consideration. Her fears about having her children removed from the home, and her low self-esteem, meant that Sue was unable to devote serious consideration to vital emotional issues. Her relationships with husband and daughters led to a vicious circle in which she was unable to respond to professionals, felt increasingly inadequate and, therefore, became increasingly unable to respond to the professional agencies.

Within the mothers' group, Sue was at first reluctant to speak and share her feelings about her circumstances. Over time, it was revealed that this hesitation to take part was because Sue held ambivalent feelings toward Tom and was fearful of condemnation by the other mothers. In fact, the reverse was true. Many of the mothers admitted to similar feelings. Encouraged by this response, she was able, in subsequent sessions, to share her wish to be reconciled with Tom at some time in the future. Sue felt the abuse had occurred as a result of a particular set of circumstances and would not be repeated. Furthermore, she felt she had contributed to these circumstances and must share some of the responsibility and owed Tom the opportunity to become part of the family again.

This was particularly significant, in terms of the role of the group, as it demonstrated that Sue had regained enough self-confidence to trust her own judgement and value herself as a mother. Sue was able to voice her desire to be reconciled with Tom to the appropriate professional authorities and pursued this intention at all times, making it clear that the safety of her children was uppermost in her priorities. One of Sue's arguments for a reconciliation with Tom was that it was Chloe's right to have access to her father. Sue held this view particularly close to her heart as Jenny's natural father had taken no interest in her, although Jenny was in regular contact with his parents, her paternal grandparents.

Jenny had made good progress in her group sessions, although the therapists felt she was wary of expressing her feelings. With two sessions left to run, Jenny made a further disclosure to the girls' group therapists. She disclosed that her paternal grandfather, with whom she frequently spent the weekend, had been abusing her for as long as she could remember. This disclosure plunged the family into another episode of police interviews, investigation and case conferences. Sue's confidence in herself, and competence as a mother, was further undermined. She had encouraged Jenny's regular visits to her grandparents believing it to be some compensation for her father's lack of interest.

This disclosure led to a court case in itself, the grandfather was accused, and subsequently acquitted, of incest. The disclosure of abuse, and the failure of the court case, further encouraged Sue to seek a reconciliation with Tom. Sue reasoned that Jenny had been sexualised by the grandfather's abuse, making her particularly vulnerable to abuse and, therefore, easier for Tom to abuse her. Jenny appeared to accept her mother's rationale and so Tom's responsibility was lessened.

This is again interesting from the perspective of developing work with mothers, it was clear that Sue had carefully examined the nature of Tom's abuse and had an understanding of the implications of sexualising a child. However, what was also clear was that there were fundamental areas regarding the nature and meaning of child abuse that Sue was unable to accept. With hindsight, it is clear that, while Sue's emotional ties to Tom were so strong, it would be impossible for her to gain a real understanding of the fundamental reasons for Tom's abuse. Although this did not affect Sue's ability to protect her children by policing them, it is clear that this weakened her position as a good role model and educator of Jenny and Chloe.

Soon after the grandfather's court case, Tom became eligible for parole. Sue had maintained her desire for them to be reconciled as a family and Tom had agreed to work toward a reunion. Jenny voiced no objections to the process of reconciliation. Work with Jenny as she has grown older informs us that this was a conscious decision by Jenny and relating to her perception of her own best interests. At the time, however, it was the general consensus of professional opinion that Jenny had been coerced or emotionally blackmailed into such an agreement. Jenny has since explained the motivation for her to accept the process of reconciliation: she felt that her mother's happiness would be greatly enhanced by a reconciliation with Tom and that this, in turn, would significantly enhance the quality of life for both herself and half-sister Chloe. Jenny felt confident that she could protect herself from Tom and that her mother's happiness would have a more profound influence than the discomfort caused to her by Tom's presence in the family home.

Whatever the views held by the family about practicalities, reconciliation was still only a possibility. A plan of action was formulated for Tom's parole. Tom was to remain living with his parents; he was to attend a sex offenders group run by the Probation Service; Sue was to attend the mothers' support group; Tom was allowed one visit a week to the family home to be supervised by Sue; the children would remain on the 'At Risk' register. It was made clear to Sue that she would need to 'police' Tom's visits and that this would be a very difficult task to undertake.

Tom's first meeting with Jenny since her disclosure was carefully planned. With guidance from his probation officer, Tom was primed to apologise to Jenny and to take full responsibility for his behaviour. The meeting took place in the family home, present were the social worker, probation officer, mothers' support group worker, Sue, Tom and Jenny. The first visits were reasonably successful. Sue admitted finding policing Tom's visit harder than she had expected but requested that the visits be increased to two a week.

Approximately four months into Tom's parole, it became apparent that things were becoming tense between Tom and Sue. Sue reported that Tom was becoming increasingly resentful of her vigilant policing, making a hard task even more difficult. He was apparently indifferent to Sue's need to ensure the safety of her children.

Meanwhile, within the mothers' group, Sue's development continued and she began to move closer to the group's vision of mother as role model and educator. It is the firm belief of those providing the mothers' group that mothers need to be strong and confident individuals, able to set the boundaries that prevent their children from becoming vulnerable to further abuse and/or becoming an abuser themselves (see Peters 1988; Briere and Runtz 1988; Young Minds 1994). A vital role of the prime child carer is to teach children how to protect themselves from further abuse and to be good role models themselves by not being abused, this is particularly poignant when figures show that many mothers of abused children are either abused by their child's abuser or were abused themselves as a child (see Gelles and Carr 1980; Browne 1994).

At six months, a review meeting was held. Tom's probation officer reported that Tom had completed his sex offenders group and had attended most sessions. However, he had not been able to contribute and had rejected all attempts to examine his behaviour. In fact, he had started to minimise what he had done – suggesting he had only pleaded guilty to save Jenny from going to court. He adopted the attitude that he had paid his due by going to prison and should be left to get on with his life. In conclusion, the probation officer said Tom must be regarded as having a psycho-sexual problem and had the potential to abuse again. In the light of this report, the meeting decided that no further steps toward a reconciliation of this family could be recommended.

Sue was angry and disappointed. She had worked hard to keep her family intact and felt let down by Tom's inability to do his share. Their relationship deteriorated rapidly. Tom sometimes missed his planned visits and turned up drunk without warning.

Unexpectedly, Sue received a visit from Jane, Tom's 15-year-old daughter from his previous marriage. She had come to see Jenny to tell her she was not alone and that Tom had abused her when she was younger. This information caused Sue to change her view of Tom completely – he was no longer a victim of circumstance but a dangerous persistent sex offender. Sue decided that he had no future role in her or her children's lives and was able to tell him and effectively end their relationship.

PROTECTION *IN* SOCIETY?

From this case study, and others derived from the mothers' group, we are able to draw a range of ideas about both the functions of the mothers' group and also about responses to child sexual abuse from other perspectives. Particularly interesting in this second category is Jenny's experience and response to the two court cases. Contrary to the general view, she did not find giving evidence at her grandfather's trial over-traumatic – it was unpleasant, difficult and something she would not wish to repeat but, nevertheless, her overwhelming feeling was positive. She almost seemed to gain a sense of achievement at having been able to do it. On the other hand, she had very negative feelings about Tom's case – partly because she had been remote from it and uninvolved. Jenny's response to his sentence was of guilt and concern for Tom's welfare. Jenny said that she had wanted the abuse to stop, not for Tom to be punished. This response is not uncommon, many children find the punishment of someone they have been close to hard to deal with when they know it is a result of their disclosure.

Although the reconciliation failed, this still had positive outcomes because Sue was able to reach the decision independently and in her own time, proving herself as a good role model to her children. Through what seemed at times a rather diverse tortuous route, Sue was able to move on from her role as her children's policewoman to become a true protector and regain her competence and confidence as a mother.

It is these elements that demonstrate why Sue's experience is such a good case to advocate work with mothers of abused children. Having been closely involved with many mothers such as Sue over a number of years, I believe that children need to learn the ability to protect themselves and need to learn the appropriate boundaries to be observed. Mothers need to be able to teach and protect their children and aid their development into adults. Children must be protected *in* society, not *from* society. Most importantly, mothers must be good role models by demonstrating how they protect themselves. These are skills that can be learned, but this is a particularly difficult task for mothers with low self-worth and self confidence, making work with mothers of abused children vital.

REFERENCES

Briere, J. and Runtz, M. (1988) 'Post sexual abuse trauma.' In G.E. Wyatt and G.J. Powell (eds) *Lasting Effects of Child Abuse*. London: Sage.

Browne, K. (1994) 'Child sexual abuse.' In 'J. Archer (ed) *Male Violence*. London: Routledge.

Gelles, R.J. and Carr, A. (1980) 'Factors affecting the successful operation of public child protective services/ agencies.' Final Report submitted to National Center on Child Abuse and Neglect. Washington: Department of Health Education and Welfare

Peters, S.D. (1988) 'Child abuse and later psychological problems.' In G.E. Wyatt and G.J. Powell (eds) *Lasting Effects of Child Abuse.* London: Sage.

Young Minds (1994) 'Child sexual abuse – key facts and recommendations.' *Young Minds, May 1994.*

PART FIVE

Young People Responding to a Changing Culture

CHAPTER 14

Violence and Young Minds

Stephen Flood and Peter Wilson

In the U.K. 100,000 children suffer from depression at any given time. Nearly 2 million children suffer from mental health problems, problems which can prevent many children from achieving their potential. Untreated mental health problems create distress not only in affected children but in those who care for them, moreover problems in childhood are associated with continuing or additional mental health difficulties in adult life.

(Young Minds, Annual Review 1994–5)

INTRODUCTION

All children have their ups and downs and go through a range of emotions as they grow up. With the help of those around them, most are able to cope well enough. Some, however, don't do so well. Without the right conditions and support, problems can arise which may have a significant impact on a young person's future and lead to serious difficulties in later life. For some children, various experiences may have rendered them especially vulnerable. For example, they may have experienced traumatic loss in early life or overwhelming abuse or cruelty, either directly or indirectly, through living in situations of domestic violence; others may have been bullied or subjected to racist victimisation at school or in the community; some children may have endured a complex and damaging relationship with a parent; still others may have been born with particular temperamental predispositions that have left them unusually vulnerable to stresses.

How these difficulties manifest themselves varies enormously and the response of every child will be different. But, for many children, these kinds of difficulties will be linked to the onset of mental health problems. Children may become unhappy at school, for example, and refuse to attend; they can have difficulty concentrating and learning; they may become withdrawn, or develop eating or sleeping problems, or perhaps take refuge in substance misuse; others may be more outgoing, more defiant and destructive. Yet these are all examples of what can be termed mental health problems. The severity of these problems varies and their causes are complex, but all mental health problems mitigate against children making the most of their lives and achieving their full potential.

Mental health problems are not uncommon. At any one time in the UK, about one child in five under the age of 16 has some kind of mental health problem. This amounts effectively to the 'two million children' described in our Annual Review and quoted above. Whilst some of these children have problems which can be categorised as mild, and which are likely to remit over time if the child receives proper love, care, understanding and support, many have problems which most professionals would consider 'moderate to severe'. These children have special needs and require extra help at school and in the community over and above that which parents and teachers can provide.

About 40,000 children, which represents about two per cent of children, have mental health problems which are serious enough to be disabling – that is, they are persistent, extreme in the way they present themselves and cause considerable distress to children and those living with them. These children need the specialist services of child psychiatrists, educational psychologists, child psychotherapists and specialist social workers. A small proportion of these children suffer from psychotic illness, usually following the onset of puberty. This affects about 10,000 children and they require specialist psychiatric services.

CHILDREN'S MENTAL HEALTH – SOME KEY FACTS

If mental health problems among children and young people are more common than we would like to think, it is worth reflecting on a few statistics which illustrate rather more starkly what some of this actually means in practice. In England, for example, in 1992, two young people aged 15–17 committed suicide each week. The Samaritans reported that in that same year, seven per cent of their callers were under the age of 15, while in 1993, 22 per cent of all new callers were under the age of 25 (The Samaritans Annual Review 1993/4). A report from the Royal College of Psychiatrists in 1995 suggested that two children in every hundred under the age of 12 are seriously depressed, and a further four or five are showing signs of significant distress and could be said to be on the edge of depression. The rate increases considerably as children get older, with about five per cent of teenagers being seriously depressed and twice that number showing signs of significant distress (Graham and Hughes 1995).

In recent years there has been heightened concern, too, about the levels of anti-social and aggressive behaviour of young people. In 1993, by the age of 14, one in twenty males in England and Wales had either been cautioned or found guilty of an indictable offence, while offenders under 21 years of age were responsible for 45 per cent of all known crimes (Social Trends 24). In 1994, a public policy debate, 'Storing Up Trouble', held jointly by Young Minds and The Child Psychotherapy Trust, revealed that of the children found guilty or cautioned before the age of 15, three out of four go on to commit later offences (Child Psychotherapy Trust 1994). The debate called for greater emphasis on early intervention. It was argued that helping to build relationships and child and adolescent mental health service provision can lead to long-term savings in health, social and prison services by drastically reducing family breakdown and preventing damaged children becoming criminals in later life.

THE EFFECTS OF VIOLENCE ON CHILDREN'S MENTAL HEALTH

The causes of mental health problems in children and young people are complex, but, in an effort to draw attention to the extent of those problems and how they are most often rooted in a combination of social, environmental and biological causes, Young Minds ran a major campaign during 1994 to highlight the effects of violence on the mental well-being of children and young people. The Campaign, 'Violence and Young Minds', had three key aims:

- to raise awareness of the effects of different forms of violence on the mental health of children

- to promote early intervention and highlight examples of the way children and young people suffering the effects of violence can best be helped

- to encourage the provision of a national network of properly resourced, effective multi-professional child and adolescent mental health services.

The campaign focused on various aspects of violence and was launched with the publication of a report on bullying which examined the implications of bullying behaviour for the mental health of children and young people. Subsequent phases of the campaign looked at the initial and long-term effects of child sexual abuse; violence in the family and its effects on the mental health of children; the effects of war on child mental health; and the relationship between televised violence and children's mental health. The outcome of the campaign was a series of reports, debates and workshops, including a day-long symposium which focused on practical measures to prevent family violence (Hankin 1995). The 'Violence and Young Minds' campaign looked at how experiences of violent behaviour, whether subtle or explicit, can contribute to a *culture* in which aggressive behaviour is tolerated and can become a significant factor in the development and persistence of children's mental health problems. The focus on bullying at the start of the campaign was a case in point.

BULLYING

Why it matters

For children, bullying is one of the most commonly experienced forms of violence, yet parents and teachers can easily underestimate the depth of misery and distress suffered by a bullied child. Certainly, falling victim to the school bully is widely feared – four out of ten primary school children who took part in a Gallup survey for BBC Education in 1993, for example, were worried about being bullied when· they moved on to their new school. Yet, despite its prevalence, or perhaps even because of it, bullying has not always been taken seriously. Only within the last ten years has a sound body of research into bullying emerged. What that research makes clear is that bullying is very common, it causes a great deal of distress and, rather more encouragingly, there are effective practical strategies that schools can put in place, both to prevent much of the bullying happening in the first place and also to deal with it when it does occur.

What is it?

Bullying behaviour can be said to have the following defining characteristics:

- it causes physical pain or emotional distress, sometimes both, through the deliberate use of aggression
- the aggression can be physical, verbal or psychological
- the aggression is repeated, not just an isolated incident
- there is an imbalance of power in favour of the bully or bullies.

It is particularly important to recognise that bullying is not restricted to overt physical aggression. Whereas boys tend to bully physically, girls usually rely on more subtle methods, such as spreading nasty stories or socially isolating the victim (Ahmad and Smith 1994). These behaviours are just as hurtful, although teachers and pupils may be less likely to regard psychological victimisation as bullying (Boulton and Hawker 1996). In short, bullying is a continuum of aggressive behaviour which includes name-calling, teasing, ostracising, threatening, hitting and kicking, through to vicious assault.

How widespread is bullying?

Aggressive behaviour is not an unusual feature of childhood. All children are likely to behave aggressively at some time and studies have found that many children admit to having bullied others. A study of over 900 pupils in 10 Scottish secondary schools, for example, found that 44 per cent confessed to having bullied other children (Mellor 1991). The most extensive research into levels of bullying in the UK was carried out by a research team headed by Peter

Smith, then Professor of Psychology at the University of Sheffield (Whitney and Smith 1993; Smith and Sharp 1994).

Based on the pioneering work of Professor Dan Olweus, who was instrumental in the launch of a nation-wide anti-bullying campaign in Norway in 1983, the Sheffield study used anonymous pupil questionnaires to establish levels of bullying and involved 6758 pupils in 24 Sheffield schools in November 1990. An average of 27 per cent of primary school pupils and 10 per cent of secondary pupils report having been bullied at least sometimes that term – 10 per cent and 4 per cent respectively said they were bullied once a week or more. There was a steady decline in levels of bullying as children got older but, although the percentage of victims fell almost year-on-year, the percentage of children bullying others was more stable. This suggests many bullies carry on bullying – they just have fewer victims.

If the Sheffield figures were replicated on a national scale, then as many as 350,000 school children aged 8–12, and over 100,000 pupils at secondary school, could be victims of regular weekly bullying. If those who are being bullied occasionally are also taken into account, then as many as 900,000 children aged 8–12 and 250,000 secondary age pupils may be suffering bullying (Flood 1994a).

Who bullies?

Traditionally, the stereotypical image of a bully has been that of a burly and unpopular coward who picks on the weedy and bespectacled class swot to disguise his own insecurities. As with most stereotypes, the reality is rather more complex. Many bullies are actually no less popular than the average child, although there is evidence from longer term studies in Norway that their popularity declines as they grow older and move through school. Such bullies tend to be self-assured, confident and physically strong, with a positive attitude towards aggression and violence. They are aggressive towards adults as well as peers, are unlikely to see their behaviour as problematic and their feelings of empathy for the bullied child are limited. Olweus found no justification from his extensive research to support the view that apparently self-confident bullies are actually insecure 'under the surface'. Using personality tests, and even stress-hormone level tests, he found that, if anything, many were rather more secure and contented than the average child (Olweus 1993).

Of course, not all bullies are so content and self-assured. To some extent, the 'anxious' bully is rather closer to the traditional stereotype – more anxious and neurotic than other children, likely to be impulsive and easily provoked, a poor performer academically and not at all popular. They are also more likely to display other forms of general anti-social behaviour. A study of over 1000 pupils in 26 primary schools in the north-east of England found that anxious bullies account for about one in five of children who bully. They also found that teachers reported 'anxious' bullies to have few likeable qualities (Smith and Stephenson 1987).

What makes a bully?

There is, of course, no formula which creates a bully, but a number of factors are likely to influence the development of bullying behaviour. Where parents are permissive or tolerant towards displays of aggression, for example, then aggressive behaviour is more likely to develop. Left unchecked, it can escalate and become routine. The use of power-based disciplinary measures, at home or at school, promotes aggression as an acceptable way of resolving conflict, while a lack of warmth and involvement in the child's early years has long been associated with later aggression and hostility. The school environment and the wider local community can also exercise an important influence, either in promoting or suppressing aggressive behaviour (Olweus 1993).

The 'whole-school' approach

The individual culture and ethos of each school is crucial in determining levels of bullying. In a study across ten Scottish secondary schools, rates of those who had recently been bullied varied between 2 and 15 per cent (Mellor 1991). Olweus found that children in some Norwegian schools were four or five times as likely to be bullied as children in other schools within the same community (Olweus 1993). In the Sheffield study, significant variations were found not only between schools but also between different classes within the same school. Schools where teachers openly disapprove of bullying and act promptly to deal with it tend to have the least bullying.

Although specific programmes to counter bullying vary, there is now general agreement that successful approaches embrace the 'whole-school' concept. This requires everyone involved with the school – teachers, playground supervisors, parents, pupils, dinner staff, governors – to work together to develop a positive school culture which openly disapproves of bullying. It is particularly important that schools develop a culture in which 'telling' is seen as positive – only the bully benefits from the secrecy which traditionally surrounds bullying. Even where conditions in the home or community encourage aggression, a school can still promote countervailing standards.

Olweus' research in Norway underlines that prevention and intervention strategies can work. A nation-wide anti-bullying campaign was launched in Norway in 1983 and follow-up research has shown that school intervention programmes can reduce bullying dramatically – over two years, there were falls of up to 50 per cent in both direct bullying, such as physical attack, and indirect bullying, such as ostracising. The fall in bullying was matched by a drop in other anti-social activity, including vandalism, theft and fighting, and children reported also that they enjoyed school more (Olweus 1993). Further follow-up research, though, sounds a note of caution. A school must have an ongoing commitment to its anti-bullying stance and tackle bullying through stable routines; a 'now and then' approach to bullying may even make the situation worse (Roland 1993).

The Sheffield Bullying Project

Of the 24 schools that took part in the Sheffield study in 1990, 23 agreed to take part in an extended Department for Education-sponsored project to measure the effectiveness of different strategies for dealing with bullying. All undertook to implement a whole-school approach, but each school also adopted a more specific intervention. Levels of bullying were measured two years later so that comparison could be made between the different interventions. Most schools were successful in reducing bullying, some considerably (Smith 1994; Smith and Sharp 1994).

The outlook for the bully – does bullying matter?

Although more research is needed to establish the impact of bullying behaviour in influencing the long-term development of both bully and victim, there is evidence that aggressive behaviour which is not effectively challenged in early childhood can carry through into adulthood. A study by David Lane compared 50 disruptive secondary school pupils not involved in bullying with 50 who were generally disruptive but also bullies. Nearly twice as many in the second group had a criminal conviction as young adults. Furthermore, 22 per cent of the convictions of the disruptive/bullying group were for crimes against the person, compared to only 1.3 per cent of the convictions of the disruptive-only pupils (Tattum and Lane 1988). There is also now clear evidence that boys who bully tend to go on to father children who bully (Farrington 1993). Olweus' long-term assessments of bullies in Norway reveal that those who bully are more likely to be involved in general criminal behaviour later in life. Olweus found that 60 per cent of those who were school bullies at age 12 had a criminal conviction by the age of 24. More worrying still, between 35 and 40 per cent had three or more convictions, compared to only 10 per cent of a control group (Olweus 1993).

The outlook for the victim – does bullying matter?

Less is known about the lasting effects of being bullied. Certainly the experience of being bullied can contribute, in the short-term, to increased anxiety, loss of self-belief and interference with academic achievement. Moreover, the experience of being bullied is likely to leave a young person much more vulnerable in the face of adverse life experiences (Rutter 1987). In his twelve-year follow-up of children involved in bullying, Olweus found adults who had been bullied as children had similar problems. They were more likely to suffer from anxiety, depression and to have low self-esteem, although it is difficult to isolate the impact of being bullied from other contributory factors (Olweus 1993). Being bullied can also presage other difficulties in adult life. For example, Gilmartin's study of heterosexual men who had difficulty forming relationships with women found that four out of five had been bullied as children (Gilmartin 1987).

Bullying: a summary

Bullying does matter. Recent research demonstrates that bullying is pervasive and causes very real suffering but there are effective prevention strategies and interventions which schools can put in place. In the short-term, being bullied can cause a lot of unhappiness, affect concentration and academic achievement and can discourage victimised children from attending school. There is evidence, too, to suggest that those children who are aggressive and bully at an early age will often continue to bully if nothing is done. Inaction for fear of making things worse does nobody any favours – all the indications are that bullying will continue if left unchecked. The longer it continues, the more entrenched the aggressive behaviour will become and the more prolonged will be the loss of self-esteem suffered by the victim. As with other forms of violence against children, indications are that doing nothing can reap a bitter harvest in later years.

VIOLENT VICTIMS

Any link between bullying and the later perpetration of violence by the victim of such bullying is neither clear cut nor established, but it can be argued that it contributes to experiences of oppression in a young person's life to which they may not be resilient but react in later life in violent ways. If causal chains are not established, recent research by Dr Gwyneth Boswell of the University of East Anglia suggests early experiences of abuse should not be trivialised or disregarded in their developmental significance.

A report for the Prince's Trust looked closely at the cases of 200 'Section 53 offenders' (Boswell 1995). Children and young people who kill or commit other grave, usually violent, offences are often known as 'Section 53 offenders' because they are sentenced under Section 53 of the Children and Young Person's Act 1933, which makes special provision for juveniles convicted on indictment for murder and other serious offences. She found 72 per cent had experienced emotional, sexual, physical or organisational/ritual abuse, or had been subjected to a combination of these. She also found that 57 per cent had suffered a 'significant loss' of some kind, either through the death of someone important or through the ending of contact with someone important, most often a parent. In only 18 of the 200 cases were there no recorded or personally reported evidences of abuse and/or loss.

CHILD SEXUAL ABUSE

If abusive childhood experiences, particularly physical and sexual abuse, are part of the histories of many adults who violate others, research over the last twenty years has made us uncomfortably aware of just how common those experiences can be. The broadcast in the UK of the BBC *Childwatch* programme in 1986 attracted an audience of 16.5 million, and its launch of the children's telephone helpline, *Childline*, swept away a great deal of ignorance and complacency. It is sobering to recall now that as recently as 1955, in his classic study of incestuous behaviour, Weinberg estimated that there was only one case of incest per million persons per year in English speaking countries (Weinberg 1955).

Reviewing research, Smith and Bentovim (1994) estimate that between 15 and 30 per cent of women in the UK are likely to have been subjected to an unwanted experience of sexual contact as some time during their childhood. This means that between 50,000 and 100,000 of today's 16-year-old girls are likely to have suffered at least one incident of contact sexual abuse at some time in their lives. Similarly, about 19,000 to 38,000 16-year-old boys are likely to have experienced sexual abuse involving bodily contact at some time (Flood 1994b).

Abused and abusers

Community surveys have generally found that the victims of child sexual abuse are fairly evenly distributed across all social classes, with girls outnumbering boys by about 2.5 to 1 and, while the vast majority of abusers are men, recent research suggests that as much as 5–15 per cent of the sexual abuse of children is perpetrated by women acting alone (Smith and Bentovim 1994).

Children and adolescents as abusers

Increasingly, however, evidence suggests a good deal of abuse is perpetrated by other children or adolescents. A study in the USA (Davies and Leitenberg 1987) found one in five of all rapes and between 30 and 50 per cent of all cases of child sexual abuse could be attributed to adolescent offenders. A more recent UK study found that one in three of all males convicted for rape were under 21 (Lloyd and Walmsley 1989). Studies of adult offenders indicate that at least 50–60 per cent committed their first offence as adolescents. Until the last few years, little attention had been given to abuse by peers or older children and adolescents, but community adult surveys have shown that many who had an unwanted sexual experience at the hands of a peer or older child also suffered distress and mental health problems. It is worth noting, too, that research indicates that something like one in two adolescent offenders have themselves been sexually abused (Williams 1994).

EFFECTS OF CHILD SEXUAL ABUSE

Factors associated with increased impact of child sexual abuse

When considering the effects of child sexual abuse, it is important to bear in mind that a number of factors have been consistently associated with a more serious impact on mental health. Abuse which involves body contact is generally associated with a more serious impact on mental health. Abuse which involves bodily contact is generally associated with more serious outcomes than that which does not, while abuse involving penetration, abuse perpetrated by a father/step-father or other trusted adult and abuse where violence or force is used are likely to be particularly damaging. Repeated abuse which endures over a long period is also associated with a more serious impact. Russell (1986) developed criteria for classifying the seriousness of child contact sexual abuse. In ascending order of seriousness, her categories are: kissing and sexual touching while the child is dressed, direct genital touching and digital penetration, oral-genital contact and penetration.

Initial effects of child sexual abuse

The initial effects most frequently associated with children who have been sexually abused include: fear, depression, withdrawal, sexualised behaviour, guilt, sleeping problems, somatic complaints and aggression. Post-traumatic stress disorder and dissociation are not uncommon. For adolescents in particular, truanting, running away, eating disorders and substance abuse are common reactions to abusive situations (Beitchman et al. 1991).

Whereas most emotional and behavioural problems associated with child sexual abuse are also common to general clinical groups of children, inappropriate sexualised behaviour is more specifically linked to a history of sexual abuse. Abused children may display sexually provocative behaviour towards adults because they have come to expect a sexual response and this can itself expose them to risk of further abuse. Depression is often associated with powerful feelings of anger directed at an offending parent, a non-offending parent or even at social services agencies, while anxiety can manifest itself in a number of ways – such as somatic complaints, bedwetting, disturbed sleep patterns, nightmares and experiencing flashbacks. Guilt sometimes develops well after the abuse has taken place and can coincide with disclosure rather than the abuse itself or when, for example, an abusive father has to leave the family home. If the abuse has been coercive and non-aggressive, the abused child may feel partly responsible for what has happened (Flood 1994b). Not surprisingly, child sexual abuse often precipitates a deterioration in academic performance (Tong, Oates and McDowell 1987).

Long-term effects of child sexual abuse

As with other forms of violence, however, the effects of child sexual abuse can continue, at least in some form, over time. Many studies have found an association between sexual victimisation in childhood and a range of difficulties, including complex and persistent mental health problems, in adult life. Most early studies set out to assess the long-term impact of child sexual abuse on clinical populations – such as psychiatric in-patients or psychotherapy patients – but, over the last ten years, community surveys have confirmed that mental health problems persist into adulthood for many survivors of child sexual abuse, not just those who present for treatment (Beitchman *et al.* 1992).

Depression and suicide

Depression is probably the adult mental health problem most commonly associated with experience of sexual abuse in childhood. For example, a community survey of mothers in Islington found that 9 per cent of the women reported having been sexually abused (defined as involving physical contact) before age 17. Of those who had been abused, two-thirds had experienced clinical depression in a three-year period, compared to one-quarter of the rest of the group. Moreover, depression was most common for those who had experienced the most severe abuse (Bifulco, Brown and Adler 1991). A study of clients attending a counselling centre in USA found women with a history of child sexual abuse were 21/2 times as likely to have a history of suicide attempts when compared to those who had not been abused (Briere and Runtz 1988).

Sexual functioning, relationships and marriage

Women who have been sexually abused as children appear to be more at risk of experiencing problems in their sexual relationships, and in partnerships in general, and have reported fear of men, frigidity and promiscuity (Meiselman 1978). Not surprisingly, the effects appear more pronounced where women have been abused by their fathers and in cases which involve penetration and/or physical force. A community survey in New Zealand found that although victims of child sexual abuse were not more or less likely to marry than a control group of those who were not abused, they were twice as likely to have their marriage end in divorce or separation (Mullen *et al.* 1988). Some studies have found an increased tendency to be involved in prostitution and substance abuse amongst those who were sexually abused as children (Silbert and Pines 1981).

Re-victimisation

A particularly disturbing finding suggested by research is that women who have been sexually abused in childhood are more likely than non-abused peers to experience subsequent sexual assault and violence. The reasons for such an association are not clear – it could be that women who have been abused in childhood are forced into more vulnerable lifestyles because they have to leave the family home. Alternatively, given that sexual abuse can adversely affect self-esteem, women may become more vulnerable to sexually exploitative men. An American study of 383 female college students found that there was a significant relationship between sexual abuse in childhood and subsequent coercive sexual experiences – even after the data was assessed to take account of the impact of poor family support for the abused child, child sexual abuse still made a unique contribution (Fromuth 1986).

Cycles of abuse

There is increasing evidence, too, that many of those who sexually abuse children start to do so at an early age. Whilst it must be stressed that only a small number of victims go on to victimise others, studies of child abusers do show that many have been abused themselves. Kevin Browne (1994) cites retrospective studies of adult sex offenders which show that 60 per cent or more of molestors began abusing children as adolescents and that over 50 per cent of paedophiles report having been themselves abused as children. Further, women who have been sexually abused as girls have been found less able to offer adequate protection to their own children, sometimes inadvertently attracting child sexual abusers into their homes.

CHILD SEXUAL ABUSE AND MENTAL HEALTH

The effects of child sexual abuse, then, can be enduring, and when they carry through into adulthood they are not restricted to the early years of adult life. Community surveys have found that women of all ages disclose similar responses, suggesting that the effects of abuse cannot be assumed to remit or ameliorate with the passage of time. Of course, it is important not to underestimate the resilience of children; the consequences of child sexual abuse cannot be easily predicted and no outcome is inevitable. All children are different and individual reactions to abuse vary. But, by providing the right kind of support, and ensuring that support is delivered as early as possible, the chances of a good outcome increases significantly. A number of factors indicate the likelihood of a more positive outcome: that the child is believed, that the child has a positive relationship with an adult – be it the non-offending parent, a grandparent or other carer – that the offender accepts responsibility for the abuse and that the child is not involved in protracted legal proceedings (Flood 1994b). The provision of properly resourced multi-professional children's mental health services is essential for helping children to deal with their experiences, to help them develop into mentally healthy adults and to ensure that the sufferings of one generation are not passed on to the next.

WAR AND REFUGEE CHILDREN

If bullying, domestic violence and child sexual abuse are, sadly, all relatively common experiences for children and young people, it is important not to forget that a small number of children are exposed to other extreme forms of violence. Research carried out by The Refugee Council in 1994 found that there were 24,000 refugee children living in the UK – more than 9 out of 10 living in London (Flood 1994c). There is probably no life experience to compare to having one's home engulfed by war. Direct experience of natural disasters can be profoundly traumatic for children, but the added element of deliberately engineered human catastrophe inherent in armed conflict can damage a child's fundamental faith in humanity. The individual experience of every refugee child is different, but all children who have fled a war zone need practical and emotional support, stability and, above all, they need to feel safe. To meet these children's needs, it is essential to develop a policy that provides support and stability, not only for those children themselves but also for their families, their communities and their schools.

CONCLUSION

This chapter has outlined the incidence and effects of various forms of violence on young minds and examined some of the implications for later adult behaviour and mental health. Some experiences of violence, such as war, we may feel powerless to prevent. But, whatever experiences children have, we can help them cope better and, by appropriate interventions, some forms of violence can actively be prevented. In a volume which looks at resilience in children and young adults, it is worth sounding a note of caution: children are not always as resilient as we might think and their lives are not as unproblematic as we would like them to be. An increased awareness of the short-term consequences on the lives children live might make us more sensitive to listening to them and more vigorous in developing the various ways we can protect them and provide for their full ability to participate as full and responsible citizens in our society.

At Young Minds, our research continually points to the need for a properly co-ordinated national network of child and adolescent mental health services. Research on child and adolescent mental health service provision was commissioned by the Department of Health and published in 1994 (Kurtz, Thornes and Wolking 1994; Hankin 1994). The researchers found that local service provision was patchy, was largely historically determined and was rarely matched to a rigorous and systematic assessment of local need. Whether or not the mental health services were in place to meet the needs of a child and family was largely a matter of luck, dependent on where they were living.

Since then, the Department of Health and the NHS Health Advisory Service have issued valuable guidelines on the provision of child and adolescent services, recommending that services should be jointly commissioned by local health, social services and education authorities in accordance with their carefully evaluated needs (NHS Health Advisory Service 1995; Department of Health 1995). It is vital that the guidance contained in these documents becomes a reality. As we said at the beginning of this chapter, all mental health problems mitigate against children achieving their full potential and making the most of their lives. If we fail to provide adequate services to support children with mental health problems, we are letting them down badly; a mentally healthy child is an empowered child.

For more information about Young Minds, write to 102–108 Clerkenwell Road, London, EC1M 5SA, tel. 0171–336 8445.

REFERENCES

Ahmad, Y. and Smith, P.K. (1994) 'Bullying in schools and the issue of sex difference.' In J. Archer (ed) *Male Violence*. London: Routledge.

Beitchman, J.H., Zucker, K.J., Hood, J.E., da Costa, G.A. and Akman, D. (1991) 'A review of the short-term effects of childhood sexual abuse.' *Child Abuse and Neglect 15*, 537–556.

Beitchman, J.H., Zucker, K.J., Hood, J.E., da Costa, G.A. and Cassivia, E. (1992) 'A review of the long-term effects of childhood sexual abuse.' *Child Abuse and Neglect 16*, 101–118.

Bifulco, A., Brown, G.W. and Adler, Z. (1991) 'Early sexual abuse and depression in adult life.' *British Journal of Psychiatry 159*, 115–122.

Boswell, G. (1995) *Violent Victims: The Prevalence of Abuse and Loss in the Lives of Section 53 Offenders*. London: The Prince's Trust.

Boulton, M. and Hawker, D. (1996) 'Emotional and psychological bullying.' *Young Minds Magazine 26*, 8–9.

Briere, J. and Runtz, M. (1988) 'Symptomatology associated with childhood sexual victimisation in a non-clinical adult sample.' *Child Abuse and Neglect 12*, 51–59.

Browne, K. (1994) 'Child sexual abuse.' In J. Archer (ed) *Male Violence*. London: Routledge.

Child Psychotherapy Trust (1994) *Storing Up Trouble*. London: Child Psychotherapy Trust.

Davies, G.E. and Leitenberg, H. (1987) 'Adolescent sex offenders.' *Psychological Bulletin 101*, 417–427.

Department of Health (1995) *A Handbook on Child and Adolescent Mental Health*. London: Department of Health.

Farrington, D. (1993) 'Understanding and preventing bullying.' In M. Tonry and N. Morris (eds) *Crime and Justice 17*. Chicago: University of Chicago Press.

Flood, S. (1994a) *Bullying: Why It Matters*. London: Young Minds Trust.

Flood, S. (1994b) *Child Sexual Abuse: The Initial and Long-term Impact on Mental Health*. London: Young Minds Trust.

Flood, S. (1994c) *War and Refugee Children: the Effects of War on Child Mental Health*. London: Young Minds Trust.

Fromuth, M.E. (1986) 'The relationship of childhood sexual abuse with later psychological and sexual adjustment in a sample of college women.' *Child Abuse and Neglect 10*, 5–15.

Gilmartin, B.G. (1987) 'Peer group antecendents of severe love-shyness in males.' *Journals of Personality 55*, 467–489.

Graham, P. and Hughes, C. (1995) *So Young, So Sad, So Listen*. London: The Royal College of Psychiatrists.

Hankin, J. (1994) 'Purchaser and provider: a national picture.' *Young Minds Newsletter 19*, 2–4.

Hankin, J. (1995) 'Family Violence: Breaking the Cycle.' *Young Minds Newsletter 20*, 4–5.

Kurtz, Z., Thornes, R. and Wolking, S. (1994) *Services for the Mental Health of Children and Young People in England: A National Review*. London: South Thames Regional Health Authority.

Lloyd, C. and Walmsley, R. (1989) 'Changes in rape offences and sentencing.' *Home Office Research Report No. 105*, London: HMSO.

Mellor, A. (1991) 'Helping victims.' In M. Elliott (ed) *Bullying: A Practical Guide to Coping for Schools*. Harlow: Longman.

Meiselman, K.C. (1978) *Incest: A Psychological Study of Causes and Effects with Treatment Recommendations*. San Francisco: Jossey-Bass.

Mullen, P.E., Romans-Clarkson, S.E., Walton, V.A. and Herbison, G.P. (1988) 'Impact of physical and sexual abuse on women's mental health.' *Lancet 1*, 841–845.

NHS Health Advisory Service (1995) *Together We Stand: The Commissioning, Role and Management of Child and Adolescent Mental Health Services*. London: HMSO.

Olweus, D. (1993) *Bullying at School: What we Know and What we Can Do*. Oxford: Blackwell.

Roland, E. (1993) 'Bullying: a developing tradition of research and management.' In D. Tattum (ed) *Understanding and Managing Bullying*. Oxford: Heinemann Educational.

Russell, D.E.H. (1986) *The Secret Trauma: Incest in the Lives of Girls and Women*. New York: Basic Books.

Rutter, M. (1987) 'Psychosocial resilience and protective mechanisms.' *American Journal of Orthopsychiatry, 57*, 317–331.

Silbert, M.H. and Pines, A.M. (1981) 'Sexual child abuse as an antecedant to prostitution.' *Child Abuse and Neglect 5*, 407–411.

Smith, M. and Bentovim, A. (1994) 'Sexual abuse.' In M. Rutter, E. Taylor and L. Hersov (eds) *Child Psychiatry – Modern Approaches.* Oxford: Blackwell.

Smith, P.K. (1994) 'School bullying – what can we do about it?' *Childright 106*, 17–19.

Smith, P.K. and Sharp, S. (1994) *School Bullying: Insights and Perspectives.* London: Routledge.

Social Trends 24 (1994) London: HMSO.

Stephenson, P. and Smith, D. (1987) 'Anatomy of the playground bully.' *Education,* 18 September, 236–237.

Tattum, D. and Lanes, D.A. (eds) (1988) *Bullying in Schools.* Stoke-on-Trent: Trentham Books.

Tong, L., Oates, K. and McDowell, H. (1987) 'Personality development following sexual abuse.' *Child Abuse and Neglect 11*, 371–383.

Weinberg, S.K. (1995) *Incest Behaviour.* New York: Citadel.

Whitney, I. and Smith, P.K. (1993) 'A survey of the nature and extent of bullying in junior, middle and secondary schools.' *Educational Research 35*, 1, 3–25.

Williams, M. (1994) 'The young abusers project.' *Young Minds Newsletter 18*, 12–13.

CHAPTER 15

Protection Through
the Prevention of Exploitation
The North Devon Project on Drugs

Will Palin

INTERVENTION

The influence of illegal drugs on our everyday lives cannot be underestimated. Open any newspaper, tune in to any radio or television channel and, almost daily, one will read, hear or see news about the drugs problem. The problem – but seldom the solution.

The problem – the increasing strain on our health, prison and probation services and the massive proportion of time our police force and courts spend in solving drug related crime. That is to say nothing of the complete devastation that drugs can, and do, cause to family life.

By the very nature of exploitation, those who are being exploited are largely unaware of their circumstances. The Children's Rights movement, along with all those representing exploited groups, faces a constant dilemma about where to draw the line between intervening to prevent exploitation and intervention for the 'best interests' of the exploited group as arbitrarily determined by those who wish to intervene.

THE EMERGENCE OF THE YOUTH TRUST

The Youth Trust is a registered charity working in North Devon who have tackled this dilemma head-on. The Trust has a deep conviction that where the use of illegal drugs is concerned, intervention is the only viable option. Unlike many other campaigns, the 'Drugs Free' message promoted by The Youth Trust is credible with young people because it comes from a base that respects the views and values of 1990s young people and is blatant in it's aim to prevent the exploitation of young people by adult, organised drug manufacturers and dealers – not to criticise the aspects of young people that make them vulnerable.

The Youth Trust creates a direct link to young people on their streets, on their terms and that is a partnership that is vital in the battle against drugs.

The Trust starts from a conviction that demand reduction is the only long-term solution to the drugs problem. By addressing the causes of initial experimentation, and by reaching the young through role models in sport and popular music, The Youth Trust and its Young Management Team provides a foundation on which young people can take their stand against peer pressure and dealers, to produce a healthy and exciting alternative to the drugs culture.

The Trust is not alone in suggesting an urgent need for a reduction in the demand for drugs and believes that this can only be achieved by some radical rethinking of the problem. A whole counter-culture has developed around the drugs scene in this country, and this has been actively supported by some of the less responsible elements of the art, music and pseudo cultures.

THE AIMS AND OBJECTIVES OF THE YOUTH TRUST

Standing beside the efforts of existing institutions, authorities and agencies, The Trust believes that initiatives have to be taken at street level, where they can be presented as clear and credible alternatives to the drug culture. The Trust, therefore, proposes to offer, initially to the young people of North Devon, a series of projects which they can support and whose success will be dependant upon their own efforts. In parallel with this, the engagement of high-profile artists and sportsmen (the so-called 'cult heroes' of the young) will both fire the imagination and attract the attention of young people and, hopefully, cause them to heed the anti-drugs message which such heroes will deliver. It will be an important feature of the Trusts approach that the Young Management Team will be drawn from the ranks of those who have fully kicked the habit and from those who have not yet been tempted to acquire it. Already, reformed addicts, who can relate to the young, are helping The Trust in the development of its proposals.

In offering to play its full part in the development of actions to combat the drug problem in this country, The Youth Trust sees the need for flexibility of action and a constant flow of information and initiatives from Government to street level and back.

To achieve the objectives of The Youth Trust, a clearly defined line of separation is drawn between the illegal drug user and the non-user. The Youth Trusts primary role is to get to young people before the drug dealer does and to support the fully reformed ex-drug user.

The Youth Trust is already working locally with The Prince's Trust and other charities in a combined effort to relieve the drugs problem and hopes to establish a mutually supportive relationship with Devon Youth Council. Additionally, The Youth Trust recognises and complements the sterling work that is undertaken by other agencies with a broader remit, such as the recently announced Devon Care Trusts 'Devon Against Drugs' campaign.

Although not in the business of rehabilitation, The Youth Trust already works closely at local level with Counselling and Rehabilitation Centres as part of its multi-agency approach. Thereby it creates a two-way referral route for the fully reformed drug user to re-enter the community and for the simply inquisitive, the experimenter or newly addicted to receive professional advice at an early stage.

THE ROLE OF YOUNG PEOPLE IN THE YOUTH TRUST

The Youth Trust has researched into national and international strategies that attempt to reduce the numbers of young people involved in the use of illegal drugs. More importantly, The Youth Trust has consulted directly with young people themselves to seek the reasons why young people turn to drugs. Defining and addressing what causes young people initially to experiment with illegal drugs points, although not exclusively, to the following:

- boredom (lack of prospects)
- lack of incentive and opportunity through employment
- curiosity
- peer pressure
- fashion.

Another major contributory factor, specifically effecting the 14 – 17-year-old age group, is the lack of places to meet. In consequence, members of this easily influenced age group are illegally drinking in pubs, attending raves and night clubs or gathering in the parks and on the streets. This is the drug dealers market-place (the battlefields in the war against drugs).

THE YOUNG MANAGEMENT TEAM

The essential element in the war against drugs are the young people at the front line of the problem – the people who are themselves most at risk. To counter the influence of the 'drugs youth culture', young people need a high sense of confidence and self-worth and clear, honest information to guide their choices. The skills of gaining self-confidence and esteem take time to develop and a great deal of commitment is required by young people to learn all the facts about drugs. To aid this process, and to better inform and guide the direction of The Trust, The Youth Trust incorporates a 'drug free' Young Management Team made up of young people drawn from a cross-section of society. These 18 and 19-year-olds are the role models to whom younger teenagers look for guidance. Together with media-created sport and music heroes, they have, collectively, the greatest influence on the young. It is intended that by giving young people the skills and confidence they need, and by sparking their imaginations with an opportunity to create their own social environment, the alternative to the drugs culture will rapidly take shape.

The conditions of membership of The Youth Trust are that all new members must be known to, and be proposed by, two existing members and that a pledge be signed not to misuse or deal in drugs. If any member of The Youth Trust is found to have done so, then he or she must undertake to seek advice and counselling from a local rehabilitation centre. If not, membership of the Trust will be withdrawn and the member expelled – thereby drawing a clear dividing line between the illegal drug user and the non-user protecting the drug free environment from the dealer. These rules are particularly significant because they are devised jointly by adults and young people and apply equally to both.

THE YOUTH TRUST: ACTIONS!

By tackling the problems that cause drug abuse from the consumer end of the market, the causes and demand can be addressed by separate, but self-supporting objectives:

1. The production, from a primary project, of a commercial and visual educational package for schools, projected by youth's heroes in sport and music and by ex-drug users. The Youth Trust will create a direct conduit to the young, with the aim of halting the very first steps taken in drug experimentation.

2. The raising of public awareness of the risks involved to the young, by reducing peer group pressure and by establishing the basis for a national team-based organisation that supports youth and community at the local level. The Youth Trust will, at the same time, offer levels of training, employment and entertainment to the young, and provide urgently needed recreational facilities at street level.

3. The Youth Trust will encourage young people to initiate, develop, manage and expand such projects with practical support, training and the provision of resources. In this way, young people can conceive an idea, be shown how it can be made viable and be given the opportunity to plan and build that idea into reality. At the same time, they can be employed to learn new and interesting skills, thereby creating a team environment which will involve the local community and give the young people of each locality the opportunity to get off the streets and self-manage their own meeting places as an alternative to 'raves', pubs and the counter-culture of the street.

The founders first met in 1992 and worked part-time for some 18 months on the mechanics of The Youth Trust. It soon became apparent that a very well structured organisation was needed to cope with the enormity of the problem.

The Legal Department of the National Council for Voluntary Organisations was consulted and charitable status was applied for in September 1993. In early February 1994, the Countess of Arran accepted the Presidency of the Trust, the founding board of Trustees was established and a Management Committee was appointed. In May 1994, a headquarters was established in offices in Barnstaple and the Executive undertook to address the initial problems of core funding necessary for the realisation of the Trust's initiatives. The Youth Trust was registered as a Charitable Company on 22 July 1994.

To take the Trust forward, a basic presentation of aims and objectives was produced and, together with a précis, was distributed to potential supporters. A broad-based structure of supporters was built, which included such respected and influential people as Joss Ackland, Phil Collins, Roger Daltry, Rolf Harris and Cliff Richard. All recognised the seriousness of the problem and willingly offered help. Support continues to grow, almost on a daily basis.

Numerous hurdles were overcome in those early days. The nominal rent of the offices had been deferred for six months by The Concert Travel Company and was furnished with desks, built by local carpenters on Community Action and TEC placements, from timber donated by a local North Devon company (Caberboard of South Molton). Office chairs were lent from Office Services and filing cabinets given by the local Green Lanes shopping centre. State-of-the-art computer equipment was donated by Bruce Robertson, Chairman of Trago Mills. Local accountants, lawyers, marketing and PR companies all gave their services free of charge. Meanwhile, the founders and trustees continued to underwrite the ever increasing communication costs.

THE YOUTH TRUST'S JUNIOR GOLF PLAYER OF THE YEAR

Knowing that established forms of funding are thinly spread and widely sought after, it was decided that The Youth Trust should concentrate its efforts on independently resourcing its initiatives through a series of fund-raising events.

A Junior Golf Challenge was held at the Manor House Golf Course (free of charge) at Moretonhampstead. Hosted by the Countess of Arran, the pro-am golf event was staged on 24 August 1994 and supported by 12 sponsored teams. Each team's professional golfer nominated his choice of junior player – the winner receiving The Youth Trust's Junior Player of the Year Shield. The day was a great success grossing over £5,000 for The Youth Trust and concluded with a black tie Gala Dinner with entertainment provided by Rolf Harris.

CONCERTS

As news of The Youth Trust spread, Woody Woodmansky, a well-respected musician, explained the aims of The Youth Trust to Cas Warner, President of Warner Sister Productions in Los Angeles. She sponsored a concert in aid of The Youth Trust and subsequently raised a substantial four-figure sum.

LOCAL SUPPORT

Following continued press, radio and television coverage, a fashion show was staged by Green Lanes, Barnstaple, with Lantern Radio of North Devon nominating The Youth Trust as its chosen charity. This was a great success, with members of the Young Management Team taking to the cat walk. 'No Sweat' of Barnstaple donated a Trek Mountain Bike to the Trust, with Lantern Radio selling lottery tickets. Meanwhile, the Young Management Team competed in the annual River Taw Raft Race (donating their sponsorships to the North Devon Hospice Trust). They won an award as the 'Funniest Raft in the Race' and made front page local news.

THE YOUTH TRUSTS NEAR TERM GOALS

The primary objective of the first Young Management Team in Barnstaple is to develop ever wider and stronger links with its 14–17-year-old peer group in North Devon. Equally important is the development of the team itself, and the support which it will come to expect from the Trust's Executive, Management Committees and Trustees. A team-based, matrix-structured organisation is already in place, with the first 15 team members ready to introduce more young people to the Trust.

Clearly the expansion of membership is of paramount importance; the more young people involved in the safer environment of an anti-drugs culture, the better the prospects for the success and expansion of the Trust itself. Of equal importance in this process is the development of a bold project which will excite and hold the attention of the Trust's young members. Acting as a pilot scheme for future tasks, the so-called 'Market Inn' project in Barnstaple will be the near-term focal point for The Youth Trust. It will offer tangible proof that multi-agency, community-based action can succeed and will provide young people with employment and skills training – at the same time as inculcating the basis of drug awareness education.

THE MARKET INN PROJECT IN BARNSTAPLE

Research has indicated that as many as 1500 young people between the ages of 14 and 17 are potential targets for drug dealers in Barnstaple alone. The town has few facilities designed exclusively for the young – who are thereby reduced, by boredom and peer pressure, to gravitate to those areas in which they become ready prey to the drug-pushers.

The Market Inn currently comprises two ground-floor bars, with two floors above and an original slaughterhouse and seventeenth-century barn to the rear. It is proposed to convert the property into: office accommodation for the Young Management Team, a coffee bar and restaurant, a general purpose activity hall and music venue, a music workshop and recording studio, rooms for snooker and pool, a computerised entertainment centre and workshops for photography and art. There is also potential for Youth Theatre groups to work in conjunction with the adjacent (and newly refurbished) Barnstaple Queens Theatre.

This is without doubt an ambitious, but viable, project. To convert the property to its maximum potential, and to meet all the required safety and environmental standards, will require an estimated capital investment of some £350,000 – of which £250,000 would be for structural work and the remainder for equipment. This requirement will be resourced in two stages:

1. Income from concerts, corporate endorsements and charitable foundations, with the possibility of top-up funding from Government and European Union and the National Lottery.

2. Sponsorship support by the regional business community for general equipment and by the music industry for instruments, sound, lighting and recording equipment.

A business plan, supporting the ideas of the Young Management Team, is being developed. Professional and technical expertise is being sought in such trades as carpentry, plumbing and electrical work – which it is hoped will also offer properly supervised skill-training to young members of The Youth Trust.

SUPPORTING YOUNG PEOPLE

Together with Lantern Radio, The Youth Trust has launched the 'Nathan Stanley Appeal' to raise the £4000 required for the purchase of a trampoline. Nathan, an England under-18 champion, is currently forced to make a 200 mile round trip to Plymouth for Trampoline training. He has a very promising career in the sport and is more than happy to adopt The Youth Trust ethos of 'Proud to be Drug Free'. He is looking forward to helping and training other youngsters in his chosen sport, and to promoting the drugs-free culture.

The Plymouth-based youth band 'Real Steel' has achieved remarkable progress since its formation in 1991. An all-girl steel percussion band, with members aged between 14 and 17, they have emerged from an undistinguished estate on the edge of the city and a background of limited cultural horizons and little or no musical tradition. The band has captured the imagination of many local youngsters and has provided a focus for positive achievement and pride in the community. Importantly for The Youth Trust, the members of Real Steel are keen to operate under the 'proud to be drug free' banner. In recognition of the mutual publicity and potential impact which this sort of association may have on a broad cross-section of the young people in Devon, The Youth Trust is helping to arrange an international youth exchange with Barbados. The financial target for this project is £10,000.

CONCLUSION, THE MIDDLE ROAD

This chapter is a case study of a charity trying to protect young people within a philosophy that the people best able to protect young people are the young people themselves. This has been achieved by developing a Young Management Team that undertake some responsibility for all aspects of the initiative – presenting in public, co-ordinating fund-raising activities, involving themselves in publicity stunts and helping manage the budget and building plans for their own social centre. The balance between involving young people in all aspects of a project and not allowing them to fall into traditional roles of tokenism is hard to manage, as is the balance between aiding the development of a youth culture alternate to the drugs culture without exploiting young people in the same way as drug dealers have done. However, The Youth Trust believes that the threat to young people of drugs is significant enough to risk relying on young people (once trained and confident) to defend their own rights and secure an appropriate role for themselves within the organisation.

CHAPTER 16

Teaching Hieroglyphs with Authority
The Roles of Primary School Teacher, the Pupil, School Culture and Local Community in Rural Mozambique[1]

Mikael Palme

Mozambican primary education is in urgent need of a qualitative and sociologically reflective approach to the question of the quality of teaching. This
means that educational planners and policy makers, education officers at
national and regional levels, instructors engaged in teachers pre- and in-service
training, primary school teachers and, not the least, educational researchers
themselves must learn to address cultural aspects of teaching and schooling.

CLASSROOM INTERACTION: RITUALS AND HIEROGLYPHS[2]

Classroom observation shows that teaching in Mozambican primary schools is
characterised by remarkably little pupil participation in verbal exchanges or
other classroom activities (Palme and Xerinda 1992). An estimate is that the
teacher, on average, occupies more than 90 percent of all time used for speech.
In lessons in grade 1 and 2, the probability is that an individual pupil will speak
once every second day. It should be remembered that these speech acts most
probably consist of ready-made sentences (that is of repeating the teacher's
sentences or sentences from the text book) with few words. As regards reading,

---

1   When I was finalising this paper, I started reading Robert Serpell's *The Significance of Schooling*,
    a book that offers a much more profound discussion of most topics dealt with here. Since the
    present text, to a certain extent, can be said to present Mozambican examples of some of the
    problems Serpell addresses, I have, at the last moment, and at some points, made references
    to his book.
2   This section, and the following one, borrow heavily from a previous text: Palme, M. (1993)
    *Final report and recommendations from the Evaluation of teaching materials for lower primary education
    in Mozambique. I. General issues*. Mimeo, INDE: Maputo.

the probability is that an individual pupil will read aloud in the classroom (on average for less than 1 minute) once in three weeks.

If listening to the teacher is the dominating pupil activity, then the next one in importance is waiting. Pupils spent approximately one-third[3] of their time in the classroom waiting. They waited for the teacher to begin the lesson, to write the name of the school, the title of the lesson or various other texts on the blackboard. They wait for their classmates to finish exercises they themselves have finished a long time ago or, at least as often, for others to finish an exercise they themselves have not been able to understand. They also wait for others to be corrected, so that their turn will come.

The third activity in order of importance is copying. Perhaps the major part of all time used for written tasks was occupied by copying the exercises as such (most often sentences) from the blackboard. A minor part is left for actually doing the exercise. In fact, classroom observations confirm that many pupils never reach the phase of executing the exercise itself. When they have managed to copy it to their text books, the teacher and the best pupils have already reached the stage of correction.

The dominant classroom interaction pattern, then, seems to be that of overwhelmingly passive pupils whose activities are limited to be almost entirely reproductive in character. In a second part of the classroom study, the main objective was empirically to test this hypothesis by using an observation scheme that focused entirely upon the polarity between, on the one hand, reproductive activities, and, on the other, what we can call creative ones, considering several dimensions of classroom interaction.

The results confirm that teaching is normally routinised and demands a predominately passive or reproductive participation by the pupils. Questions asked by the teacher are predominately closed in character: the answer is given and other answers would be regarded as incorrect. Moreover, questions normally demand answers that should either be taken directly from the pupil's text book or from what the teacher has previously said. Also, teachers rarely ask questions that refer to experiences outside the school context or the context of the text book.

Verbal interaction consists almost entirely of either monologues from the teacher or exchanges between teacher and pupils of the well-known question-answer-evaluation type. The explanations given by the teacher rarely go beyond what is said in the pupil's text book. Moreover, teachers tend to use the exact words or formulations found in the text book or in the teacher's manual.

---

3   The percentage of time used for waiting has not been possible to calculate, since the classroom observation study did not use methods that were sufficiently sophisticated for this purpose. The figure is a pure estimation based on observation of a number of lessons. The question is, of course, what should be considered as 'waiting'. Does it include all situations when individual pupils obviously are 'inactive', for example because other pupils are being interrogated by the teacher?

Finally, there is little or no individual attention. Teachers normally address themselves to the entire class. Even corrections, which occupy a considerable time in teaching (on average about 13 per cent of teaching time), are rarely characterised by giving *individual* help to the pupils (for example by explaining mistakes), since teachers normally only have time for checking whether answers are correct or not.

It is not surprising, then, that perhaps the most striking feature of teaching in Mozambican primary schools is its strong ritualisation. The teacher asks questions and organises exercises, the pupils listen to the teacher, answer the questions and do the exercises, but, in doing all this, they focus not so much upon the content of what is being said of the answer or of the exercise. Instead, the main attention is upon formal aspects of the interaction. There are a number of rules for classroom behaviour that work independently of any content. Pupils learn early, for example, that one basic rule is that it should not be expected that what the teacher says is necessarily understandable. Teachers learn the corresponding rule that pupils are often far from likely to understand what is being explained and certainly not to communicate their problems of understanding. The rule says that unintelligibility is not a justified reason for the teaching not to continue or for the pupils to interrupt the teacher with questions. Classroom ritual, then, has it that even if a considerable part of the teacher's explanations are likely not to be understandable for the pupils, either because the language is too difficult or because the subject matter is or both, teaching goes on as if everything was all right. A strikingly open form of classroom ritual is the often criticised but much used chorus answers. In normal Mozambican primary school class rooms, pupils repeatedly confirm that they are present, that they are listening and that they understand by saying 'sim!' ('yes!') or 'não!' ('No!') in response to the teachers explanations, often encouraged to do so by a rhetoric question from the teacher (for example 'estão a perceber?', 'Do you understand?'). Another common form of ritual confirmation that everything is going well is when teachers pause before uttering the last word of a sentence, so that pupils can fill in the missing word (or missing end of a word). In this case, the missing word is normally evident from the context, so pupils do not have to listen carefully to the meaning of what is being said to be able to produce the missing end of the sentence. When, as sometimes happens, the correct answer is not known or evident from the context, at least one or two of the best pupils or repeaters will know what kind of answer is required. When the teacher repeats the question, everybody, just through listening to these pupils, will know the expected answer and the ritual can fulfil its purpose of confirming that the teaching goes on normally. Yet another form is a purely rhetoric question which requires either a confirmative chorus answer ('Sim!') or a non-confirmative one ('Não!'). In such cases, the pure intonation used by the teacher indicates whether the answer should be confirmative or non-confirmative. Thus, pupils can participate in the ritual without understanding much, or anything, of the content of what is being said.

Even if these rituals are obviously pedagogically contra-productive, it is important to understand their functional value. Above all, they permit teaching to go on – even when conditions for real learning do not exist. If pupils had not learnt that it is a rhetorical, ritualistic question when the teacher asks if they have understood, and if they did not know from experience that this question, according to the ritual, demands a positive answer ('Sim!'), then they would impose on the teacher at least some of their real problems of understanding and learning. The teacher then would have to choose either to give up the demands of the teacher's manual and the curriculum and try to deal with these problems, or to go on with the syllabus in spite of the difficulties. Existing rituals make it possible to suppress the enormous problems that normally exist in Mozambican primary school classrooms. This is vital, since taking these problems seriously often would mean going back to the syllabus in the very early grades in primary education. There is, for example, evidence that many pupils up to grade four still use counting on their fingers and toes as a dominant method in Mathematics. To solve such problems, teaching would have to go back to what was supposed to be learnt in grades one and two. In grade three and onwards, text books and instructions in the teacher's manuals count with pupils who are more or less able to read and write. This, however, is often not at all the case and many Mozambican primary school teachers confront the impossible task of teaching pupils as if they have mastered these skills when in fact they have not.

Closely linked to the ritualistic character of classroom interaction and classroom behaviour is the question of what kind of learning existing teaching practices encourage. Since so many factors – the demanding curricula, the little time available, the abstract character of the knowledge to be learned, the ritualisation of class room interaction, just to mention some of the most important – make it very unlikely for pupils to achieve substantial learning. Pupils have to develop alternative strategies in order to satisfy the demands of the teacher and to survive in the classroom. Many of these strategies have to do with pure survival. Pupils will learn to master the rituals governing classroom interaction, for example to say 'sim!' or 'nâo!' in the right situations. They will also learn to wait for the repeaters or the best pupils to answer questions. Moreover, they will try to memorise – making use of a competence that is probably much more developed in illiterate societies – entire sentences or even entire texts and try to make use of them in the proper situations. Rote learning dominates. It was discovered, in tests made among grade four and grade five pupils in Science and Geography, that a high proportion of pupils were able to repeat memorised abstract definitions without being able to give any meaning to these definitions. In a reading test, Grade three pupils turned out to have memorised entire texts just from hearing them being read aloud in the classroom. In the test situation, they repeated these texts from memory, pretending to read, but without being capable of reading.

A result of the teaching practices described above, and of the survival strategies of the pupils, is a growing discrepancy, from grade one and onwards, between, on the one hand, the level of pedagogical transmission (the teaching as it is described by the curricula, the text books and the teacher's manuals and as it is carried through by the teachers) and, on the other hand, the level of reception, that is the understanding and assimilation of the pupils.

FACTORS DETERMINING LEARNING[4]

Pupils' mother tongue and the language of instruction

Perhaps the most striking aspect of classroom interaction is the restraints on communication set by the pupils' language proficiency in Portuguese. Outside proper urban schools, pupils, even in grades three, four and five, have difficulties in understanding the explanations given by the teacher. When interviewed after lessons, pupils often cannot relate the essentials of what the teacher has said. Moreover, pupils' texts in the teaching materials normally surpass the reading proficiency of the pupils, not only in rural and suburban schools but generally (Luis 1992). Data suggest that what is particularly problematic is the assimilation of concepts, especially abstract ones, which often are assimilated in vague or confused ways. The consequence of pupils' difficulties in writing is that classroom activities that include writing take excessive time and often do not achieve what was planned (Hyltenstam and Stroud 1993).

But that is not all. Low proficiency in the language of instruction puts dramatic constraints on verbal exchange within the classroom. Text books and teacher's manuals put little emphasis on what we can call 'dialoguing as a pedagogical method', aimed at creating links between the pupils' previous experiences and conceptions and the new subject matter. The small possibilities there are for verbal exchange are normally reduced to a minimum because of what we have called the ritualisation of class room interaction. One particularly important factor in this context is the fact that pupils rarely master the language of instruction sufficiently to express themselves and participate in any kind of dialogue. Instead, pupils will do their best to try to satisfy the teacher by repeating memorised sentences which they imagine are demanded by the speech situation or the context. This is what, at times, produces the kind of

---

4 More profound cultural factors determining school learning – such as the culturally framed conceptualisations of education and learning among specific ethnic groups discussed, for example, by Serpell (1993) or by Paul Riesmann (1990) – are not discussed here. The Mozambican studies referred to were more limited in scope and did not directly address such questions.

absurd, nonsensical and out-of-context contributions from pupils who make a mistake either about what is the context or what, in a given context, should be the expected kind of answer.

The constraints put on classroom interaction are particularly important since the distance between pupils' experiences and previous conceptions on the one hand, and the subject matters and new concepts on the other hand, probably is far greater than for schoolchildren in the industrialised world. Language is an indispensable means for creating the necessary links, that is for creating conditions for a reasonable dialectic between assimilation and accommodation, to put it in Piagetian terms.

The studies made within the evaluation project have, among other things, come to focus on the very different linguistic situations in, roughly, three social settings. In rural areas, in the studies represented by three rural schools in Nampula, Portuguese tends to be spoken only in school. Children are linguistically socialised in their mother tongue, which they learn to master as any other member of the local community in which they live. In properly urban schools, most pupils have Portuguese as their mother tongue and will know words or expressions from Mozambican languages only occasionally. In suburban areas, however, the linguistic situation is confused. Tests and interviews with pupils testify that children are brought up in a linguistic context in which neither their original mother tongue nor Portuguese is totally dominating. As a result, a specific suburban language seems to develop, which takes most of its characteristics from traditional regionally-dominating languages (in Maputo Ronga and/or Changana) but which, at the same time, does not include all the vocabulary and linguistic subtlety of the language of origin. Hence many Ronga or Changana-speaking children in suburban Maputo do not master their mother tongue sufficiently for describing phenomena around them using the richness of this language. Instead, they will make use of Portuguese words or expressions without mastering the language as such. An example of this specific linguistic competence, produced by urbanisation, is that a majority of interviewed suburban pupils in grades four and five used the word 'rio' ('river') for describing any assembly of water, being ignorant of the various words available in their mother tongue and also of the specific Portuguese word for such things as 'river', 'canal', 'beach', 'lake', etc. (Chiau 1992).

Which are the possible options? Taking a long-term perspective, there is the possibility of using Mozambican languages as the medium of instruction in the first years of schooling. This possibility, which is well in line with international research, would, however, need to gain political and social acceptance among the national élites. Currently, bilingual approaches are celebrated on a purely rhetorical level, but in practice there is no substantial input into such programmes. There seems to be little point in insisting never to use expressions or words from the mother tongue for elucidating new concepts in, for example, Science, if not deliberately to create repetition and drop out.

Pupils' experiences

Interviews made in relation to the text books in Science and Geography have highlighted the pedagogical problems arising from the simple fact that pupils' experiences of the world are limited, at least when seen in relation to the subject matters that are taught. There are obvious problems of this kind, for example in teaching about the thermometer, an unknown phenomenon among the majority of Mozambican children (Palme and Eliasson 1992). But there are less obvious instances. It was, for example, discovered that a considerable proportion of pupils in the Maputo suburbs have difficulties in grasping the notion of river, since they have never seen any. Makua children in the inland of the Nampula province, for the same reason, often have difficulties in assimilating the concept of 'sea'.

The question of the limitations to children's factual experiences of the world and the specific obstacles these limitations create in learning processes is present in all teaching and has been constantly confirmed by pupil interviews on all kinds of subject matters. Let us here put forward three aspects of this question.

As in the two examples mentioned above, factual experiences obviously have an important impact on the formation of concepts. In the study on pupils' conceptions of phenomena dealt with in Science teaching, it was, for example, shown that children's factual experiences of vapour condensing into water in the air had a strong impact on their understanding of concept of vaporisation. Since few of the interviewed pupils had understood that vapour, properly speaking, is invisible, many of them proposed other explanations as to how water could disappear from a bowl put in the sun (the most common explanation being that the water disappeared into the walls of the bowl or into the ground). Basing her argument on her own experience, a girl in Grade five in a rural school insisted that clouds were formed by water coming from cooking utensils (the only source for vapour) and that the heavy rains during the last year could only be explained by the fact that much cooking had been done in people's homes. This conviction was challenged by a classmate who argued that clouds could also be formed in early mornings above small lakes (Chiau 1992; Linha, Palme and Xerinda 1992).

Second, it should be remembered that pupils' experiences, as in the case of the understanding of rivers and the sea, are determined by geographical and social factors. In interviews on pupils' perception of alternative visual perspectives of an object, it was obvious that, for example, the representation of a house or hut from above was more easily understood by urban children, who either had come across photographs or television images using this perspective or had themselves climbed up high buildings. Similarly, in interviews on children's conception of the form of the earth, the few pupils who expressed ideas similar to the explanation given in the text book had seen pictures of the earth in space on the television, television sets being extremely rare outside urban middle class areas.

A third aspect to stress in this context is, once again, the question of language. Since teachers' explanations are given in a second language, pupils are all the more dependent on their factual experiences for understanding new concepts. Grasping very little of the teacher's explanations about the water cycle, Makua-speaking children in rural Nampula schools try to give meaning to words like 'vaporisation' and 'condensation' by making use of their own experiences and previous ways of conceiving similar phenomena. When they have no personal experience of the phenomena that the teacher and the text book try to explain, chances are small that their understanding will come anywhere close to what teaching hopes to achieve.

Pupils' culturally- and linguistically-framed conceptions

Existing curricula and text books are badly adapted to school-aged childrens' previous conceptions of the world. This bad adjustment is further strengthened by the predominantly passive role given to the pupils by the instructions in the teacher's manuals. Since real teaching practices, with few exceptions, give an even more passive role to pupils (because of the teaching conditions that the teachers have to confront and because of existing conservative teaching traditions), pupils cannot assimilate new concepts. If learning is seen as an active process in which pupils construct new concepts, negotiating between their previous conceptions and experiences on the one hand and new experiences and information handed to them in the classroom or by the text book on the other hand, then existing programmes, text books, manuals and teaching patterns clearly do not favour learning (Hewson and Hewson 1984; Hewson 1988).

Let us refer to two different examples. In the teaching of the water cycle – one of the dominating themes in Science in Grades three and four – one learning difficulty for children from the Makua-speaking province of Nampula is that they tend to understand the vaporisation of water in a different way (Palme, Linha and Xerinda 1992). The expression used in the mother tongue for describing that water disappears, *owelela*, normally has the connotation that it disappears *into* the ground (as water in rivers might appear to do) or *into*, for example, the walls of a bowl. This connotation further strengthens a natural tendency for children not to believe things that they cannot see, such as invisible vapour. As a result, many Makua-speaking schoolchildren have greater difficulties than Mozambican children elsewhere to grasp the notion of vaporisation. Now, if the syllabus, the text book and the teacher manual would have been more conscious of the importance of these children's previous conceptions as regards how water disappears, more stress might have been put on finding ways to surpass this difficulty.

Another example will be taken from a study on pupils' conceptions of the earth. Interviews with pupils in Grade five and six showed that a majority of school-aged children at this level in Maputo suburbs conceive the earth either as a flat circle surrounded by water (the dominating conception in suburban Maputo) or as a circle inside which human beings as well as the sun and the moon are to be found (a conception that is more common in urban areas). The very short time dedicated to teaching the form of the earth – a few lessons – and the way this time is used, is far from enough to convince these pupils to negotiate their previous conceptions for the ones taught in school (Chiau 1992).[5]

'Culture' in teaching

The simple point to be made in relation to this short presentation of studies on classroom interaction and learning in the Mozambican primary school is that there seems to be no short cut to more 'effective' teaching. In order to address cultural obstacles to learning, curriculum developers, writers of teaching materials, instructors at teacher training colleges and in teacher in-service training, and, most of all, the primary teachers themselves must be equipped with at least some instruments enabling them to identify and understand the cultural and linguistic mechanisms that shape the teaching process. Perhaps the only asset the primary school teachers possess, along with the pride they still may have in their profession, is their familiarity with local social, linguistic and cultural traditions. Among the many factors that block the use of this resource, at least one belongs to the realm of the changeable – namely the priorities and constraints set by national educational planners and decision-makers as concerns strategies for quality improvement. Striving for modernity, and legitimising their positions by claiming to be more modern than the ones that they are set to rule, the national élites normally have little understanding and interest in what they tend to see as 'particularistic' and generally backward local or regional traditions. Instead, educational planners tend to identify modernity with the models of thinking inherent in the Western management-oriented culture represented by the donor community (that is the providers of fanancial aid) and its international experts. It is highly unlikely that the cultural blend[6] arising from the meeting of the donor society and the national administrative élite would be productive for the creation of better conditions for a cultural adaptation of school to the end-users of schooling.

---

5   In fact, the two conceptions described here can also be seen as a negotiated compromise on the part of the pupil with what the teacher has tried to teach and with what is said in the text book. That would explain that most pupils insist that the earth is circular, even when they believe we live inside this circle (as in a sphere) or when they conceive of the earth as flat.

6   I am well aware that the somewhat loose use of the word 'culture' here is dangerously essentialistic, but it is intended metaphorically.

THE 'CONTEXT': SCHOOLING IN A MATRILINEAL RURAL SOCIETY[7]

The ritualistic character of primary school teaching and its extremely low 'output' in terms of pupils' learning should also be understood in the context of what schooling means in the specific community in which the school operates. In traditional rural society, school is in many ways a marginal institution with little significance for people's life and future. Rural children live in a world dominated by the cycles and demands of agriculture. Work, family education, religious ceremonies, initiation and other rituals, and often semi-institutionalised educational agencies such as Koranic schools educate children and prepare them for the future. Even though school may be regarded as an educator, in the broad, moral sense of the word, it is just one of several educational agencies – and, in reality, by no means the most important one. In fact, dropping out of school is not a sudden event but the result of a process that normally has been slowly going on since Grade one. For the few who have success in school, continued formal education may be an alternative. For all the others, leaving school is not a dramatic event. Their future is well prepared for and their participation in important activities much needed. Going to school means, in a way, artificially prolonging the state of childhood and postponing such things as contributing more fully to the survival of the family through work, getting one's own *machamba* or getting married. When school comes into conflict with more trustworthy and impelling principles for social reproduction, such as marriage or working for the survival of the family, it is abandoned – and for good reasons. If formal school can be of doubtful interest in the eyes of parents or families, it is, of course, even more so for the children themselves. Being able to read and write, the most basic goal in formal education, is not of an obvious value in rural societies where children not only can survive very well without this competence but also have very little or no use of it since there is so little to read and so little to write.

The problem of the significance of schooling was focused in a sociological study of families' educational strategies in the general context of social repro-duction in a rural, matrilineal community in northern Mozambique. Peasant families were generally unable to ascribe any meaning to what was taught in school in terms of content. Subject matters – concepts, factual information and even skills such as measuring – in subjects like Geography, Science or History were not merely badly understood, they were seen as belonging to a closed universe to which ordinary people had no access and that, further, had no significance whatsoever for normal life. Instead, schooling was basically as-cribed a pure functional value, that of opening up the door leading to modern

---

7   Most of this section is borrowed from Palme (1993).

society and its well-being. But even in this respect, the relationship to schooling was ambiguous.

On the one hand, getting educated meant the possibility of leaving the peasant condition, of getting employment and a salary and eventually being able to live in the city where signs of wealth such as electricity, running water, cars and even television sets, at least according to rumour, were so abundant. Having a son or a daughter achieving this would not only be an honour for the family but secure its well-being in future. Villagers thought, in a general way, that having access to school would improve their conditions in future and, more specifically, that education was one of the few available means for individual social mobility upwards.

On the other hand, the peasant families knew from experience that the road to success was long, costly and insecure. It would be far from enough to send the children to the neighbouring school, within walking distance, where Grade six was taught. Leaving school at the end of Grade six would not be sufficient and it would be necessary to arrange for continued studies in the suburbs of the city. This implied finding a home where the son or daughter could stay. Arrangements of this kind could only be made using the extended family and its network of solidarity ties. The educational ambitions of most peasant families had to stop here. They had no contacts whatsoever in the cities and boarding schools became increasingly rare when state expenditure for education was cut down. A family with the good fortune of having close relatives in town would be well off. More often, the children, if they could be sent to anyone at all, had to stay with distant relatives and in households where they might be treated as servants – as was confirmed by interviews with young men who had returned to the village after a year of humiliation and starvation in the city. No one had been able to complete Grade seven.

Sending one's daughter to town in order to continue her studies could turn out to be a most dangerous strategy. Separated from the extended family, which in normal circumstances would function as a moral safeguard, the young woman might be unable to confront the radically different social environment that town life offers. Probably (no interviews have been made which support this hypothesis), the fact that moral values and teachings of traditional rural family education were too distant from town life reality to be adequate in the new surrounding, might lead to a moral confusion that resulted in pregnancy and enforced school drop out (On this point, see discussion on pregnancy below). It should not be forgotten that when a peasant family sends a child to town it will, in a sense, lose the child to an unknown society whose 'secrets' are unfamiliar to the parents themselves and within which they do not feel at ease. The picture of the humble peasant father waiting for hours outside a suburban school to get a word with the teacher about his child being expelled for alleged truancy or some other problem, is an illustrative one. Finally, sending children to town in order to continue school meant economic sacrifices that could be substantial.

The family not only lost a productive member but had to send food (and money) to town, which was a time consuming and often expensive undertaking.

The educational project was not only costly and hazardous, it was also contradictory. Receiving education meant leaving the peasant conditions and finding the way to modern society and its fortunes, which would, in turn, give the means to support the original group, the family, in future. But those who managed to succeed usually changed. From the point of view of the village, a person of the city, an educated or a rich person – someone who belonged to the modern, urban world and who automatically would be considered to have many profitable contacts – was named a *mkunya* (a 'white person'[8]) regardless of his or her colour of skin. This expression was often used both ironically and critically, but basically expressed both superiority and the fact of the city person being different – 'not one of us' as an interviewed peasant put it. Getting one's daughter married to a *mkunya* was an honour because it meant getting connected to another, and probably superior, world where wealth was available. But the undertone of irony or criticism in the use of the notion of *akunya* (plural form) was equally important. In traditional peasant society there is little room for individuality: the individual cannot exist alone, outside the pattern of family relations to which he belongs and where his position, to a great extent, is defined from birth. Education, though, by definition puts the individual in the unknown community of *akunya*, a world out of control from the original group, transforming him into something different. This transformation did not necessarily threaten solidarity ties to the group of origin – at least not according to harmonious ideals set up by some peasant families that were interviewed – but was far from unproblematic, as witnessed by numerous stories of ungrateful relatives whose behaviour, once they had disappeared to the city, showed little respect for their group of origin and its needs. The 'secrets' of school and of formal education, to which the educated young man (or woman) were considered to be initiated, then, also represented a potential danger to the moral values which guaranteed the unity of the group.

This transformation might be accepted for boys but represented a considerable risk for girls. An educated girl would not be able to marry a man with less education than herself. Uneducated men would not dare to approach her and, in any case, such a marriage was generally seen as unhappy and unstable, since the woman would know secrets that her husband did not know. This would severely limit the range of potential suitors and put the family in a situation where it became dependent on unknown suitors whose intentions and behaviour were equally unknown. Matrilineal tradition had it that the married woman should stay in the area of her family of origin and her husband build the family hut there. This was seen as a guarantee for stability and future reproduction, since children were to be brought up in proximity to the extended

---

8   Literally, 'a Portugese-speaking person.'

family to which they belonged, that is that of the mother. The educated woman, then, might either continue as unmarried (and be a burden and a shame for her family) or marry men who were likely not to respect tradition, but without representing any other visible advantage such as wealth or high social position. In either case, the whole base upon which family reproduction rested was put at risk. It was also generally thought that the educated girl would change her attitudes, become less respectful to her parents and to traditions and rituals and lose her taste for manual labour in the fields. The education of girls thus threatened social reproduction and, since the perspective of any real advantage coming out of schooling was so uncertain, families were less inclined to go for continued education.

In order to understand these facts, we must consider the structure of the Makua matrilineal society – clarified by Christian Geffray (1991) in his analysis of the crucial role of girls or young women in the whole logic of social reproduction of this society. Traditionally, family economy is based upon the labour force provided by the young men who marry into the family, even though the wealth produced by this labour is not understood as a product of their work but as the rightful property of their mothers-in-law, who 'feed' the family and see to its well-being, that is redistribute the products of labour to family members.[9] The household of the senior mother – the 'mother of mothers' – is the central one in the family network, even if the real chief of the family conglomerate would be her brothers or maternal uncles. As her own children grow up and her daughters can be married, the young woman passes from being junior – which implies subordination to her own mother (and her mother's brothers or uncles) – to the group of senior women who, benefiting from the labour of their sons-in-law, can guarantee the well-being of their family network. It is also important for her to give birth to daughters at an early stage of her social career, since she can, as Geffray shows, later on in life, rightfully 'adopt' one or several of her granddaughters – thus reproducing a situation in which, by marrying these adopted daughters, she can benefit from the suitors' labour force, without which she would have difficulties to survive. Becoming a respected and influential senior woman is the accomplishment of the social career of a young woman.

It is crucial, then, that a family conglomerate (comprising several generations) produces girls and that these girls, as future women, stay closely attached to the family in order to guarantee the inflow of new suitors or husbands and their labour force. The status of the woman, then, makes her immobile. If she

---

9   This is the image of the often maternal head of family or clan shown in many Makonde 'family tree' sculptures. The head of the female ancestor appears on top of a 'tree' of bodies that cling to her, representing the dependence of family members on the (female) ancestor as the physical incarnation of the family/clan itself, outside of which they cannot socially exist, as well as their physical dependence on her as 'feeder'.

were to leave with her husband, she would not fulfil this function or later benefit from her position as a senior woman.

It is in the interest of the elder generation[10] that a young girl marries and starts giving birth to children (daughters). But it is also very much in her own interest, namely if she wants to gain social respect and simultaneously create conditions for her social and material survival as a senior and, later, elder woman. School, then, does not fit well with the conditions for social promotion of women.

For boys, education was a less contradictory project. The main responsibilities of husbands were to secure the reproduction of their wife's lineage by making them pregnant, constructing a house for the family and securing its material well-being. Within their own lineage, for example as brothers (to their sisters) and uncles (to their sisters' children) or as nephews (to their maternal uncle), they assumed wider responsibilities. They would supervise the education of children (including their integration in rituals and ceremonies guided by the local *mwene* or his substitutes) and protect the interests of the family in questions of marriage or disputes over land. Belonging to 'the same stomach', the same *nloko*, meant considering nephews and nieces as one's own children, thus assuming full moral and material responsibility for their well-being and future. Being both husband and brother (nephew, uncle, etc), the man must procure the means for the survival of the group.[11] This, of course, was normally accomplished through agriculture[12], but might very well include such things as selling his labour, travelling, or getting educated and entering into modern society. In doing this, the man should, traditionally, act as a representative of the group, contrary to being an individual fortune seeker, and act on its behalf and for its benefit. Individual achievement, either in education or in professional careers, was ideally an accomplishment of the group itself. The educational project, then, became less contradictory as such. Educating sons, male nephews or male grandchildren was to educate an organic member of the group and a means for the group to secure its future well-being.

---

10 Geffray means that whereas production is controlled by women, reproduction is the domain of men, especially through their role as *maîtres du mariage*. By orchestrating the alliances between families and by seeing to it that junior women with a specific hierarchical status in one family marry junior men with a specific hierarchical status in the other, the *maîtres* of marriage, normally the maternal uncles on both sides, secure hierarchical positions within the world of men.

11 Geffray (1991) shows that marriage strategies are often oriented towards a strengthening of the alliance between the family conglomerate of the man, where he as brother or uncle can influence the marriages of his sisters or his nieces, and the family into which he has himself once been married – thus uniting two groups and extending the sphere of influence of the man himself.

12 As a junior (suitor or newly married man) his labour would, however, primarily be put at the disposal of the family into which he is married.

This was, roughly, the ideal representation of things.[13] However, peasant families were aware that often reality was different. The transforming force of education was a visible one. School-leavers from higher grades who had returned to the village because of lack of opportunities had a more or less openly problematic relationship to their social surrounding of origin. They had been forced to return and they wanted nothing other than getting away once again. They had lost much of their faith in the values that build up traditional peasant life. They questioned or ridiculed the secrets of the elders which were transmitted through initiation and other rituals. New categories of thinking had entered their minds and they would typically express themselves, at least in the social situation that the interviews constituted, using oppositions such as: old fashioned/modern, superstition/science, local/ universal, eventless/eventful, etc. The uneasiness they felt embraced all aspects of daily life, such as the lack of taste and variety of traditional food, the poor houses, the hard and never-ending work in the fields, the unattractiveness of local women, the dullness of entertainment activities, the oldfashionedness of rituals, etc. They were, to use an expression by Pierre Bourdieu, people whom school had put in a warped position in history (*une position en porte-à-faux*). They belonged neither to the peasant society they came from nor to the modern world they aspired to. Facing the sociologist, as an impersonation of modern society, they had to conceal the extent of their participation in traditional beliefs and practices. Being back in their village of origin, they equally had to keep under cover some of the beliefs or attitudes acquired in the city – because of their blasphemous or irreverent character. Their doubt of the values of traditional peasant society, in particular the belief in the cult of the ancestors, put indirectly into question its very base, the unity of the group, by challenging the way of understanding solidarity ties between members of the same group. Hence, education, as the vehicle for this transformation, tended to threaten the whole base upon which traditional society rested and give way for an individualism which was its very opposite.[14]

Thus peasant families were aware of the changing force of education. The contradictions of the educational project were, perhaps, most openly visible in this double attitude: wanting education as an instrument to improve the condition of the group but mistrusting the effect of education as a danger to the solidarity of the group.

---

13 It should be stressed that the anthropological field work underlying these reflections was far too short to produce anything else than general descriptions. The author is well aware that details may be wrong or put into a somewhat badly understood context.

14 Geffray (1991a) tells about all young men he met in distant rural villages during his research – young teenagers who had finished school and wanted nothing else than to get out of the village, at any price. It is interesting that some of these young men, who had been eliminated from secondary school (or at the edge of entering secondary school), were the only persons who at least talked about making agriculture in a new way, with paid manual labour and regular commercialisation of products.

THE RURAL PRIMARY SCHOOL TEACHER:
A STRUCTURALLY AMBIGUOUS POSITION

An understanding of the cultural mechanisms determining the quality of primary education cannot overlook the primary school teachers themselves. The social image of the primary school teacher is typically dualistic. On the one hand, he[15] is often presented as a type of hero in the development process, fulfilling his modernising mission under harsh and unfavourable conditions. On the other hand, he is at least as often given most of the blame for the poor quality of primary education. Classroom research and interview studies with primary school teachers certainly confirm their pedagogical shortcomings, but a wider perspective should be formulated here. Who is, culturally and socially, the rural primary school teacher?

A recent study on mainly rural Mozambican primary school teachers showed that almost all teachers are themselves of peasant origin (Baloi and Palme 1995). With their relatively high educational level, normally Grade six, they often represent an exception in the family and hold a position of responsibility in the family network, taking care of younger family members as far as concerns clothing, accommodation or education. In some cases, the socially upward mobility of teachers of modest social origin had been part of a general change in the position of the family generation to which they belonged: their brothers would equally have reached secondary school and their sisters would have tended to marry into the modern sector of society.

Because of his ascending social trajectory, the group of origin often invests a collective expectancy in the teacher – hoping for him to improve its living conditions. In view of the present unfavourable economic situation of teachers, such hopes are very rarely satisfied. However, even if the rural teacher does not have the economic means to meet such demands, this is partly compensated by the social and symbolic capital he possesses – being regarded as an educated man who deserves respect. The rural teacher continues to be the most important mediator between the rural world and its inhabitants and the modern world, functioning both as interpreter and messenger.

But if the primary teacher is respected in the rural community for his educational and cultural level, modern society tends to disrespect him for the

---

15 For social reasons, the rural primary school teacher is with very few exceptions a man. Rural teachers are often transferred from one school to another and it would be against the logic for social reproduction in a male-dominated society that women were mobile in this way. Since men are not expected to marry with women with a higher social or educational stand, female teachers cannot marry locally, as rural male teachers do. Instead female teachers are mainly found in urban or sub-urban schools, and are married to men belonging to the little modern sector. In fact, an interesting phenomenon is that the teacher training colleges for primary teachers now recruit more than 50 per cent girls, which would point to a possible future radical change in the definition of the rural primary school teacher.

same reason. Being of modest social origin, holding a modest educational diploma and receiving a low salary, the primary teacher does not correspond to the criteria for social distinction in the modern society. Probably, this ambiguous position explains the social frustration from which so many teachers suffer.

The frustration of which so many primary teachers give witness also depends on the gradual degradation of their material conditions during the last 15 years. The dramatic poverty imposed on rural areas by the war has also destroyed the old system of local community support to teachers. As a result, the primary teacher does not have the means to give a physical presentation of himself that corresponds to what he would feel to be that required by his position. What seems to be at stake when the teacher is obliged to face his pupils wearing ragged trousers and badly worn shoes, or to receive parents being dressed in a torn shirt, is the whole social definition of his identity.

In fact, the question of clothes crystallises much of the typically intermediary position of the rural teacher. Interviewed teachers stressed the importance of dressing in a civilised manner, even under harsh conditions. Wearing a clean shirt and ironed trousers was one of the ways through which the social distance to the peasant society was maintained. Dressing up was, in this sense, totally parallel to the civilised use of Portuguese that teachers aspired to and distinguished them from their peasant surrounding. These corporal relationships to the world are important because they so clearly express one fundamental aspect of the position of the rural teachers: that of being the farthest outpost of the modern society and its legitimate culture, language and values. Defending the correct use of a language, Portuguese, that they themselves badly mastered, and insisting on performing classroom rituals in the local school in a basically unsympathetic environment, these teachers, in a sense, fought barbarism on behalf of a modern civilisation – in which they themselves, ironically, are to be found at the very low end of the hierarchical scale. A similar structural position is held by the teacher training colleges and in a way that threatens to turn them into obstacles for any development programme aiming at improving primary education. Since these colleges primarily recruit students and instructors who have, respectively, been excluded from secondary school and higher education and whose social ambitions are oriented upwards (becoming a teacher candidate or an instructor also keeps the door open to future studies), they tend, in various forms, to develop despise for low prestigious primary teaching. Interviewed instructors usually understood their present condition as temporary and further emphasised that their role was to give the necessary 'theoretical' foundations for sound teaching, not to inform the candidates on how practical teaching could be done. Thus, reproducing the division between 'theory' and 'practice', they also managed to free the social image of their own profession and position from the suspicion of being in any sense close to that of the primary school teachers.

However, the role as a defender of civilisation is only one aspect of the position of the rural primary school teacher. Being themselves of peasant origin and surviving in an almost totally rural environment, all interviewed teachers were, at the same time, firmly integrated into the rural community. Marrying locally, they were obliged to respect the rules of behaviour in the matrilineal society. Most interviewed teachers had, for example, not been authorised by the *humu* (the head of the family of their wives) to move their spouses and children out of the area of influence of their families. The incongruity of the modern education system, in which teachers are regularly transferred from one school and area to another, with the organisation of matrilineal society thus often imposed on the teachers a form of bachelorhood and isolation. In their own extended families, counted on the side of their mother, they would also be submitted to the authority of the elected *humu*. Teachers who had accumulated respect in their families of origin would also, after retirement, be likely candidates for becoming *wahumu* (plural form). Confronting an interviewer who, by all appearances belonged to the higher levels of the education system, interviewed teachers would also try to conceal their participation in local religious practices. However, several in-depth interviews revealed that teachers share most religious and so-called animistic beliefs of the community into which they are inserted.

The structurally ambiguous position of the primary teacher sheds light on the question of how school knowledge relates to – and could, eventually, differently relate to – local systems of knowledge. The interviewed teachers obviously experienced the conceptual universe of school and modern society, on one hand, as totally separate from that of the traditional society, on the other. They also recognised that the modern 'scientific' explanations of natural phenomena, that they themselves tried to teach in school and that were to be found in teachers' manuals and text books, probably were incompatible with the explanatory systems used in daily life. Their practical solution to this contradiction was to claim that one conceptual system was valid in school and another one in the surrounding society and that, in practice, these systems rarely, or never, met as antagonistic or competing explanatory systems. In this way, the contradiction was resolved by operating with a categorisation of 'in-school knowledge' and 'out-of-school knowledge' which also well corresponded to the marginal role of school in the daily life of the local community.

The interviewed teachers normally had few reasons to challenge this state of affairs. Since what was taught in school was by and large incomprehensible in the local community or else reduced to the surface value of tangible skills such as reading, writing or counting, no one would dare to question the content of teaching. In fact, the local school – as a sort of physical representation of modern society and its secrets – was regarded almost as foreign territory by peasant parents who normally would feel insecure in these unknown surroundings.

The point to be made here is that serious attempts to culturally adapt teaching to local needs, and to culturally- and linguistically-determined conceptual systems, would create a dramatically new situation – demanding a new definition of the role and position of primary school teachers in relation to the local community, its social structures and practices.

On the other hand, many obstacles or challenges remain. First, the primary school teacher himself must be assisted in redefining his conception of school knowledge and its relationship to other conceptual systems. Liberating teachers' cultural competence and turning it into a resource in school development would, however, imply that the hierarchically-structured education system itself – from the donor agencies and national education officers to regional education directorates and teacher training colleges – is able to recognise and respect both the complexity and the importance of regionally differing cultural systems, so as to promote such aspects of teaching in curriculum development, the writing of teaching materials and the design of teachers pre- and in-service training. Second, the cross-cultural communicability between supposedly modern knowledge systems and 'traditional' or local ones would need to be explored in practice. If we, with Robert Horton (1993), regard traditional beliefs and conceptualisations not as pure products of fantasy but as explanatory systems that are quite functional in their context and not different in nature from those of modern science, modern concepts would have to be negotiated in relation to these alternative explanations. The difficult social aspect of such a negotiation is that different age groups and different layers in the local community necessarily would tend to differ substantially in their willingness to accept it and, consequently, that the proper process of negotiating would tend to create new social tensions. Third, any attempt to adapt the contents of teaching to local needs and local conceptual systems would have to face the problem of convincingly showing that school knowledge really does have any user's value in the local community.

CONCLUSION: 'CULTURE' AND EDUCATIONAL EFFECTIVENESS

What, above all, is needed at various organisational levels of the education system is a greater awareness of the cultural aspects of teaching and learning. Without such an awareness, it is highly unlikely that national curricula will ever be more fruitfully adapted to the conditions of teaching, that teaching materials will be developed that are operational in the classroom or that teacher pre- and in-service training programmes will ever be able to address the key problems of education.

At the national level, the urban upper middle class that is dominating state administration, including the Ministry of Education, must be manoeuvred into a position in which the defence of its privileged position does not necessarily imply a refusal to recognise regional cultural differences and the suppression of a regional competence that, necessarily to some extent, goes beyond the cultural capital currently held by the national élite itself. This applies, perhaps above all, to the question of language policies in education.

The current strong trend of adapting the national élites in the education sector, including the small research community, to the models celebrated by the donor community (survey techniques, statistical analyses at macro level, internationally produced and imported instruments such as the IEA assessment programme[16]) must be balanced by a donor input recognising and encouraging other kinds of investments more specifically oriented towards elucidating the national cultural complexity that is determining primary teaching.[17] At one level, this simply means spending more money on exploring linguistic and cultural conditions for successful teaching[18] and on experimental pilot projects linked to curriculum development and teacher pre- and in-service training. In assessment, this means developing a proper national assessment competence designed to satisfy the need of identifying weaknesses in curricula, teaching materials and teaching – in order to inform curriculum reform and the design of teacher in-service training programmes.

When the quality of education and teaching is discussed, one fundamental question is normally omitted, namely that of the social actors, or better, the social agents, who deal with and define not only how educational policy is being developed, but also what are the legitimate ways of thinking about and discussing educational matters. For an extremely poor country like Mozambique, what are the chances for the small national élite to develop a national competence that goes beyond the need to satisfy today's definitions of what are legitimate problems of education? This is a serious question. Tendencies are that the national élite – if this sociologically vague terminology can be accepted

---

16 For a criticism along the lines of the IEA programme, see Vedder (1994).

17 For a more detailed discussion of the shortcomings of traditional macro and planning approaches, see Serpell (1993).

18 Even though some of the trends in school effectiveness research lately has come to acknowledge the fundamental importance of context-related social and cultural differences between schools (see, for example, Proudford and Baker (1994)), the statistical means and simplistic categories to which educational realities tend to be reduced in this kind of approach makes it rather useless for qualitative improvement, for example through teachers pre- and in-service training. However, since macro-level research of this kind perfectly corresponds to the world-view of most educational planners and decision-makers and since school effectiveness traders are not missing on the market, school effectiveness research obviously is a growing business in third world countries. Since the field of educational research in low income countries is so limited, this new importation is seldom balanced or tempered by other research traditions.

– orients itself primarily in relation to the international donor society and its organisations. It is not only that this is where benefits can be obtained, for example salaries compared to the ones of expatriates, it is also important that this is the only visible landscape. It is very unlikely that there would exist a large academic field, for example, as in Western countries where various traditions can live and develop and within which young researchers and future education officers can be trained. What normally exists is much more of a monolithic situation, where the currently prevailing ideas of the donors define what can be discussed. Even if, today, quality is on the agenda, it is unlikely that the selection mechanisms of those among the élites who will deal with educational questions, not only now but also in future, are favouring the kind of investments that are needed for the development of a real national competence in this respect. Such a competence would imply profound knowledge of the particularities of regionally different national languages and cultures, as well as interest in, and respect for, low prestigious primary school teachers and their problems. This kind of knowledge is not likely to become a serious criteria for the selection of élites. Do not the acculturation effects that are so obvious and visible in the national education system – the basic experience of becoming different by and through education and the entrance into modern, 'civilised' society (basically the 'akunya' effect) – in conjunction with the additional effects of having to adapt to the world of the donor-ruled elite, favour other basic qualities, such as forgetting or suppressing one's cultural origin and opening oneself to the language, the values and the ways of thinking and being of the really dominating culture – that of management, statistics, English, planning – thus making of oneself the African copy of the organisational culture of the dominating donor agencies that these agencies so much need in order to manage education in Africa?

REFERENCES

Baloi, O. and Palme, M. (1995) Vocação ou exclusão. Um estudo sobre o professor primário recém-formado (Vocation or exclusion? A study of the recently trained primary school teacher). Forthcoming in *Cadernos de pesquisa*. INDE: Maputo.

Chiau, S. (1992) Pensamentos dos alunos e aprendizagem na disciplina de Geografia na 5a classe. Análise das concepções dos alunos e das suas relações com o livro escolar e com o ensino como está previsto no manual do professor. Cadernos de pesquisa, No 7. INDE: Maputo, 1994 / Projecto de avaliação pedagógica do livro escolar, Relatório 16. Inde, Maputo

Geffray, C. (1991a) *La causes des armes au Mozambique. Anthropologie d'une guerre civile.* Paris: Karthala.

Geffray, C. (1991) *Ni pére, ni mére. Critique de la parenté: le cas makhuwa.* Paris: Seuil.

Hewson, M. (1988) 'The ecological context of knowledge: implications for learning Science in developing countries.' *Journal of Curriculum Studies 20*, 317–326

Hewson, P. and Hewson, M. (1984) 'The role of conceptual conflict in conceptual change and the design of science instruction.' *Instructional Science 13*, 1–13.

Horton, R. (1993) *Patterns of Thought in Africa and the West. Essays on Magic, Religion and Science.* Cambridge: Cambridge University Press.

Hyltenstam, K. and Luis, M. (1992) Aspects of Writing in the Mozambican Primary School. *Projecto de avaliação pedagógica do livro escolar, Relatório 7. INDE, Maputo.*

Hyltenstam, K. and Stroud, C. (1993) *Final Report and Recommendations from the Evaluation of Teaching Materials for Lower Primary Education in Mozambique. II: Language Issues.* INDE Research Report Series, no 3, INDE: Maputo.

Linha, C., Palme, M., and Xerinda, C. (1992) O ensino de Ciências Naturais e as concepçâes das crianças. Um estudo sobre o funcionamento do livro escolar na disciplina de Ciências Naturais e as suas condiçâes. Projecto de avaliação pedagógica do livro escolar, Relatório 18. INDE, Maputo.

Luis, M. (1992) O Português das crianças bilingues nas escolas primárias de Moçambique visto através dum teste de recontagem. Projecto de avaliação pedagógica do livro escolar, Relatório 5. INDE, Maputo.

Palme, M. and Eliasson, Y. (1992) *Teaching the Thermometer. A Comparison Between Mozambican and Swedish Text Books and a Commentary on Pedagogy in Mozambican Primary Education.* Projecto de avaliação pedagógica do livro escolar, Relatório 19. INDE, Maputo.

Palme, M. and Xerinda, C. (1992) *O que se passa nas aulas? Um estudo sobre os padrôes de interacçâo na sala de aula no ensino primário em Moçambique. (What's happening in the classroom? A study of interaction structures in Mozambican primary education.)* Projecto de avaliação pedagógico do livro escolar, Relatório No 4, INDE. Maputo.

Palme, M. (1993) *The Meaning of School. Repetition and Drop out in the Mozambican Primary School.* Education Division Documents, No 60. Stockholm: SIDA.

Proudford, C. and Baker, R. (1994) 'Looking at school improvement from a contextual perspective.' *School Organisation Vol.14,* 1, 21–35.

Riesmann, P. (1990) 'The formation of personality in fulani ethnopsychology.' In M. Jackson and I. Karp (eds) *Personhood and Agency. The Experience of Self and Other in African Society.* Uppsala Studies in Cultural Anthropology, no 14. Uppsala: Almqist and Wiksell International.

Serpell, R. (1993) *The Significance of Schooling. Life-journeys in an African Society.* Cambridge: Cambridge University Press.

Vedder, P. (1994) 'Global measurement of the quality of education: a help to developing countries?' *International Review of Education 40*, 1, 5–17.

CHAPTER 17

Truancy
The Greenstreet Detached Truancy Project

Tuaneri Akoto

INTRODUCTION

The London borough of Newham is one of many boroughs which make up London as a whole. It also is the poorest borough in Britain. With high unemployment, poor housing, crime and drug abuse, it also has it's fair share of domestic and social problems and issues.

Newham was formed in 1965 by the joining of two former boroughs. It has a population of 217,000, of which 49.1 per cent is under 34 years of age. There are estimated to be 32,326 young people aged between 10 and 21 – this being the age range which Newham Youth Service caters for.

Newham Youth Service is a council-owned service which caters to the needs of young people in the borough. The Youth service aims to 'enable young people to fulfil their potential as active citizens in the groups and communities in which they live through a process of informal education.'

THE GREENSTREET DETACHED PROJECT

The Greenstreet Detached Project has been in existence for over three years. It is the property of Newham Youth Service and originated out of a need to work with young people who are unattached to any youth provision.

As part of the detached project's natural development, in catering to the needs of young people, the truancy aspect was developed. This, in effect, meant working with young people who, for various reasons, refuse to attend school – this act being called 'truancy' – or who were excluded from school.

The truancy project's primary goal is to reduce acts of truancy and exclusion by providing a programme of alternative educational activities which are of interest to young people, while maintaining the basic elements of learning through reading, writing and arithmetic. The secondary goal, should the first one fail, is to get young people back into education.

The pivotal point of the project is the use of youth workers; the reason being that youth workers operate and teach in an informal manner in comparison to schools. This style of educating young people we know to be very successful.

YOUNG PEOPLE ON THE PROJECT

The young people accepted on the truancy project had to meet certain criteria, the main one being absenteeism from school. There was to be a maximum of 15 students but this was cut down to 10, this being a more realistic number in order to give each student the attention they required.

Each young person is given a folder containing:

1. Aims.

2. Objectives.

3. Code of conduct contract.

4. Rules and regulations.

5. Timetable.

6. Day/week learning experience sheets.

7. Profile data sheet.

8. Core skills development chart.

9. Youth worker/school contact sheet.

THE COURSES

The courses were, and are, designed in a manner in which young people are educated while they enjoy themselves. The courses are based on activities and subjects which the young people choose, want as a career and staff feel they need.

International dimension

Because education is something which is taught and delivered in many different ways and manners, we felt that the delivery of education by another country should be looked at by the students. This basically meant the organising of a youth exchange as part of the truancy project's arsenal in order to educate young people. The exchange was to introduce to the students international methods of combating truancy and delivery of education – formal and informal – but from a perspective which they could question, challenge, share experiences and learn from.

METHODS OF TEACHING

The Greenstreet Detached Truancy Project has paid great and detailed attention to what young people have said are their main dislikes of school and aspects of it, these fit under five categories:

1. The environment.
2. Teachers.
3. Peers.
4. Subject material and content.
5. General pressure.

The environment

In order to create and facilitate an environment that was conducive to easy, but effective, teaching and created, or had, an atmosphere for pleasant, easy and stress-free learning, it was decided that out-of-school premises would be more appropriate. Sites that bore all the hallmarks of the above mentioned criteria were prevalent in Newham, these being youth centres. Due to space, size and learning facilities, the Little Ilford Youth Centre was chosen.

Teachers

Teachers came under heavy fire from young people during the research stages, the two main reasons being: how they teach and their negative and disrespectful manner.

How young people are taught is almost as important as what they are being taught. This is an aspect of education which, to a great degree, is a one-sided event in favour of 'formal teaching'. One has but to look at three quarters of the schools in one's locality and observe that this is the prevailing way in which young people are taught. This style of educating, we know, fails many young people – young people who want to learn but cannot come to terms with the manner in which they are taught.

Based on past experience, youth work projects and youth exchanges, we have used informal teaching to great effect as a primary method in the educating of young people. Some aspects of this involved:

- Lessons being taught in group circles
- students constructing their own timetable based on subjects of their and the teacher's choice
- students being responsible for their own learning
- students partly involved in the administration of the truancy project

- students evaluating all aspects of the project on a weekly basis and then making changes, if necessary and beneficial.

There is an old adage that states: 'it's not what you do, it's the way that you do it.' It is one that we have used and have learned from in order to assist in the educating of young people.

The negative and disrespectful manner, which some teachers communicated towards young people caused the most damage between teacher/student relationships. We are fully aware of the trials and tribulations that teachers undergo with young people, but, in terms of trying to build up a relationship which encourages young people to want to learn, one has to consistently set positive examples for young people to emulate – if not learn from.

In order to assist the development of positive teacher/student relationships, several measures were adopted and these had to be agreed by all teachers or tutors who were to be accepted on the project. Some of these measures are:

- Everyone, students and teachers, referred to on a first-name basis
- all students respected and treated as young adults
- no disciplinary measures or actions be administered in front of, or discussed with, fellow students
- teachers/students do not swear, curse or embarrass one another
- there be no favourtism towards the educating of particular students over any other student.

Peers

An escalating problem in combating truancy is one of peers, yet, at the same time, it is peers that assist in the process of combating truancy. Less than a third of young people in schools are a negative influence. Attending school is a social activity: it is a place where young people go to learn together, share together and be together. As well as being a place of positive influence, it is also a breeding ground and congregation point for negative influences. Many problems faced by young people, in terms of truancy, are related to their fellow students. Problems such as bullying, theft, drugs, friend/relationships, negative pressure and enticement are all activities peers encourage amongst themselves.

The above mentioned problems and past-times which young people indulge in are regarded as social and peer issues by the truancy project. As a result of this, we have incorporated into their timetable, as part of their learning, issue-based projects and lessons. These projects and lessons are primarily based on showing young people the short- and long-term effects and dangers of activities that they indulge in. Additionally, the students are shown how to positively challenge and refuse what are generally regarded as negative aspects and activities of their peers.

One of the benefits of having the truancy project away from the young person's school site is that it removes the students from the problems, traumas and negative influences that they are confronted with in the school. This, in itself, is exactly what the young person is, in effect, doing when truanting.

Subject material and content

A major contributor to young people being bored at school is that lessons that appear to have no immediate or future use are regarded, by them, as not essential and therefore not of interest. This is not to say that the subject and content are not important for their future possible job prospects or general life. But, if it is perceived by young people as not needed, then it becomes a problem to teach.

We have surmounted this problem by subtly involving arithmetic, reading and writing into projects that we know young people are interested in. Projects such as singing, photography, art and design, cooking and sport.

General pressure

Pressure is an all-important aspect in the refusal of education by young people. It is something that can and does confront many young people at every corner they turn in life. It can be, and is, fatal in some cases. Social pressures, domestic pressures, peer pressures, parental pressures, educational attainment pressures – the list is endless. These are pressures that may never go away for some young people. The only way out for some is to truant. This, in itself, is a partial remedy as it doesn't solve any of the problems or issues young people are confronted with and by. Truancy was thus used as a solution, by young people, to many social, domestic and peer problems – problems and issues that were minor and some that were very serious.

Knowing that some pressures and issues are beyond the scope of our skills as youth workers, the truancy project involved the use of counselling. This had a far greater effect in combating truancy and educating young people who attend the truancy project than we could have ever imagined. Most of the reasons ascertained from young people for truanting were actually smoke screens hiding deeper and more severe reasons.

THE SUBTLE ART OF EDUCATING

Educating young people is a skill that has to be taught or acquired along the way of life. What you teach, and how you teach it, are what makes the difference in what a young person will learn and wants to learn. As we have already covered the manner in which we teach young people, it follows suit that the next important step is the content and how it is delivered. Formal deliverance of education tends to involve a very disciplinarian method that is not suitable to many young people, some tolerate it while others totally and utterly rebel against it. It is this type of young person that we find attends our truancy project or is frequently sent to us.

Formal deliverance of education fails many young people, not just in Newham but nation-wide. This method of deliverance of education is fine for those who find it suitable, but for those who do not, there is no alternative in the schooling system. Youth centres educate young people from a premise of informal education focused on social, domestic and personal issues. It is from this premise that the basis of deliverance of education to young people was formulated by the truancy project.

For some young people, sitting down in front of a desk and studying something that means, or is of, precious little consequence to them is a major contributing factor for less or practically no educational attainment. We, at the truancy project, concentrate on what are the foundations for education while, simultaneously, educating young people on any given subject. This, in essence, means we primarily concentrate on the what is commonly referred to as the '3 rs': Arithmetic, Reading and Writing.

The truancy project runs several set lessons or activity-based projects which incorporate the '3 rs'. These lessons are what young people have chosen and what the staff know will develop key life skills, as well as provide the educational and career subject content needed by the young people.

The canteen project

This was the most successful project as it involved all aspects of formal and informal education. The students were required to cover every aspect of running the youth centre canteen for 2 hours a day, 3 days a week. This not only meant cooking and serving, but also making the decisions on what to buy, purchasing the stock, working out the prices and being responsible for 'their' canteen.

If the subject to be learnt is taught in a manner and style which young people can relate to and it has, to them, an immediate use, then they will and do learn it. This project alone covered arithmetic, writing, reading, social and peer interaction and decision making. The students never once looked upon it as 'Oh God, maths' or 'God, boring writing'. The canteen project meant something to them. Arithmetic, on these occasions, had an immediate use, it was something they needed now in order for the canteen project to succeed and not make a loss, not something they would have no need of later on in life because they were not going to get a job that required maths.

Centre management course

Of all the projects, this was the one which presented young people with their biggest problems. The course required the development of various aspects of inter-personal and administration skills. Although the course was designed to cover, amongst other topics, programme construction, face-to-face work and inventories, book-keeping was withheld because arithmetic was already covered in the canteen project. A bigger emphasis was placed on administration.

In terms of improving the students' English, grammar and spelling, they were asked to type letters, memo's or one or two sentences about things they most disliked about the staff and the truancy project. This they did eagerly, while asking how to spell this or how to spell that or how to structure the letter or memo. Once again, not being aware that they were actually undergoing a dual learning process, it was a process which they liked.

Once the students were confident in the art of letter writing they started asking to write letters to their parents, friends and social workers. Other students soon followed suit. This was not discouraged as it was our indicator that learning was taking place. Plus, for some of them, it was the starting point in communicating, regardless of what was being written, with parents and friends whom they had, at one stage, refused to communicate with.

This style of development of inter-personal skills and educational knowledge was used extensively, for example, answering the 'phone and writing down messages for 30 minutes a day in order to develop communication, writing and spelling skills. The choice of material and content in order to educate the students in this course are plenty.

Cuisine project

This session was primarily aimed at the development of a domestic life skill, it is something that all schools do. The difference with how we at the truancy project assisted in teaching young people how to cook was that we allowed them to come up with the ideas of what to cook. Also, we attempted to teach them to cook foods of their parents' nationality/ies. This aspect of the cuisine project lead to it being very successful in terms of everyone taking part because, once again, if it is of interest to the young people or it has an immediate use in their lives, it will be learnt.

Youth exchange 'London – Paris'

Because young people from differing cities and environments do not live in this world alone, it is imperative that they should be given the opportunity to meet, speak, share views, life experiences and issues together on a face-to-face basis.

At the Greenstreet Detached Truancy Project, we believe that international experiences for young people should not be an 'opportunity' or an experience that some parents can afford and call holidays, but a standard feature in their general education. Because of this belief, we try, and do, organise youth exchanges with differing cities in Europe – the latest one being to Paris. This exchange was organised around issues of truancy and the deliverance of formal and informal education. In order to continue with the education of the students, not just by attending lessons, they were involved in the general administration and organising of the exchange. This meant that they were involved in the selection of issues to discuss, communicating with the French staff, the programme construction, making the ground rules and recording and leading the discussions.

These are all points of learning which the students started when they first attended the truancy project. This in itself is concrete evidence that the students were learning from the project's methods of teaching and it's style of delivering education. In terms of educating some young people, education should not be about learning something quickly or by pressuring someone to learn something. It should be about assisting young people to learn with pleasure, of making the subject and it's contents mean something to them – otherwise education will be treated like anything else in a young person's world that is horrible or causes unnecessary pressure, they will simply move away from it or rebel against it.

CASE STUDIES

The success of the methods used by The Greenstreet Detached Truancy Project can only be measured in terms of its impact, change of mentality and the willingness to learn of the young people who attend. A young person simply returning to school cannot be an accurate measure or indication for total success in reducing truancy; it shows no change in their mentality or the environmental factors which initially caused them to truant. If these factors do not change, and change for the better, then the return to school, or the enforced return to school, will be short-term.

The Greenstreet Detached Truancy Project uses five indicators or points to measure it's effectiveness on the lives of young people who truant:

- Domestic conditions
- social conditions
- peer relationships
- schooling conditions
- deliverance of education.

We discovered, very early in the initial stages of the truancy project, that truancy was an end result of a long equation of negative conditions:

> domestic conditions + social conditions + peer relationships + school conditions and system = truancy

> (a breakdown in any one of these situations can lead on to truancy).

Young people were using truancy as a solution to all, if not some, of the conditions in the equation.

As a result of this discovery, counselling was introduced into the project. This was introduced by way of one-to-one discussions and group discussions and by using their work as a platform to introduce new ideas, concepts and analogies with which to view their problems and solve them (if possible).

Charlene (fictitious name)

Charlene, 15 years of age, comes from a single parent family. Her parents separated when she was six years old. She is the only sibling living at home with her mother. Her sisters and brother have all moved out and go on living their own lives and raising their own families. Charlene has said that she truants because school is boring, that the teachers have no respect and that she does not get on with other young people. Charlene gets on okay with her mother but says that her mother always nags her. Charlene also baby-sits for her sister's daughter and other people's children. She is also having problems in her existing relationship.

Once the underlying issues were ascertained, the real work with solving or administering to Charlene's situation began. The first was to solve the relationship problems with her boyfriend, as she spent a great deal of time depressed about it. This was initiated by getting Charlene to send her boyfriend a valentine card. Without realising it, Charlene was already back on the road to education.

In order for Charlene to do this card, she had to design the graphics for it, think of what to write – with correct spellings and grammar – and how to express what she felt constructively. She became enthusiastic about learning how to use the 'stupid computer' in order to produce a high quality end product. Yet, without being aware of the educational aspects and learning, Charlene gave her all in order for her card to be perfect.

Dealing with the baby-sitting was not so much a problem as we discovered that it was something she attended to when she was bored while truanting. Because Charlene was now doing something she liked – attending the truancy project – and being genuinely interested in the work set, there was no need for her to baby-sit as a pastime activity.

Charlene's enthusiasm and commitment towards finishing any piece of work soon began to get her praise, not just from the truancy staff but also from her education welfare officer. Much to our surprise, during the third week of attending the truancy project she asked if she could take her folder home to show her mum the work she was doing and had done. Charlene returned the next day with a broad smile on her face and explained that her mother was proud of the work she had done and that she was now attending an educational project every day.

Charlene's mother's pride was given another boost as Charlene and some of the other students were photographed and interviewed by the local newspaper about their involvement in the truancy project's youth exchange to Paris. When the paper was published, Charlene's mother took the newspaper around to all her (Charlene's mother's) friends' houses.

In this particular case, although Charlene point-blank refused to go back to school, tackling and assisting in the coming to terms with her social and domestic problems led onto getting her back into education. Charlene now takes part in every lesson set whether she likes the lessons or not because each lesson has an immediate use and meaning to her.

Donald (fictitious name)

Donald is the oldest in his family. He lives with his mother, stepfather and younger sister (who is fathered by the stepfather). He has a reasonable relationship with his mother and stepfather, this he also extends to his younger sister. Donald stated that his reasons for truanting were because school is boring, he dislikes the teachers and that he prefers to be with his dog.

As with Charlene, improving Donald's academic ability and general attitude towards education could not begin until we had ascertained the underlying reasons for his truanting.

We realised, from close observation and discussions, that Donald's main traumas were of a domestic nature. Specifically speaking, they related to his stepfather's relationship with his mother and that he vented his disapproval via his sister. Donald has, on several occasions, injured his sister, as well as set fire to her bedroom. This we ascertained as Donald's way of getting attention, as well as getting revenge for his sister receiving more attention than he thinks she should.

In order to focus Donald on some form of work relating to his domestic life, we encouraged him to design, for his mother's front door, a 'Beware of the dog' poster. This he relished and asked if he could do several. The following day he said his mother really liked it and could he do one for his sister's room. The fact that Donald's mother was now paying an interest in him and the work he was doing was the initial impetus needed to get Donald back into education.

As the days went by, Donald produced more posters for his house and room. Now, although Donald's academic abilities were poor, we gradually began to encourage him to add more text and sentences into his posters. This was one way in which we worked on improving his spelling and English. Additionally, he is now producing more work, willingly and happily, for his sister.

As part of joining the truancy project, the students sign a code of conduct contract. There were two rules which became learning points for Donald: No swearing and To talk to other people with respect whether you like them or not. Donald swears profusely and acts in a very disrespectful manner. After working with him we ascertained that he swears as a result of the company he keeps and he acts in a disrespectful manner because far too few people respect him – the latter being a case of people treating him as a kid.

After working with Donald for two months, consistently treating him as a young adult and respecting him, Donald's negative mannerisms, swearing and disrespectful nature diminished immensely – not just at the truancy project but also at home (this we found out by way of feedback from his mother and education welfare officer). Donald lives in an area of high unemployment and crime. He tends to spend a lot of time with his older friends who have left school. At present, these friends are more of a negative influence than of a positive one.

Slowly but surely we are getting Donald to appreciate that he still has an opportunity to improve his education and life prospects. But this will be a constant battle and one which we accept we may lose in the long run because, upon leaving the truancy project or when absent from the project, Donald is in, or immediately returns to, the environment/s which have such a powerful and negative influence on his life and actions.

CONCLUSION

The act of truancy in itself is not a problematic entity. Truancy is a solution, by young people, to many life factors which negatively affect them. Some factors are very traumatic, stemming from an earlier age and some minor, but the young person has no, if very little, support or assistance in dealing with the issue/s. We have found that three quarters of the reasons put forward by young people for truanting are actually smoke screens to serious complications or traumas in their lives.

These complications and traumas, having not been solved and/or new ones being piled on top, simply add to the overall pressures in a young person's life. The simplest solution is to take time out, to have a break – truancy.

By directly attempting to resolve, and/or assist in the improving of, some of the conflicts in a young person's life – whether they be social, domestic, peers or inter-personal skills – the Greenstreet Detached Project has had a far greater influence and response in getting young people back into education. Additional to this is the fact that informal education is complementary, and as important, to formal education. It is a fallacy to believe that one should have a higher priority over the other. You cannot prepare a young person for adulthood with just academic attainments and, in a similar vein, you should not prepare a young person, in an industrial society, without career development.

Benefits

The Greenstreet Detached project has had many benefits from using informal education and informal teaching as the main way forward in the reintroduction of education to young people.

Treating young people as adults, with respect, courtesy and friendliness, and as human beings, eliminated virtually all of the hatred and dislikes that were aimed at teachers and school. This, coupled with an informal and almost pressureless environment, provided an ideal atmosphere in which young people found themselves to be prepared and willing to learn.

Showing young people how to, directly and indirectly, effectively and constructively, confront, challenge and question the issues and problems they face in their daily lives created a bond of trust and faith between the staff and the young people. These, in turn, laid down the foundations upon which staff assisted young people in coming to terms, or dealing, with many of life's social and domestic issues and problems.

One of the most striking benefits of the truancy project was the positive feedback we received from the parents, relatives, schools, education welfare officers and the students themselves. Not only did the feedback encourage the parents to continue sending their children to the project, but they were also overjoyed to see them taking part in something educational that the student liked and attended regularly – this being proof that informal teaching and informal education should have a higher priority in the education of young people.

Eradicating or alleviating the domestic and social problems in young peoples lives, as well as building up their general confidence, makes all the difference to their self-worth, self-confidence and how they contribute, interact and feel in the society and community in which they live.

Disadvantages

The main, and most important, disadvantage to young people attending the truancy project is that, at present, it cannot provide formal educational qualifications. This, in itself, is not a self-defeating issue because our primary goal is to get young people back into school where they can continue with their formal education. But, more often than not, the young people who attend our truancy project refuse point-blank to return to school. Our secondary goal is to get them back into education, suffice it to say not in a school and preferably not on a school site.

Another disadvantage, discovered as the project progressed into its second year, is that long-term attenders become accustomed to the informal methods of teaching and informal education. Although this system is suitable and conducive to their learning does it present a problem when some of the students return to school. Formal education, and the manner of teaching, is not always the most appropriate way for some young people to learn.

Age, and the legal age to leave school, proved to be a major disadvantage in terms of trying to educate young people. It arose that being 15 years old, or being near to the school leaving age, gave the young people an attitude of 'Well I'm leaving soon so it doesn't matter'. It was discovered that the majority of students that we accepted aged 15–16 were relatively harder to teach because of this 'I'm leaving soon' attitude. The nearer they were to the school leaving age and date, the harder it was to teach them and get them involved in any activity

Truancy projects, by their very nature, provide a safer, more relaxed, less stressful and welcoming atmosphere, when compared to most schools. On the one hand this is exactly what is required to entice the reintroduction of education to young people. But, on the other hand, it is also an easy option out of school for those who generally would not truant (regardless of the education system failing them) or who have a lower rate of truancy.

RECOMMENDATIONS

1. An alternative measure needs to be incorporated into the education system where informal education and teaching are available to those whom formal education fails and it be treated as a natural part of standard education for young people.

2. That informal counselling should be incorporated into schools as a life and learning evaluation lesson with a minimum of half an hour a week, thus allowing young people a platform on which to air, and focus on – either on a one-to-one basis or in a group setting – problems, issues and concerns that are important to them.

3. That the education system should not primarily concentrate on the '3 rs' but also, amongst others, inter-personal development and social interaction.

4. That a system which can identify the 'possible' signs of potential truancy be set up in order to solve, if not attempt to alleviate, the situation before it comes into fruition.

5. That, in order to meet and assist the needs and problems young people are consistently facing, there should joint support and a work committee between:

Agency	Assistance in
Education department	Formal education
Youth services and youth provisions	Informal education
Social Services	Domestic and personal problems
Education Welfare Officers	Identify truants and potential truants
Colleges/Commercial Business	Training and work experience
Police	Crime prevention initiatives
Tenants' Associations/shops	Ascertaining locations of truants
Parents	All aspects of the young person

Further information can be obtained from:

Mr Tuaneri 'Tui' Akoto, Project Co-ordinator, The Forest Gate Youth Centre, 1 Woodford Road, Forest Gate, London E7 ODH. Tel No: 0181–519–7820, 0181–471–3468

PART SIX

Strengthening the Human Spirit

CHAPTER 18

The Truth of Single-Parent Families

Children from single-parent families
[Mercy Ojelade, Courtney Weston and Benjamin]

INTRODUCTION

This chapter is not written by adults that have no idea about what being a child in a single-parent family is like, it is written by children in single-parent families for all children. Read this and take our advice. We understand.

We made a radio programme about single-parent families (see McCrum 1996) but we couldn't say everything we wanted to say because it was only twelve minutes long, so we decided to put as much as we could here.

IS IT MY FAULT

Sometimes children feel that it is their fault that they are in a single-parent family. Do not feel this way because your parents should know, and you should too, that it is not your fault. When I was younger I thought that it was my fault that my father had died. Now I realise that it was not my fault at all. I am sure that eventually you will feel the same. Don't worry if you wait and wait and you still don't feel this way. You're not the only one.

Henrietta said: 'Once I did think it was my fault. When my mum was pregnant she had a lot of stress and my mum was a bit ill. I thought that was why they split up. I thought it was my fault as well because I am the youngest. Now I understand that it isn't my fault because lots of children have mums and dads that split up and their mum wasn't stressed or ill.'

HOW TO COPE

If you find yourself in a single-parent family, don't worry if you begin to cry in front of your friends. Just tell someone like your teacher. Talking can help a lot. It lets you express what you feel, so don't bottle it up, tell somebody. Some of the time mums get to look after the child and sometimes dad. Whoever looks after you, they love you as much as they can. It sometimes means helping around the home. You know both parents love you. You will someday understand why your parents split up. Whatever happens, you are the most important person, so work hard at school and make a success of your life and try not to make the same mistakes as your parents.

DIVORCE

Parents get divorced because they begin to drift apart. It is very pitiful for the child. It makes a mark on the child. After the divorce comes the custody case. Custody is the case about who is going to look after the child. Sometimes the dad gets custody but most of the time the mum (but men can look after children too). It is very hard for the parents as well as the child.

Court cases and Judges – that is what parents have to go through, but it is the children I think that have the hardest time because they do not know which parent will look after them. It is very harrowing for them. Sometimes, if one parent has been looking after the child for a long time, the jury will order that parent to look after the child.

WHAT DO YOU THINK ABOUT BEING A SINGLE-PARENT FAMILY?

'My dad and mum are not divorced but are split up. I would like to go on holidays with my mum. My mum and dad do get on but not as much as I want. I would like people to understand a bit more and to take me seriously. I'd rather talk to people in the same situation.'

'At first I kept it to myself. When I told everyone, they didn't believe me. Usually I blame my dad but I don't really mean it. My mum left my dad and sometimes I try talking to her about it.'

'I feel very upset because I have not got a dad around and it feels different.'

'It's different to live with dad. I'd like to see more of dad. I like living with my mum. I would never like to live with my dad. I would like to have both of them at the same house.'

'My dad is stricter than my mum. I always have to have my dinner at the table at my dad's house. But at my mum's house (where I live), I can eat on the floor. My dad tells me off if I do a little thing wrong but my mum says "don't do it again". I don't mind being in a single-parent family because I live with my mum, but my dad gives us money and we see him every weekend and I go on holiday with him. I would like him to live with us.'

'If I get teased, I just ignore them because they tease me a lot and I feel different and I feel upset. They tease me that I live with my mum and not my dad. Sometimes I take it personally.'

'My mum has never talked to me about it.'

'I never lived in a two-parent family because my dad died when I was small. Sometimes I wonder what it would be like to live with two parents. But I enjoy living with my mum because she tells me things my friends don't know.'

'I want a different dad. We do not get much money from dad. I would like to be in a two-parent family. My dad has a drink problem. He kicked the front door down once. I want a gentle dad. I think if dad would have looked after me, I would be in care. I was two when they split up. It has changed me. I go to bed late sometimes. I have to help around the house. My mum is a good cook.'

DO YOU THINK BEING IN A SINGLE-PARENT FAMILY IS DIFFERENT TO BEING IN AN ORDINARY FAMILY?

'Yes, because there is one person in your family and they are always busy. And you used to have both of them and it seems strange.'

'A single parent family *is* an ordinary family.'

'Yes, because you get more love with two parents.'

'Yes, because of not having a dad to help you.'

'There's no such thing as an ordinary family.'

MY DAD AND I

'I feel it's not very fair, but everyone says life's not fair. The world is for women with children. It's not a men's world. If a man is with a child he gets suspicious looks. My dad is a much better cook than my mum. He does nice healthy food. He doesn't drink much and he takes me out and talks to me. He teaches me about things my friends don't know, like genetics, history and science. He's got good plans for me and he's got my future in his mind all the time. He hasn't got much money for the work he does with children. People often think men can't look after children because of the way they are. I think women are expected to look after the children because they get pregnant, but it takes two people to create a child, so a man is heavily involved as well.'

'It's good for me, as a boy, to live with my dad because he has been through puberty and he can tell me what it feels like. I think men can look after children and they can be gentle and firm, a bit like a lion in a pride of lions. My dad's had to look after three children and they all enjoy their time with him, because he cares, and I think that most men care about their children.'

WHAT YOU FEEL ABOUT OUR RADIO PROGRAM

We have asked children what they feel about our radio programme. This is what they said:

'I think this is important because it helps children who are in a single-parent family.'

'This is also important to those who aren't in a single-parent family.'

'I liked the way that they told you not to worry about other people.'

'I liked the bit where they talk about who loved you most. People need to know what it is like to live with one parent.'

'I feel that if I was in a single-parent family, this programme would cheer me up.'

We then asked them whom they would recommend this to. Their answers were:

'I would recommend this radio programme to parents to see how it would be if they were to split up and how the children would feel.'

'People who have never seen their mum and dad.'

Then we asked them on what occasion they thought of this subject:

'The thought came up while I was talking to my mum.'

'I think of this when I see children walking with their parents and I look at myself, with my mum.'

'When my mum and dad have a disagreement.'

The last question we asked was how they feel about it:

'I feel quite good now I've had someone to talk to.'

IF YOU NEED HELP...

Childline:
0800 1111.

Stepfamily (produces a newsletter for children in stepfamilies):
Chapel House, 18 Hatton Place, London EC1N 8RU. Tel: 0171 209 2460 (for general enquiries); 0990 168388 (for counselling).

The Children's Legal Centre:
The University of Essex, Wivenhoe Park, Colchester, Essex CO4 3SQ.
Tel: 01206 873820

Youth Access:
1a Taylors Yard, 67 Alderbrook Road, London SW12 8AD. Tel: 0181 772 9900

If you feel lonely, there are over two million children in single-parent families in this country.

Reference

McCrum, S. (1996) 'A Voice in the Media: Radio – Children Speaking For Themselves.' In M. John (ed) *Children in Charge: The Child's Right to a Fair Hearing. Children in Charge 1.* London: Jessica Kingsley Publishers.

CHAPTER 19

The Rights of the Child
in a Paediatric Oncology Unit

Penelope Cousens and Michael Stevens

INTRODUCTION

The Royal Alexandra Hospital for Children is located in the inner-city and was built in 1869. Due to the efforts of our parents, the Oncology Unit is probably one of the most modern in Australia. We have over 900 patients on our clinic books. Many of these would be children visiting the clinic on a six-monthly or annual basis for checkups. Our ward has 10 beds which, unfortunately, is often insufficient – meaning that children have to be accommodated in other wards of the hospital making ward rounds something of a trek occasionally. Nevertheless, cancer in children is rare and we should point out that there are only two major paediatric oncology units in New South Wales. We have been attached to the Oncology Unit for seven years; for the past three years Penelope has been working full-time as psychologist in the Unit. Although successes far outnumber failures in the Unit, there are, of course, times when a child relapses after all attempts have been made to cure the disease and it is this small group of children that this paper is about. We have noticed that in some cases the decision to cease treatment and to begin palliative care has been left to the child, and everyone – parents and medical staff – has obviously been content to do this. We have often wondered what it is about that child, and possibly that family, that allows the medical staff to feel comfortable about this. This chapter outlines the results of our enquiries.

> 'Children are protected legal persons only capable of providing limited consent to medical treatment until they attain the age of majority. An exception exists under the "mature minor rule". If a child has reached that stage of intellectual development where it has sufficient capacity to understand the nature and effect or consequences of the proposed treatment, then the child is capable of giving a valid consent.' (Uniacke 1991, p.56)

We have begun our chapter with a quotation from a legal journal because, although it discusses the legal position with regard to commencing treatment, it applies equally well to the cessation of life-sustaining treatment in the case of malignant disease. We do not intend to dwell on legal issues but would point out that on 17 August 1992, the *Medical Journal* of Australia published an article outlining guidelines for the management of terminally ill patients. These guidelines state that the patient has the right to request, refuse or negotiate modification of treatment. They also state that the person must be 'competent' to make decisions. It is the matter of competence that we wish to discuss. We would like to explore what 'competence' means when we are discussing children and their ability to make critical decisions.

It seemed to us that the best way to start was to ask colleagues in the Oncology Unit for their views on the subject. A brief questionnaire was prepared and staff members were asked if they would mind answering the questions in an interview. The length of time required depended very much on the respondent. The basic questionnaire needed 10 to 15 minutes but it was found that many of the respondents became quite involved and the time varied. Everyone approached agreed to participate and 18 questionnaires were completed altogether. Six doctors, five nursing staff and seven non-medical staff were interviewed.

Everyone agreed that there are times with an adult patient when it is desirable to cease treatment and concentrate on relieving distressing symptoms, even if this means shortening life. Responses to the question: 'Under what circumstances would you be likely to recommend such a step?' included: 'when the patient asks for treatment to be discontinued' (5 cases) and 'when the treatment is adversely affecting the quality of life remaining to the patient and there is no longer hope of cure'. Most of the respondents agreed that the decision is basically one of balancing benefits of continuing treatment versus the burdens of such treatment. They also agreed that they would have answered the questions similarly if *child* was substituted for *adult* in the previous questions.

Having established that none of the respondents felt that treatment should be continued on moral and ethical grounds regardless of possible final outcome, the questions then addressed issues more pertinent to the subject being explored.

'Who do you believe should be responsible for a decision to stop treatment in the case of a child?'

Most respondents felt that this was a decision to be left to the parents, with the understanding that they were fully informed by the doctors of all possible alternatives and their consequences, but that older children should be included in the decision-making process. One nurse felt that children should be present at this time, whatever their age, and one doctor pointed out that it was important that a balance be maintained so that parents felt involved in the process but were not placed in the position of taking sole responsibility for the decision.

'In your experience, have you encountered a situation where the parents have left such a decision to the child?'

Respondents were equally divided on this question. Two doctors felt that, though it appeared that the children were making the decision, in fact parents were prepared beforehand. In other words, the decision has been made jointly at an earlier time.

'What if the parent and child disagree?'

It was agreed by all that intervention is needed in this case, the goal being to reconcile the parents and child. The importance of this reconciliation was emphasised for everyone's peace of mind, both before and after the child's death. It was pointed out that in cases where the child wants to cease treatment and the parents want to continue, it may be because the parents have not accepted the fact that their child is dying. It was also pointed out that recommendations from doctors may reflect their own philosophy (based on religious beliefs, financial considerations, etc) which may not always concur with the views held by parents. The need to maintain the close relationship between child and parents was seen to be of prime importance, regardless of whether or not the staff agreed with the decisions made.

All respondents agreed that there have been occasions when they felt the child should have been included in the decision-making process and where the parents had not maintained open communication with the child. Those who had not actually known of such a case were convinced that this was a possibility.

All respondents, except two non-medical staff, felt that there may be cases where a child's expressed preference is unduly influenced by parents and where the child may not have a full understanding of the implications of stopping or continuing treatment. The two respondents who did not agree felt that this was unlikely to occur because of the emphasis in the Unit on providing full information to families from the time of diagnosis.

When asked how this situation might be dealt with, intervention was again recommended. The importance of reconciling the views of the child and parent was again emphasised. Open communication between parents and child would be encouraged but where parents insisted that the child not be told of the seriousness of their illness, all respondents agreed that, while the parents' wishes must be respected, parents should be told that if the child asks the staff direct questions about their illness, then they will have to answer those questions honestly.

Many of the responses to the previous questions had been qualified by the child's age. When asked if there is a particular age at which children are competent to make important decisions for themselves, a wide range of ages was mentioned – it was felt that children aged seven years and over should be involved in decision-making and that some children are capable of making critical decisions at eight years of age. Critical decisions included decisions like ceasing treatment for most of the respondents.

'Are there characteristics of a child's behaviour that would make you feel a particular child is competent to make critical treatment decisions?'

All agreed there were and they are listed in order of frequency as follows:

1. *Understanding:* It was felt that children demonstrated their understanding of their illness by the types of questions they asked their parents and medical staff. An ability to communicate openly and honestly with adults was also seen to demonstrate maturity. The child who does not ask questions and does not show an interest in their illness and treatment procedures was considered to be either using excessive denial or immature.

2. *Independence:* Medical staff were of the opinion that the child must show some evidence of independence from the parents, some individuality and have demonstrated confidence in their own decision-making process.

3. *Emotional Maturity:* Calmness and appropriate expression of emotion at times was thought to demonstrate emotional maturity. Evidence of emotional involvement on the part of both parents and children and the ability to support each other was felt by two respondents to be important. The child who shows empathy for the distressed parent and is supportive was thought to be mature.

'Are there characteristics of the parent-child relationship which would make you feel comfortable about leaving critical treatment decisions to the child?'

Again all agreed there were as follows:

1. *Open, honest communication:* This was seen to be the most important factor. The parents' ability to convey information at the child's level of understanding and their willingness to include the child in medical consultations and answer their questions were thought to be indications of this type of communication. Conversely, in cases where parents specifically asked that the child not be given information about their illness, it was acknowledged that the children know very

well what is wrong with them and appreciate the seriousness of their illness but are denied the opportunity to discuss it openly.

2. *Emotional maturity of family:* It was felt that the family which is able to maintain open honest communication with their child is also likely to be emotionally mature and will have expressed their emotional responses appropriately while supporting each other and being able to accept each other's unhappiness and pain. Mutual respect for each other's opinions and feelings was also a consideration. One respondent felt that occasionally parents can become so emotionally involved that the intellectual process may be overridden. In such a case, the child may be more competent to make decisions.

3. *Independence:* One respondent commented that some families encourage their children to be independent from an early age. This can be demonstrated by parents allowing their children to make minor decisions for themselves regarding treatment and care.

'Is the history of the parent-child relationship since diagnosis relevant?'

This was felt to the case even if not at a conscious level. Characteristics mentioned were:

1. *Coping Styles:* This was mentioned by most of the respondents as being the most important aspect of the family history. It was felt that the way a family coped with diagnosis was likely to persist throughout the illness unless intervention took place. Again, open communication between parents and child was seen to be most important.

2. *Family Relationship:* Warmth, closeness and the ability to provide a safe environment for the child were all aspects of the family's history that were considered important. The disruption of a stable environment by the arrival of an estranged parent, particularly one seeking involvement in the decision-making process, was mentioned by one respondent. Again, the issue of whether the child has been encouraged to make decisions regarding treatment and care was raised. It was felt that if previously all decisions had been made by the parents, then it would not be fair to the child to expect them to make a final decision of this nature.

The final question addressed the issue of whether or not children who have been treated in the Oncology Unit differ in their level of maturity to children in other departments of the hospital and in the community. This was a more general question and responses were applicable to all paediatric oncology patients.

Respondents were reluctant to compare with other departments of the hospital because of lack of knowledge. Non-medical staff felt that while younger children often regressed (possibly because of over-protection from their parents), older children were reported by parents to be more sensitive to other people's feelings and kinder. It was felt that because cancer is such an emotive issue, children are treated differently. A concern was expressed that they may become more materialistic than their peers in the community. Others were described as being more mature generally with an appreciation of everyday things. One of the nurses pointed out that cancer is unlike other chronic diseases, for example cystic fibrosis, as the patient's experience of illness is much more compressed with peaks and troughs while other diseases tend to ripple along and extend over a long period of time.

Children who are dying were described as being more withdrawn, thoughtful and more insightful as their condition worsened. Death and dying were felt to be much 'closer' for oncology patients with an early realisation that 'it can happen to me'. Most respondents agreed that, emotionally, children seem to mature at an accelerated pace but not cognitively, although familiarity with medical terminology may give this impression. There was doubt that the understanding of the irreversibility of death is more advanced than for healthy children.

Returning to the characteristics of the child that our colleagues feel are indicative of sufficient maturity to allow them to make critical decisions for themselves, we will examine each briefly in a theoretical context.

One important characteristic was the independence of the child. Winnicott (1965) says that one of the tasks of childhood is the attainment of autonomy and independence while Erikson (1982) stresses the concepts of industry and the building up of a sense of competence in the school-age child leading to the search for identity of the adolescent. These are not easy tasks for the child and are facilitated by the ongoing care of the parents in normal circumstances. The dying child in the Oncology Unit is often completely dependent on parents and medical staff in a physical sense and sometimes in an emotional sense as well. We say 'sometimes' because it seems to us to be possible for children to maintain a sense of self, despite their desperate situation. The wish to have parents close by in a physical sense does not necessarily imply emotional dependence. Parents who are able to recognise this, respect the child's right to make minor decisions thereby fostering a sense of autonomy and helping the child to maintain a sense of self.

A second characteristic that respondents mentioned was emotional maturity. Although this has been touched on in the previous section, we feel it is important to look at this issue more closely. How does one assess emotional maturity and, more particularly, how do we assess emotional maturity when the child's environment is the antithesis of the ideal for normal development? What are we talking about when we talk of emotional maturity? Generally speaking, it seems to mean the ability to express and handle our own emotions and those of people close to us. We feel that the respondent who said that what she would be looking for was the child's ability to empathise with the parent's grief and be supportive was particularly perceptive. That child would seem to have reached a level of maturity often not attained by adults. If we can be permitted a little poetic licence, we would describe this child as 'emotionally decentered'. By this, we mean the child has reached a level of moral maturity which enables him or her to empathise with others. Hogan (1973) see moral development in terms of five basic concepts: moral knowledge, socialization, empathy, moral reasoning and autonomy. The child who is not only able to empathise but also to support grieving parents must surely be described as emotionally mature, particularly when it is remembered that the source of the grief is the child himself. We see examples of children protecting their parents often in Oncology.

Finally, the most important characteristic mentioned by our colleagues was the child's understanding of their disease. Although it is common in the Oncology Unit to hear children as young as three and four years of age using sophisticated medical terminology, their understanding of this terminology is often very superficial. For example, a child may say: 'I'm having a lumbar puncture today' but, when asked: 'What does that mean?' they will reply: 'It means I am going to see Bart today and he'll tell me some funny jokes' (Bart being our pain nurse consultant). In fact, working with children in the Unit, it has become clear to us that it is not until children are functioning at the concrete operational level (using Piaget's stages of development) that children are able to begin to understand their illness.

When asked to draw their understanding of their disease, children with leukaemia aged from seven years will often draw 'good' and 'bad' cells being attacked by rockets representing chemotherapy. Similar concepts are used to describe treatment for tumours. These children will certainly understand what it means to be told that the chemotherapy is not working. However, the full implications of this may not be fully appreciated as children of this age are likely to be irresolute about the irreversibility of death. This is not the case for children aged 12 years and older, who understand that death is permanent.

There are two issues about understanding that worry us, however. One is that our colleagues felt that the type of questions the child asks indicates their level of understanding. We would question this as we have met several children who would be most unlikely to ask questions at all but who have a very good understanding of their disease and its implications. These children have chosen not to seek out information but to use denial as a defence and have found that this is the only way they can cope. We would argue that while many children use intellectualisation as a defence, it does not necessarily mean they are more knowledgeable or, indeed, more mature.

The second issue is: what are we wanting and expecting the children to understand? We suspect that what we are really talking about is the child's understanding of their own death. Lansdown (1989) maintains that children with cancer progress through stages of understanding as follows:

> 'I am very sick.
> I have an illness that can kill people.
> I have an illness that can kill children.
> I may not get better.
> I am dying'. (p.33)

It is our belief that at the time of diagnosis even pre-verbal children have some understanding that they are very sick, which they acquire from the reactions of those closest to them. As treatment progresses, the older child soon learns that not only does the disease kill some adults but that children also are not immune to its effects. They must hear of other children's deaths, some of whom they may even have been friendly with. At the time of relapse, the seriousness of the situation and, again, the reactions of those around them, bring a realisation that they may not survive this illness. Finally, it becomes clear that they are dying.

The title of this chapter is 'The Rights of the Child in the Paediatric Oncology Unit', the focus being on the right of the dying child to make the final decision to cease treatment. We have attempted to gather together the thoughts of our colleagues in this regard. The child who has maintained some independence and sense of self, who is able to empathise and support grieving parents and who understands that his or her own death is a possibility and then a certainty, is surely capable of making critical decisions regarding cessation of treatment and has the right to do so. As adults, we are continually striving to understand the inner world of the child. It is our task to try and understand the inner world of the dying child as well.

REFERENCES

Erikson, E.H. (1982) *The Life Cycle Completed*, New York: W.W. Norton and Co.

Hogan, R. (1973) 'Moral conduct and moral character: a psychological perspective.' *Psychological Bulletin 79*, 217–232.

Lansdown (1989) In D. Judd *Give Sorrow Words*. London: Free Association Books.

Uniacke, P. (1991) 'Children's consent to medical treatment.' *Law Society Journal*, 56–57.

Winnicott, D.W. (1965) *The Family and Individual Development*. London: Tavistock Publications.

Winnicott, D.W. (1971) *Playing and Reality*. London: Tavistock Publications.

CHAPTER 20

Learning Rights
A Fundamental Prerequisite
for Protecting Oneself and Others

Gael Parfitt

Work in this chapter seeks to examine the relationship between learning rights and self-advocacy, and draws upon professional experience in schools and qualitative research findings with young people in order to illuminate some relevant issues.

INTRODUCTION

How do young people learn to protect their rights and respect and support the rights of others? How do they learn to take charge of their lives? I believe that active learning experiences can help young people to represent and protect their interests and concerns. This is more likely to happen if learning processes are democratically experienced, so that young people's rights are fully acknowledged and 'lived' in classroom interactions. Respecting them in the learning situation means they are much more likely to respect themselves. If they are encouraged to initiate, problem solve, and make sense of their own learning processes, they are more likely to feel actively involved. Active learning of this kind, which explicitly focuses upon children's rights in practice, can enable young people to develop the skills and abilities to express and defend themselves. So what kind of learning journey is this which could offer support for self-protection and self-advocacy?

Equal access to an enabling education seems to me to be a children's right. I saw many young people struggling with various kinds of discrimination and economic disadvantage. Some found ways of achieving and became more empowered as a consequence. Others fell back. One such young person was Sharon.

Sharon was eleven when she joined my Humanities group in 1984. She had already been moved from another class because of her 'behaviour' and this was her 'last chance' in the school. She found it difficult to concentrate and I found myself spending a good deal of time with her once the other members of the class had settled down to the task in hand. Other teachers, and some school students, soon complained about Sharon. School students claimed that Sharon received a disproportionate amount of teacher time and attention and some of her teachers said that she was impossible to teach. Sharon didn't want to leave, but she accepted and abided by the decision to move her to a special school. She did not express any concerns. She shrugged her shoulders with an air of courageous defeat. Her parents were not articulate and they were not around. What rights did Sharon have? How could she become involved in the quest to identify and support her best interests? Was the planned move the right one for her? How might she be supported? Few curriculum subjects in the school ventured to make a contribution to this aspect of Sharon's education. The 'problem' of Sharon's future was absorbed into the domain of the pastoral care system and the Year Head dealt with it. No doubt sensitive discussions took place. This is, in my experience, normal procedure in UK state schools. But could Sharon make a case for herself? We heard later that Sharon had been put into care (supervised state residential provision). She died in her bath, choking with chewing gum and electrocuted by the fire that had fallen into the water. Sharon was barely thirteen years old when she died. Her old classmates did not seem to be troubled by the news.

It was my work as an Humanities teacher with Sharon, in the early eighties, that first led me to consider rights issues in the learning process itself. Recent legislation has made it clear that children have a right to be consulted. But this same legislation presupposes that young people know 'how' to make an informed judgment and express their views. The Gillick judgment, set out by Woolf and endorsed by Scarman (1986), states: 'a child under sixteen can give a true consent depending upon her maturity and understanding and the nature of the consent required'. This surely presumes the existence of an enabling education. Equally, Department of Health guidelines for those working in child protection (Department of Health 1988), have stressed that professionals must recognise that children have a right to be consulted and their views taken into account. In addition, the Children Act 1989, following recommendations in Articles 12 and 13 of the UN Convention on the Rights of the Child, intends that account be taken of the views of young people concerning their future well-being, but it is often difficult for them to express and refine their views without appropriate learning support. How do young people get the support they need to develop the skills and attributes of analysis and self advocacy?

In this chapter I draw upon two research case-studies to illuminate the relationship between learning rights, assertiveness and self-protection. The first is only referred to briefly. This was a whole-school evaluation of a method of learning assessment called 'Profiling' (Parfitt *et al.* 1990). The crucial thing here was that young people were invited to comment upon their own learning achievements. The second is an ongoing research study of self-reflection in learning, and this enquiry also pays close attention to views of the young people involved.

THE CURRENT EDUCATIONAL CONTEXT

Support for a national curriculum grew in the UK during the 1980s. The idea of a broad and balanced curriculum entitlement in which every child could make continuous progress and development appealed to all sides of the political spectrum. But the new English National Curriculum of 1988, which every state school (though not the private sector) was required to adopt, was designed to focus on core traditional subjects with a nationalist focus and was, hence, one-sided. It was modelled on an old school curriculum of 1904 – technology was the only additional feature. Social Studies, as it had been known, was not identified as a subject area, nor were any of the other 'new' subjects. Teachers were required to cover an enormous factual content in these traditional knowledges. Despite the committed recommendations of educational working parties (Cockcroft 1982), the active engagement of young people in pro-grammes of enquiry and problem-solving was somewhat restricted.

Schools had now been caught in an educational 'free market' in which success and survival were measured by test results in the traditional subjects and, of course, self-reflective practices were time consuming and difficult to measure. Future funding to schools now depends upon successful recruitment. School student test results of these subjects are aggregated and published as indicators of each school's success (this list of schools has been called a league table and likened in this way to a competitive football result scenario). This inflated test score 'currency' massages uninformed public judgment; parents are then encouraged to use these results as a means of evaluating and selecting schools for their children. So-called parental choice becomes pivotal in school recruitment and resourcing exercises, which are then orchestrated by the testing of mainly passive, traditionally-focused learning. As Jeff comments:

> During a decade and a half in which a torrent of legislation has sought to reshape the administrative structure, ethos and content of our education system, it is impossible to isolate a single reform, clause within an Act, or ministerial directive designed to extend the capacity of young people to influence or exercise some measure of control over their own education. (1995, p.25)

So the traditionalists (aided by the 'free market' enthusiasts) had won out over the egalitarians, but teachers still continued to try to make the learning process interactive and enabling. Committed members of the educational community constantly tried to incorporate active reflection in assessment procedures. Working in the late 1980s as an Evaluation Consultant, I saw for myself that insight into the 'how of learning', as part of an active and enabling learning programme, was crucial for learning development and self-esteem but difficult to implement in the current climate.

THE FIRST RESEARCH STUDY

In this small-scale evaluation research study, I was supporting four teachers inquiring into the usefulness of a school student assessment profile pilot in a large inner city comprehensive school. A cross-section of school students aged between 11 and 16 were invited to comment. Methods of assessment usually seek to determine 'what' has been learnt. But some also consider 'how' learning is taking place for diagnostic purposes. The aim of these profiles, known in the UK as Records of Achievement (R.o.As), had been to engage students in the *control of their own learning*. The plan was that school students could be encouraged to reflect upon their studies with their teachers in a running record of interviews and informal chats. In this way they could play an active part in the diagnosis and remedy of their learning errors. However, this early attempt exposed a number of practical difficulties. A substantial number of teachers at the school felt that there just was not enough time or funding for this initiative, alongside the new demands necessitated by the implementation of the National Curriculum. It was felt that much of the work was reduced to a summary programme in the rush and clamour for publishable test and examination results.

Not surprisingly, the evaluation study revealed that the majority of students in the school did not know what these profile records were for. The teacher-researchers gained the impression that the young people had not been effectively informed. The school students interviewed mainly experienced the record keeping as 'boring tick box time'. This kind of comment was typical and referred to three weeks of work on self-assessment questionnaire responses. This was almost the only time in the school year when formal recognition was given to self-reflection. But the questionnaires merely asked such questions as:

How well do you think you have done in mathematics? Well? Very well? Not so well? There was little to indicate that the school students were engaging in an ongoing analysis of learning processes and they clearly hadn't received an induction into this kind of thinking. There was little real self-reflection. Nor were they feeling empowered. However, one teacher was managing to develop a more complex approach to school student review and self-reflection.

Opportunities for funding were rare and difficult to obtain at this time. However, this colleague had the good fortune to obtain resourcing for video-recording facilities, and time out to evaluate this practice. He encouraged young people in one class to reflect upon their learning progress. As he replayed video footage of classroom interactions he observed that some young people seemed less involved in the tasks to hand. Rather than restricting himself to the usual classroom discipline strategies, he asked the young people involved (of which there were six in number) to view the video-recordings with him and comment on what they saw. He also invited me to attend. He had a fair and respecting rapport with the school students. They all described particular difficulties with self-discipline. As one student put it: 'If I'm with my friend we muck about, but not when we're playing maths games' They had a number of organisational proposals to make with regard to seating arrangements for different tasks and activities.

These young people were starting from scratch. They were beginning to reflect on their behaviour in the classroom and, with guidance, I felt sure they would be able to comment upon the broader learning process. There was potential here for supported self-reflection, assertiveness and self-protection, and R.o.A. interviews seemed to provide a place for the rehearsal and development of these skills and abilities.

THE SECOND RESEARCH STUDY

When this research study commenced in 1991, I was concerned to find out what young people understood and felt about their learning experiences. I thought that a children's right to an enabling education was important but I hadn't yet seen the link between self-reflection and self-advocacy thinking processes. This connection emerged as the research work developed.

The research is theoretically rooted in a constructivist framework. In other words, it is assumed within the research that our social world, our reality, is made up of the meanings and interpretations that we construct in order to make sense of everyday life. Within this framework it is recognised that those with more power may be in a position to impose their definition of 'reality' upon others. For this reason I did not want to dictate the direction of the research. The 'how of learning' was also getting some attention within the research school, which was situated in a small town in the West of England where two initiatives were underway. The first involved a school student assessment profile called a record of achievement, like the one discussed above, in which students reflected on their learning achievements individually with their tutor. The second was a thinking skills course in which a class of children examined 'ways in which they were learning' as a whole-class and group activity.

The thinking skills course was inspired by the practical theorising of Professor Reuven Feuerstein (1990). His committed work with the learning traumas of young people arriving in Israel after the holocaust led to the development of a theory and programmes of mediated learning. He took the view that the children he was working with had been prevented from developing an apparatus with which to store and re-use the mass of information bombarding them. Social access to ways of interpreting this data help to provide the means of understanding. He designed what he termed 'Instrumental Enrichment Exercises' for these children in order to create and encourage reflective thought, thus enabling learning from experience. While acknowledging the importance of environmental factors, Feuerstein gives primary emphasis to work with cognitive deficiency. The work of the teacher, parent or other learning mediator is seen to be crucial. Such persons can help learners with a process of mental-cognitive structuration. This reflective induction into learning processes offers learners a fundamental learning repertoire. According to Feuerstein, a lack of cognitive organisation can lead to an impulsive approach to a new problem; the learner does not draw on insight from past experience or wait to listen to some kind of inner intuition but, instead, plunges into task completion in a random way. With one of Feuerstein's instruments ('the organisation of dots'), learners are given the task of connecting the dots in arrangements that vary in complexity. *Ad hoc* approaches invariably lead to meaningless confusions. The recollection of familiar geometric shapes offers a key to pattern intelligibility. The vital reflective debriefing that follows tends to counter impulsiveness and encourages the learner to look for signs of the familiar in new tasks. This learning instrument also offers a profound experience of the ordering and arranging necessary to the understanding and interpretation of other forms of knowledge. Sharron (1987) gives a detailed historical account of Feuerstein's remarkable practical study and investigation of learning difficulty. Those supported came from a range of different cultures and many began to develop cognitive survival strategies. Since that time, Feuerstein has continued to be successful in assisting young people with learning difficulties. This transformative work provided insights into the 'how' of learning, which placed the learner far more in charge of the learning process and so gave further impetus to the present research case-study.

A teacher in 'the research school' was much taken with the work of Feuerstein. She felt that the children 'needed a vocabulary' – a way of working that directed attention to the processes in which learning was taking place. This entailed 'learning about learning' in the curriculum. But this is the difficult part. She comments that: 'Some young people don't think back. Others aren't very good at formulating what they really do well, and what could be done better. They either think it's all bad, or all good. More able school students are over-confident and can't see how they can improve.' An imaginary mirror needs to be part of the learning activity, so that learning can be reflected upon as it is happening. With teachers, young people need to know what to look for, what to discern, how to analyse and the questions to raise. As one school student put it: 'How can we learn from our mistakes, if we don't know what they are.' Feuerstein had been sensitive to the need to distance the learning task from

negative personal experience. This concern to separate formal learning programmes from painful associations is very important, particularly for children
who have had horrifying experiences outside their control.

However, there is a danger that the emotional and moral side of life
experience can get completely marginalised. My colleague, the teacher in the
research school, certainly found the tasks too abstract, she felt they needed to
be grounded in some way so that they could connect with the child's personal
experience without stirring up painful or threatening memories. She challenged
the need for task abstraction that Feuerstein had fostered. Mainstream children
needed a sense of task relevance. Several attempts had been made to adapt
Feuerstein's instruments to the needs of mixed ability children in UK state
schools. One such programme, developed by a team of educational advisers in
Somerset, has become known as the 'Somerset Thinking Skills.'

SOMERSET THINKING SKILLS

A group of educational advisers working with Nigel Blagg, an educational
psychologist in Somerset have modified, extended and contextualised Feuerstein's work for use in UK mainstream classrooms. A useful pack to augment
reflective thinking has been produced. Whole classes and groups of children
can follow this programme in a developmental way. This scheme of thinking-
focused work locates the tasks in everyday scenes. Learners are here encouraged
to be detective-like, employing a form of practical reasoning to sort and reflect
on cognitive problems. As Blagg (1988) comments:

> 'The early activities offer a chance of establishing the right kind of
> working environment for "learning to learn". The intentional use of
> ambiguity creates debate. Pointing up the need for careful analysis and
> hypothesis testing, *inviting* students to move away from an impulsive
> approach to problem-solving in favour of greater reflexiveness.' (p. 4)

The teacher decided to work on this 'thinking skills course' with her tutor group
of 30 school students as they moved up the school. They have now completed
a five-year programme. I attended and videoed some thinking skills sessions. I
sought to find out how young people in the school were thinking about learning
and to see what perceptions they had about learning relationships. The enquiry
was not hypothesis driven. This issue of the 'how of learning' was, so to speak,
approached sideways. I decided to use draw-on experiences of the second
initiative, which all students at the school undertook. Here they had a one-to-
one discussion about their learning achievement with their tutor. I hoped they
would be reflecting upon how they were learning. If I focused my research
interviews with them on perceptions of different kinds of assessment, including
these records of achievement, I would be providing an opportunity for school
student discussion of thinking skills and any other aspects of learning relationship to be raised.

The method was ethnographic and principally qualitative, which meant that every attempt was made to use non-directive questions in interview and to stay with the actual words spoken so that the interviewees construct their own interpretations of their experience.

I invited some of the school students to become involved in orientating and focusing the research, and also in collecting and analysing some of the data. This attempt at collaboration did not meet with much enthusiasm. I think I should have spent some considerable time developing a positive relationship with the students before making a proposal of this kind, but even teacher colleagues, though interested, found it difficult to find the time to be very involved. This may be because, for both teachers and school students, the curriculum has become something of a speed track.

Ten per cent of school students were interviewed in a school population of 830 students. This research drew from a sample cross-section of young people aged between 11 and 18. The sample were selected in terms of gender, mixed ability and experience of 'thinking skills'. They were asked to comment on the old assessment reports and the new records of achievement assessment profiles. The old assessment reports offered a list of short comments from teachers about achievement in each subject area and all students interviewed had had previous experience of these reports in their present or a previous school. The records of achievement, on the other hand, were intended to involve and empower young people in control of their own learning. The questions in the semi-structured interview schedule were designed to elicit insights into the learning process drawn from this comparison between these two different forms of learning assessment, and also encouraged students to make any further observations if they felt it to be appropriate.

THE FINDINGS

Several issues were raised by the school students and a number of learning process pathways for self-advocacy were revealed. Some students focused upon the teacher/student relationships in the old reports and records of achievement. There were concerns about control, having a 'say', and queries about the relevance of questions in R.o.A.s from tutors about their home life.

Where subject departments like English were assessing school students in R.o.A.s, and in an ongoing way, there was appreciative feedback. Here a student comments that:

> A few points were brought to light that I hadn't thought about. For English I learnt that my expression could be improved and it was shown clearly what I was good at. It was also made clear that if you want to know what to do about improving you can ask the teacher.

There is already a sense of some active involvement. Some, but not all, judgments about the school student's learning come from the teacher and the student is positive about the teacher's insights. But it seems to me to be significant that the school student didn't already know that the teacher could be approached for advice about self-improvement. Young people in schools know how to seek their teacher's assistance, but getting help and seeking advice for self-improvement seem to be seen as two different things.

A third of the sample interviewed were more equivocal about whether they had a right to have a say in the one-to-one R.o.A. discussions with their teacher, yet it is clear that the student quoted below had concerns that needed to be voiced. In this example, the school student is comparing the old style reports with the more recent records of achievement:

Q: Did you have a chance to say something?

A: No, not really.

Q: Did it matter?

A: Not exactly, but I didn't like them, (the old reports) they don't
      put any good points. Some teachers, if you're not very good at their
      subject, then they don't like you. I'm stuck in a subject at the
      moment and I don't want to be in it. My tutor forced me to take it.

Here the student is also talking about being *forced* to take a subject. It seems fair to assume that the student would welcome further consultation – but at the time of interviewing, all the National Curriculum subjects were compulsory.

The manner and quality of the interaction between tutors and school students also became a focus for attention. For instance, with reference to tutor/student interviewing, students expressed surprise at the apparent interest in their personal lives: 'What's it to him (the teacher) whether I went abroad when I was seven?' or 'What's the colour of the wallpaper in my bedroom got to do with my work in school?' One student actually went so far as to claim that the teacher 'was just trying to have a bit of a nose'. The school students here are looking through language to the possible intentions of the tutors.

Several teachers interviewed said they were attempting to learn more about each young person and their learning achievement inside and outside the school, but it's easy to see how misunderstandings might occur – particularly where record of achievement guidance for teachers makes the two learning arenas of home and school formally distinct (see, for instance, the Cambridge Partnership for Record of Achievement (1988) used by the school). In this guidance pack, 'Personal Qualities and Experience' gained in and out of education are separated from 'Vocational Skills' and explanations about the relevance of both for learning analysis are assumed rather than spelled out for the teacher or the school student.

The lack of detailed attention to learning processes in R.o.A. implementation in schools across England has been pointed out elsewhere (Nuttall *et al.* 1990), so it was reassuring and impressive to find that two-thirds of the school students recounted positive experiences. As one student put it: 'The interviews made me view myself differently. It's the first time I've had to think of what I'm learning and why. I'd like more interviewing, more frequently and at greater length.'

The importance of a mutually-directed dialogue has also been highlighted. In a recent evaluation of assessment practice, James (1990) presents a transcript of an end of term tutorial conference and demonstrates the extent to which a well-intentioned and enthusiastic teacher imputes meaning to the school student, rather than encouraging the school student to voice observations, concerns, and judgments. School students need to be able to speak for themselves. An important quality of democratic dialogue seems to me to lie in the capacity of all participating parties to initiate discussion and debate through the raising of questions. It was impressive to find that the majority of school students interviewed at the research school described 'real conversations' with their tutors.

Dynamic engagements of this kind enable students to realise the worth and value of their own views. They are not just passively copying and remembering. Rather than being situated in the learning process, the students can begin *to situate themselves*. They are standing back and making judgments about what it is that affects them. Not surprisingly then, they tended to place importance upon their role in the proceedings – hence:

> I enjoyed the interview because I wanted to share my experiences and achievements. I had freedom of speech, sort of thing. I felt comfortable. it was more like a discussion. I don't really talk about myself much normally. It didn't help with my learning because it was about my personal life, not about my school life... I wouldn't change the idea of it but I'd change the organisation, and students should have the option to be interviewed by the tutor they get on with.

> Not everyone wanted to do it and those who didn't disrupted those who did. But there was a chance to say something about yourself.

> The tutor was nice, not telling us what to do, which was good.

Here we see ways in which the school students involved are beginning to identify certain learning rights. A small emancipatory shift has taken place; there seems to be a sense of an entitlement to freedom of speech and a fair hearing.

Some teachers are afraid to encourage school students to ask questions. One teacher interviewed said that questioning what's happening makes children feel insecure: 'Where will it end?' he asked. 'Supposing the children actually question why they should be in school...!' If such questions about school have been raised in the classroom, they have, in my experience, provoked important discussions about the value of schooling. Young children are very curious and soon take enthusiastic steps to explore their environments. Much would be lost if this active mode of enquiry were to get dissipated in schools. It is commendable that the majority of teachers in the research school wished to promote 'lively and inquiring minds', and this central principle guided the school's policy documents and R.o.A. practice.

The school students interviewed had participated in thinking skills coursework and this may have affected the range of comments offered:

> 'There are different ways of thinking. You need to stand back and think before acting. There is more than one way to solve a problem.'

> 'Planning is important'

> 'I don't think of questions that the teacher asks.'

> 'Now and then I question what the teacher says'

> 'Sometimes I ask questions that my teachers cannot answer'

> 'You know how much you know by how much you remember and by if you've had to answer a question and you can answer it directly and straight away.'

> 'Learning is happening all the time.'

> 'Learning is picking up easy things that are taught to you and using background reading and research to help with the difficult things.'

> 'You need to be prepared to listen'

> 'You need to develop co-operative skills for English, and organisational skills for science'

> 'I learnt to speak out in class, but I got the most from small group work. I learn from interacting with other students in small groups and it helps me feel more confident'

> 'Sometimes there's a relevance problem'

> 'Some school work is too repetitive. It needs to be more challenging.'

> 'You must take responsibility for your own learning through research, etc.'

> 'Reasoning is a key element in helping me to think and act in different situations.'

These comments are essentially practical. They engage with insights into the 'how of learning'. Obviously, these student perceptions are not in any way extraordinary, but they mark out early overtures in a reflective movement of personal thinking and argumentation. This analytical approach not only aids understanding of, and involvement in, the learning process, but fine-grained observations and expressions of judgment are being made. The students are learning to find their voices, to articulate issues that matter to them.

The teacher at the research school who introduced the thinking skills initiative, together with the colleagues who conducted the R.o.A. interviews as open dialogues and the school students who participated and shared their insights, have highlighted important aspects of 'learning about learning' in practice. They have also indicated ways in which experience of self-reflection may contribute to self-advocacy in children's rights developments.

The tutor group that took this reflective journey did markedly better in final year examinations than their peers. Many educationalists have argued for the importance of regular review in learning (see Rowntree 1985), but examples of it beginning to work in practice like this, where guidance about learning processes is provided, seem to be rare. We are getting closer to an educational situation that might have helped Sharon, and others like her, but we still have further to go.

LEARNING PROCESSES, ASSERTIVENESS AND CHILDREN'S RIGHTS

Alongside a reflective thinking course with opportunities for individual review, where rational aspects of self-reflection and self-advocacy can be practised and developed, students interviewed made comments that pointed to three further learning rights requirements:

Access to relevant ethical issues

Is it enough for young people to learn how to learn? Don't they also need to be able to identify the social influences that impact upon the way they are learning? Reflective thinking courses should protect school students from painful memories that might inhibit their progress. But, in extremis, this kind of social skimming can leave students exposed to racism, sexism and the like; it maintains a delicate balance between protection and vulnerability.

Young people thus need information about relevant ethical issues. The students weren't asked about children's rights in the research interviews, but some indicated a need for this sort of ethical knowledge. For instance, one student stated that: 'We need to understand standards and how to conduct ourselves as well as learning for academic and exam purposes.' Others seemed to infer or state a desire for fair play. For instance, one student observed that: 'I had a good experience of learning in technical drawing because of good discipline and good humour, and the teacher didn't try and make you feel small.' Professor Ronald Carter (1990) argues that young people need to understand how language works. He points out that:

> this sometimes involves seeing through language to the ways in which points of view can be manipulated. Now this happens to be something politicians are very skilled at doing... Educated citizens need to be able to see how they are being used, and how they are being constructed by users of language. (BBC TV *Panorama*, November 1991)

In 1990 the tide seemed to turn. Elements akin to early Social Studies courses described above were promoted in some National Curriculum Guidelines – 'The Cross-Curricular Themes, Skills and Dimensions'. This course offers opportunities to identify and debate relevant ethical issues, particularly in the Citizenship section, and allows a consideration of those sexist, racist and classist factors that can be a barrier to learning. The social circumstances of learning are a crucial part of the learning experience. There is more than one kind of cultural self-expression, and it is not by chance that many traditional forms of education favour some varieties and degrade others. Oppressed children need to be able to name the sources of their own deprivation (Hall 1974). A good citizenship course, like that outlined by Rhys Griffith (1996) can provide the interactive dialogue and challenge that will bring the learning experience alive to issues of social justice, so that every participant has a voice, knows how to recognise and reject stultifying dogma, and can work to improve the situation for themselves and others.

Access to collective consultation and collaboration

These features of the learning experience were repeatedly referenced in the data. Considerable emphasis was placed upon the sense of 'family' and 'community' established in the thinking skills tutorial classes:

> 'The tutor group was built upon camaraderie. It was very much a family-type group. The learning occurred in groups, so there was input from everybody. The group also volunteered for various tasks around the school'.

> 'Initially, Somerset Thinking Skills was only seen as another bit of work, but it brought us together as a team, although you weren't thinking about it at the time.'

> 'a more relaxed atmosphere in the class where you could say anything.'

There are indications here of a desired classroom and tutorial ethos constructed by school students around notions of participation, mutual respect, learning community and freedom of voice. Their observations have been inspired by the co-operative, consultative ethos taken forward by the teacher. There is then a politics of learning being articulated and a commitment by the teacher, to participative citizenship values, is finding expression in this practice. The United Nations Convention on the Rights of the Child not only stressed the rights of young people to a free education, but that the education provided should respect the values of each young person (Article 29). These ideas of democratic interaction in the classroom are not new, as those familiar with the work of Grundy (1987), Young (1989) and Freire (1989) will know. A classroom ethos in which all students are heard, respected and valued should then be a right of learning. Conditions of this kind will also help promote the collective skills and abilities necessary for self-advocacy and self-protection.

Experience of emotional self-expression

More opportunities to express the emotional side of learning were signalled. One student explained that:

'We aren't able to express ourselves, we keep it all inside and it comes out the wrong way I suppose'

Q: What happens if it 'comes out the wrong way'?

STUDENT: An angry attitude to the teacher, or you just don't get down to lessons and take it out on other pupils.

In the research school, the teacher's emotional support of students tended to alleviate this problem of a 'feeling gap', but the school student emphasis on the importance of the teacher's role in developing a sense of 'team links' and 'family' shows the stress placed by them on this aspect of learning. The heartfelt understandings of events can enable a sense of empathy and compassion for self and others to develop, something advocated by Goleman (1996). The emotional side to learning thus needs to be allowed a place in discussion. As one young person commented: 'I don't very often get a chance to talk about my brother.' His brother had recently committed suicide. He explained this quietly and without self-pity. It seemed as though the feelings about the loss had been deeply locked away. The emotional impact experienced, and insight gained from grave experiences of this kind, must surely inform the language of selfhood, self-reflection and self-advocacy.

CONCLUDING COMMENTS

This chapter has outlined insights into various kinds of reflective activity, to emphasise the relevance of this experience for self-advocacy preparation.

Richly embroidered reflective practice of this kind must clearly be a learning right and can also provide a basis for group- and self-protection. How else can deprived groups and classes of children ever win power in the system if they are educationally unprepared and unequipped for the struggle? However, learning rights are not yet seen as central to curriculum developments in the UK. Nor do they feature as key elements in the curricula of most nation states. The work with Children's Hearings begun in Norway by Kirsten Eskeland (1996) is inspirational in this respect.

THE INTERNATIONAL CHALLENGE

Meanwhile, a range of 'Fundamentalist Dogmas' are re-emerging across the globe in the run up to the twenty-first century. Dictated doctrines do not encourage reflective criticism in young people. As Spiecker (1991) notes: 'Inculcating doctrines are always associated with the suppression of the critical attitude' (p.16).

Moreover, the ethical and feeling dimensions will be needed all the more, in the growing amoral sphere of the international free market (Bauman 1992). Alongside these concerns, Baudrillard (1988) warns that the very sense of selfhood of young people is under pressure. He alludes to the way various forms of Information Technology and Pop Media create a speedy and illusive world of seductive images detached from authentic ongoing experiences of individual life. An exploding cascade of personality fragments burst across the screen and threaten the child's sense of personal uniqueness.

In contrast, a dynamic sense of selfhood can be developed as practical reflection of learning experience takes place. Points of view can evolve, and skills and abilities of self-advocacy can begin to emerge. So it is imperative that all young people are initiated into learning practices of this kind, so that they can be supported in expressing and defending their rights. We need to build such opportunities so that young people like Sharon have more of a chance.

REFERENCES

Blagg, N. *et al.* (1988) *The Somerset Thinking Skills Course. Course Booklet Module 1.* Oxford: Basil Blackwell Ltd.

Bauman, Z. (1992) *Intimations of Postmodernity.* London: Routledge.

Baudrillard, J. (1988) *Selected Writings.* Cambridge: Polity Press.

Cambridge Partnership for Records of Achievement (1988) *Personal Qualities and Experience.* Cambridge: University of Cambridge Local Examinations Syndicate.

Carter, R. (1990) *Knowledge about Language and the Curriculum.* London: Hodder and Stoughton.

Cockcroft, W.H. Chair (1982) *Mathematics Counts.* HMSO: London

Department of Health (1988) *Protecting Children:A Guide for Social Workers Undertaking a Comprehensive Assessment.* London: HMSO.

Eskeland, K. (1996) 'Voice of the children: speaking truth to power.' In M. John (ed) *Children In Charge: The Child's Right to a Fair Hearing.* London: Jessica Kingsley Publishers.

Freire, P. (1989) 'The politics of education.' In P. Murphy and B. Moon (eds) *Developments in Learning and Assessment.* Sevenoaks: Hodder and Stoughton.

Feuerstein, R. (1990) *Instrumental Enrichment: an Internvention Program for Cognitive Modifiability.* Baltimore: MD University Park Press.

Griffith, R. (1996) 'New powers for Old: transforming power relationships.' In M. John (ed) *Children In Our Charge: The Child's Right to Resources.* London: Jessica Kingsley Publishers.

Goleman, D. (1996) *Emotional Intelligence.* London: Bloomsbury.

Grundy, S. (1987) *Curriculum: Product or Praxis.* Sussex and Philadephia: The Falmer Press.

Hall, S. (1974) 'Education and the crisis of the urban school.' In J. Raynor (ed) *Issues in Urban Education.* Milton Keynes: Open University Press.

James, M. (1990) ' Negotiation and dialogue in student assessment and teacher appraisal.' In T. Horton *Assessment Issues.* Milton Keynes: Open University Press.

Jeff, T. (1995) 'Children's educational rights in a new era.' In B. Franklin (ed) *The Handbook of Children's Rights: Comparative Policy and Practice.* London: Routledge.

Nuttall, D. *et al.* (1990) 'Record of achievement: report of the National Evaluation of Pilot Schemes.' In T. Horton *Assessment Issues.* London: OUP.

Parfitt, G. *et al.* (1990) *Evaluation in the ILEA.* ILEA Code RS1284.

Rowntree, D. (1985) *Assessing Students: How Shall We Know Them.* London: Kogan Page.

Scarman Lord (1986) *The Gillick Judgment.* Gillick v. West Norfolk and Wisbech Area Health Authority, A.C. 112, Hansard.

Sharron, H. (1987) *Changing Children's Minds.* London: Souvenir Press.

Speicker, B. (1991) 'Indoctrination: the suppression of critical dispositions.' In B. Speicker and R. Straughan *Freedom and Indocrination in Education: International Perspectives.* London: Cassell Education Ltd.

Young, R. (1989) *A Critical Theory of Education.* Hemel Hempstead: Harvester Wheatsheaf.

The Contributors

Tuaneri Akoto has been in youth work for over 10 years and has operated from varying styles of work and projects according to community need. This has been in inner city areas of London, working with the less advantaged in socially deprived communities.

Rachel Brett LLB, LLM in International Human Rights Law, is Associate representative at the Quaker United Nations Office in Geneva and co-ordinator of the Child Soldier Research Project, which is being undertaken in the framework of the Graca Machel 'UN Study on the Impact of Armed Conflict on Children'. She was the originator and principal researcher of the Essex Human Rights Centre's Conference on Security and Co-operation in Europe Project. She has published extensively on the CSCE/OSCE, the role of non-governmental human rights organisations and other human rights issues.

Araceli Brizzio de la Hoz was born in Xalapa and studied for a BA in Anthropology at the University of Veracruz and for a Masters degree at the National University of Mexico. Since 1981 she has worked as a senior researcher at the Institution of Research in Psychology of the University of Veracruz, Mexico. From 1984 to 1989 she acted as a member of the Executive Council of Defence for Children International.

Judy Cashmore has a PhD in Developmental Psychology and has been conducting research in the broad area of children's welfare and the law. This research has included work (for the Australian Law Reform Commission, the NSW Child Protection Council, the National Child Protection Council and the NSW Department of Community Services) on: the use of closed-circuit television for child witnesses; systems abuse; physical punishment; difficult access cases in the Family Court; and a longitudinal study of wards leaving care. She is a member of several government committees and is currently a Research Associate at the Social Policy Research Centre at the University of New South Wales.

Ann Catchpole was born in Malaya and experienced the upheaval of a last-minute evacuation leaving her father behind, who was taken Prisoner of War. She is social work trained and has also worked for 15 years as a Samaritan. She now works as a field social worker part-time in tandem with the work she does for the Joint Agencies Child Abuse Team in Exeter which she describes here.

Children from single-parent families: These children have all given their consent to the inclusion of their paper. They are Mercy Ojelade, Courtney Weston and Benjamin.

Penelope Cousens works in the Department of Psychological Medicine at the Royal Alexandra Hospital for Children, Westmead, New South Wales, Australia as a Clinical Psychologist.

Stephen Flood has been Research and Press Officer at Young Minds since 1993. During 1994, he researched and wrote a series of reports on the impact of different forms of violence on the mental health of children. Previously he worked within the Health Promotion policy division at the Department of Health, where he was part of the small team that organised the first ever European Drug Prevention Week in 1992.

Janina Gonçalves studied for her PhD at the University of Wales Centre for Development Studies. and for her MSc at the Universidade Cândido Mendes, Rio de Janeiro. She worked for CBIA (Centro Brasileiro para a Infância e Adolescência) formerly FUNABEM (Fundação Nacional para o Bem-estar do Menor) for several years and is presently at the Ministry of Justice, which assumed the activities relative to child policy in Brazil after CBIA was extinguished, collecting and processing all documentation produced during the last years by CBIA/FUNABEM, at the National Archive.

Edith Grotberg is Senior Scientist at the Civitan International Research Center at the University of Alabama at Birmingham, Alabama, USA. She was Director of Research for a US Government Agency concerned with children, youth and families at risk.

Marianne Hester is a Lecturer in the School for Policy Studies at the University of Bristol. She has carried out a variety of research in the area of violence and abuse against women. One of her most recent research projects has been on Domestic Violence and Child Contact in England and Denmark, in collaboration with Lorraine Radford. Her publications include *Lewd Women and Wicked Witches* (Routledge, 1992) and *Women, Violence and Male Power* with Liz Kelly and Jill Radford (Open University Press, 1996).

Mary John (Editor) is a psychologist whose research work has largely been with minority rights groups. Early work was with John and Elizabeth Newson as part of their longitudinal study on child-rearing. Since then she has acted as a psychological consultant to Head Start in the United States, an expert adviser to the Centre for Educational Research and Innovation, OECD, Paris and, later, on disability matters to the EEC. She is a Professor of Education and a Deputy Vice Chancellor of the University of Exeter.

Etta Mitchell worked for 20 years as a Barrister's Clerk. In December 1994 she was appointed by Victim Support to set up the Crown Witness Service at Exeter Crown Court. She is married with two children.

Manuel Martinez Morales has been a researcher at the University of Veracruz, Mexico since 1981. He received his PhD in mathematics from Texas Technology University in 1994. His research interests are in Statistical Models of Behaviour and Bayesian Networks.

Will Palin entered the music industry in 1969 as a sound engineer (David Bowie, Lou Reed, etc), becoming a tour manager and event co-ordinator specialising in Third World concert tours and charity fund-raising events. He co-founded, with Ian Walker, The Youth Trust. Instigated in 1995, The Devon Consortium Partnership (S.C.O.D.A. funded) is training 23 young people in Plymouth and Barnstaple as Peer Educators.

Mikael Palme is a sociologist at the Institute of Education in Stockholm, Sweden. He has worked extensively in the developing world and is currently directing a SIDA-funded research collaboration between his Institute and the Mozambique National Institute for Educational Development (INDE) in Maputo.

Vanessa Parffrey is a Lecturer in Education Studies at the School of Education, University of Exeter and is a qualified Educational Psychologist. She is currently working with schools to develop inclusive policies for children with behaviour difficulties and with the Children's Society to promote self-advocacy amongst socially excluded young people.

Gael Parfitt is a Lecturer in Curriculum Development and Evaluation at the School of Education, University of Exeter. She has undertaken research into teaching and learning at national and local levels and is committed to the principle that all young people be entitled, by right, to an education that offers equality of access and an active engagement in a developmental and self-fulfilling learning journey.

Chris Pearson is a Research Associate and a member of the Domestic Violence Research Group at the University of Bristol. She is a qualified social worker and has worked, for many years, with women and children who have experienced domestic violence and abuse. She is currently working on a national survey of court welfare and mediator practice in relation to domestic violence funded by the Joseph Rowntree Foundation.

Michael Stevens is a paediatric oncologist and is Senior Staff Specialist and Head of the Oncology Unit, The New Children's Hospital, Westmead, Sydney.

Wendy Thomas is the Director of Population Concern, an agency working mainly with young people in developing countries. She was formerly Director of London Brooke.

Sheila Townsend is a group therapist. For eight years she has worked in a Health Agency providing a statutory family and child service in Devon. Her sphere of work has focused on a support group for mothers whose children have been sexually abused.

David Treharne is a Lecturer in Education Studies at the University of Exeter and is particularly involved in Community Education and Re-Start Education.

Peter Wilson is Director of Young Minds. He trained as a social worker in the 1960s, before training at the Anna Freud Centre as a child psychologist. He has worked at Child Guidance Clinics in Brixton, Hoxton and Camberwell and was Director of the Brandon Centre (formerly the London Advisory Centre) for eight years. He has been Director of Young Minds since 1992.

Louise Williamson has worked as Director of the Children's Division at the British Refugee Council since March 1995. At the time of the conference she was carrying out research at Queen Mary's and Westfield College, London University, on policy-making for unaccompanied children. The research is ongoing, for interim reports see 'Alone in a Strange Land', *Community Care* 11.11.93, pp.26–27; 'A Safe Haven?: The Development of British Policy Concerning Unaccompanied Refugee Children 1993–93' *Immigrants and Minorities 14*, 1, March 1995, pp.47–49.

Subject Index

References in italics indicate figures or tables.

ABCD Pack 158
abortion fatality rates 102
abuse cycles 182
abused children 9, 13, 149–60
  court cases 128–9, 131, 132
  Joint Agencies Child Abuse Team 150–1
  methods of working with 155–8
  pace/coverage of work with 154–5
  personal perspective 149–50
  reasons for intervening 151–3
  timing interventions 153–4
  working with mothers of 160–7
  see also domestic violence; sexual abuse; systems abuse
abusive recruitment 53
accessibility of complaints procedures 42, 44
adolescents
  as abusers 179–80
  sexuality of 98–106
'adult disease' incidence 11
adversity, types of 24–6
Advisory Committee, International Resilience Project 19–20
Advisory Group on Video Evidence 131
advocacy
  refugees 81, 84, 86
  systems abuse 34, 41, 44

see also learning rights and self-advocacy
age limitations
  combat recruitment 52, 53–4
  employment 65, 67, 73
  first intercourse 102, 103, 104
  medical treatment decisions 240–1
agency support, excluded children 116, 122
agrarian issues, Brazil 90, 91–2
aggressive behaviour levels 172–3
akunya 206
anxious bullies 175–6
apprenticeships, Mexico 68
'armed forces' definition, child soldier studies 56
assertiveness *see* learning rights and self-advocacy
assessment profiling project 249–50
Associated Immigration Rules 81
Association of Directors of Social Services 83, 86
asylum, applying for 80–1
Asylum and Immigration Appeals Act (1993 UK) 81
Asylum Bill (1991 UK) 81, 84
'asylum-seekers' definition 86
attachment theory 42
attitude research, UK 3–4
autonomy, encouraging 27, 28

baldness, stress-related 11
Barnstaple, Market Inn Project 192–3
'Bill' definition 86
births, unwanted 102
books, abused children work 155–6, 157
'bored records', excluded children 116

boys, Mozambican education 208
Brazil, 7, 11
  marginality and extermination 88–97
Brazilian Centre for Childhood and Adolescence (CBIA) 11, 94, 96
bullies 175–6, 177
bullying 23–4, 173, 174–8
  characteristics 174–6
  effects of 177–8
  'whole-school' approach 176–7
bureaucracy problems, excluded children 122

Can't You Sleep Little Bear 155–6
canteen project, Greenstreet Project 222
'capitation' effects 110
care, abuse in 40–1
care advocates 81, 84, 86
case load problems 36–7
case study requirements, child soldier project 55–63
CBIA (Brazilian Centre for Childhood and Adolescence) 11, 94, 96
'ceasing treatment' decisions 238–45
centre management course, Greenstreet Project 222–3
chains of abuse 152
'channels' of political participation 89, 94
character building 12–13
Charlene, truancy project case 225–6
child abuse court cases 128–9, 131, 132
Child and Adolescent Statute (Brazil) 91, 93, 95, 96
child care law, UK 81–2

'child' definition, child soldier studies 55–6
child labour 9, 10–11, 64–76
  children's own views 69–71
  criteria and ideologies 66–8
  definition 67–8
  ending exploitation 73–4
  rights 71–2
  risks 68–9
child-oriented systems 41–2
child-parent relationships, medical treatment decisions 240, 241–2
Child Soldiers Research Project 55–63
Child Witness Packs 130
childbirth risks 101–2
Children Act (1989 UK) 81–2, 247
  contact arrangements 136, 141, 144, 146
children as abusers 179–80
Children (Care and Protection) Act (1987 New South Wales) 43
Children's Hearings, Norway 259
Children's Legal Centre, UK 84
Children's Rights Development Unit, UK 83
children's views
  contact with parents 144–8
  excluded 115–19, 117, 123, 124
  listening to 40–1, 124
  Mexican workers 70
  single-parented 233–7
citizenship courses 258
city schooling, Mozambican 205–9
coercive combat recruitment 53, 54

cognitive deficiency work 251
collaboration
  inter-agency 37–8, 42, 229–30
  student 258–9
'colonialist' model 89, 94
Committee on the Rights of the Child 54, 55
communication skills
  child's 29
  medical treatment decisions 241
'community' information, child soldier studies 61–2
competitiveness
  origins of 12
  UK schools 108–9
complaints mechanisms 40–1, 44
compulsory combat recruitment 56
concept understanding, Mozambican schools 201, 202–3, 212
concerts, Youth Trust 191
'conditions' information, child soldier studies 58–9
confrontation fears, child witnesses 127
consultation, student 258
contact arrangements, child–parent 14, 135–6, 140–6
  and further violence 141–4
context information, child soldier studies 56–7
continuity needs, child's 42
contraception statistics 99
Convention, UN see UN Convention on the Rights of the Child
co-operative approach, UK schools 107–8
co-ordination problems
  refugee children 83
  systems abuse 37–8
Co-ordinator for Refugee Children 83

coping styles
  medical treatment decisions 242
  single-parented children 233–4
copying activities, Mozambique schooling 196
cost issues, refugee children 82–3
counselling
  child witnesses 127, 130
  excluded children 116
  truancy project 221, 224–5, 229
Court procedures, child witnesses 127–8
court welfare officers 140, 143, 144–5
cram schools, Japanese 11–12
Criminal Justice Acts (UK) 128–9, 132
criminal offending 173
  bullies 177
  violent victims 178–9
Crown Court Witness Service 130
cuisine project, Greenstreet Project 223
cult heroes, use of 188
cultural aspects of schooling, Mozambique 195–216
  classroom rituals 195–9
  context 204–9
  learning factors 199–203
  teachers 210–13
cultural differences
  competitiveness 12
  resilience 20, 21
cycles of abuse 182

death see extermination of children
Denmark, parent contact arrangements 145–6
'Department of Health' definition 86
depression 172, 180, 181

developmental psychology approaches 6
developmental stages, and resilience 30
disabilities, children with 11, 157–8
domestic violence 135–46
  children's views 144–6
  contact arrangements 140–4
  definition 137–8
  effect on children 138–40
Donald, truancy project case 226–7
donor agency influence, Mozambique 4, 203, 213–14, 215
drug prevention project 13, 187–94
dying children, treatment decisions 238–45
  characteristics of child 241, 243–5
  parent–child relationships 241–2

Eastern Europe 5
education
  Mexican child workers 69
  reproductive and sexual health 100–1, 102–5
  see also cultural aspects of schooling; excluded children; Greenstreet Truancy Project; learning rights and self-advocacy
Education Acts (1981 and 1986 UK) 107
education information, child soldier studies 60–1
education provision, excluded children 114–15, 114
Education Reform Act (1988 UK) 108
educational psychologists, and excluded children 116, 122

Elton Report 107
emotional abuse 138–9, 143
emotional expression dimension of learning rights 259, 260
emotional maturity, and treatment decisions 241, 242, 243–4
emotions, child's management of 28, 29
'employment' information, child soldier studies 61
endings, abused children work 156–7
environment factors, Greenstreet Project 219
ethical dimension of learning rights 257–8, 260
'ethical virtue' 12–13
'Exceptional Leave to Remain' 81
exchange arrangement, Greenstreet Project 218, 223–4
excluded children 107–25, 217
  background 107–10
  provision 121–2
  statistics 110–15, 112, 113, 114, 121
  views of children and staff 115–21, 117, 120
exploitation of children, work as 73–4
extermination of children, Brazil 88–97
  conceptual overview 89–91
  from uneasiness to well-being 91–3
  welfare actions 93–7
external support, child's 26–7

family relationships, medical treatment decisions 242

Fast-track system 130, 131, 132
fathers, and single-parent families 235–6
financial influences, school exclusions 108–9
fingerprinting asylum applicants 81
forced combat recruitment 53, 56
foreign debt effects 7
foster carers, support for 39–40
Freedom's Children 3

Gardner, Juliet 150–1
Geneva Conventions 52
geographical factors, Mozambican schooling 201
Gillick judgment 247
girls, Mozambican schooling 206–8
golf player award, Youth Trust 191
Gomes da Costa, A.C. 94, 96
Goodnight Mr Tom 155
Greenstreet Truancy Project 5, 217–30
  advantages/disadvantages 227–9
  case studies 224–7
  courses and projects 218, 222–4
  methods 219–22
  participants 218
  recommendations 229–30
Guidelines on Refugee Children 80, 83
guilt
  sexually abused children 180–1
  single-parented children 233

health conditions, Brazil 90, 93, 95
help contacts, single-parented children 236–7

historical background,
   extermination in Brazil
   90, 93
HIV/AIDS statistics 99
'Home Office' definition
   86
Housing Act (1985 UK)
   82

'I Have, I Am, I Can'
   model 22–4, 26–9
immigration law, UK 80–1
'in-school knowledge' 212
inappropriate sexualised
   behaviour 180
independence, and
   medical treatment
   decisions 241, 242,
   243
induced combat
   recruitment 56
infrastructure conditions,
   Brazil 90, 91, 95
institutional abuse 34,
   35–6, 40–1
institutionalisation of
   concealment, Brazil
   93–4
'Instrumental Enrichment
   Exercises' 251
integrationist perspective
   89
inter-agency collaboration
   37–8, 42
   truancy 229–30
internal strengths, child's
   28
International Resilience
   Project 14, 19–30
international standards see
   UN Convention on the
   Rights of the Child
internationalisation,
   economic 89, 90, 95
interpersonal skills, child's
   28–9
'invisible jobs' 69
isolation of excluded
   children 119
It's Your Turn, Roger 155

JACAT (Joint Agencies
   Child Abuse Team)
   150–1
Japan, work-related stress
   11–12
Jenny, sexual abuse case
   162–6
Joint Agencies Child
   Abuse Team (JACAT)
   150–1
juvenile labour 67–8

labour see child labour
land conflicts, Brazil 90,
   91–2
language problems,
   Mozambican
   schooling, 199–200,
   202–3
learning difficulties work
   251
learning rights, and
   self-advocacy 246–61
   current context 248–9
   other needs 257–9
   research studies 249–57
'leaving school soon'
   attitudes 229
legal profession, and child
   witnesses 38–9
   see also solicitors
legislation (UK), child
   refugees 80–2
legislative background,
   excluded children
   107–10
listening activities,
   Mozambican schools
   195–6
'local authority' definition
   86
long-term effects of child
   abuse 181–2

Machel study 55, 63
Magistrates' Courts 126–7
Makua society 201, 202,
   207–8
male involvement, sex
   education 104–5
Maputo children 200,
   201, 202–3

marginal role of schools,
   Mozambique 204, 212
marginalisation of
   children, Brazil 88–97
Marginality Project 90,
   91, 96
Market Inn Project, Youth
   Trust 192–3
marriage
   Mozambican schooling
   effects 206–8
   sexual abuse effects 181
matrilineal rural context,
   Mozambican
   schooling 204–9
'mature minor rule' 238
maturity, and medical
   treatment decisions
   241, 242, 243–4
mediators 140, 145–6
medical treatment
   decisions 238–45
memorising practices,
   Mozambican schools
   198–9, 199–200
mental health and
   violence 171–86
   bullying 174–8
   key facts 172–3
   refugee children 183
   Section 53 offenders
   178–9
   sexual abuse 179–83
Mexico
   sex education 104
   working children project
   64–74
monitoring processes, and
   systems abuse 43
Mousie 154
military involvement see
   soldiers, children as
moral development 244
mothers of abused
   children 160–7
   case study 161–6
Mozambique 4, 5, 7
   see also cultural aspects of
   schooling

Nathan Stanley Appeal
   193

National Curriculum 108,
    248
national education
    planning,
    Mozambique 203,
    213–15
neglect, institutional 35–6
Newcastle Crown Court
    131
NGOs (non-governmental
    organisations)
    Brazil 91, 94–7
    sex education role 105
North Devon Project on
    Drugs 187–94
Norwegian anti-bullying
    campaign 175, 176–7
NSPCC 129–30

oncology unit treatment
    decisions 238–45
'optimal' childhoods 6
out-of-court hearings 131
'out-of-school knowledge'
    212
over-compliance 154
overlooked needs 35
'overservicing' 37

pace, abused children
    work 154
'paradigm' changes, Brazil
    95
paramountcy principle
    136, 141
parents
    medical treatment
        decisions 239–42
    police interviews 126
    responsibility principle
        141
    school exclusions 109,
        121, 123
    sex education 105–6
    see also contact
        arrangements
participation, Mozambican
    pupils 195–6
'pass the parcel' 35, 42
passive participation 196
pebble box play tool 156

peer factors, Greenstreet
    Project 220–1
peer involvement 13
    see also Youth Trust
penal custody for children
    14
personality development,
    and child labour 68–9
Pigot Committee 131
'pillar to post' 35
play, abused children work
    156
police interviews 126
police involvement,
    excluded children 118
Poppies on the Rubbish Heap
    157
'post-service' information,
    child soldier studies
    60–2
poverty 5–6, 95
    and child labour 66, 67
pregnancy rates, teenage
    99, 101–2
pressure, and truancy 221
primary school teachers,
    Mozambique 210–13
privacy rights 8–9
private sector role, Brazil
    91
problem solving skills,
    child's 29
'Profiling' learning
    assessment 248,
    249–50
programme abuse 34
programme refugees 78,
    86
proof of abuse 143
'prostitute' definition 86
prostitution, child 11
protection rights, UN
    Convention 7–14
puppets, abused children
    work 156

quota refugees 78, 86

racism
    in refuges 139
    towards refugees 82

radio programme,
    single–parent families
    233, 236
Real Steel youth band 193
'reasons for involvement',
    child soldier studies
    59–60
Records of Achievement
    (R.o.A.s) 249, 250,
    253–6
'recruitment' definition,
    child soldier studies 56
recruitment information,
    child soldier studies
    57–8
Red Crescent Movement
    53
Red Cross 53
reflective thinking
    research 248, 250–7
Refugee Council Working
    Group 78–9, 83, 84,
    183
refugees 10, 86, 183
    see also unaccompanied
        refugee children
rehabilitation of child
    soldiers 14
reinstatement of excluded
    children 118, 119
reintegration information,
    child soldier studies
    62–3
reproductive health
    99–100, 101–2
reproductive participation
    196
resilience 3, 14, 19–30,
    183
    contributory factors
        26–9
    descriptions 23–6
    importance 21–2
    language of 26
    sources 22–3
resource problems, and
    systems abuse 34,
    36–7
re-telling of abuse 151–2
re-victimisation 182
review processes, and
    systems abuse 43

rights of the child *see* UN Convention on the Rights of the Child
ritualisation, Mozambican schooling 197–8, 199–200
R.o.A.s *see* Records of Achievement
role models
  child's 27
  mothers as 165, 166
rote learning, Mozambican schools 198–9
Royal Alexandra Hospital, New South Wales 238
rules, child's need for 27
rural Mozambican schooling 200, 204–9

school exclusion *see* excluded children
schooling and culture *see* cultural aspects of schooling
science teaching, Mozambican schools 201
screens in court 129, 131
Section 53 offenders 178–9
self-advocacy *see* learning rights and self-advocacy
self-reflection research study 248, 250–7
separation, domestic violence after 138, 140
services
  access to 27, 35
  children's mental health 183–4
  inadequacy 35, 36–7
  inappropriate 35
settings, for resilience work 21
sexual abuse 9, 13, 138, 179–83
  children as abusers 179–80
  effects of 180–2
  mental health 182–3

mothers' therapy groups 160–7
sexual functioning problems 181
sexual health 13, 99–100, 101–2
sexuality, teenage 98–106
  definition 99–101
  educational approaches 102–3
  parental role 105–6
  risks 101–2
  role of NGOs 105
  training needs 103–5
sexually transmitted diseases 102
Sharon, learning rights case 246–7
Sheffield Bullying Project 175, 176, 177
single-parent families, children's views 233–7
skills, lack of 38–9
social exclusion, Brazil *see* marginalisation
social factors, Mozambican schooling 201
social services demand, Brazil 95
'social services department' definition 86
social skills, child's 28–9
social studies courses 258
socialisation, work and 66–7
'soldier' definition, child soldier studies 56
soldiers, children as 14, 51–63
  age of recruitment 53–4
  developing understanding 55–63
  international compromise 52
solicitors, and child witnesses 140, 143, 145
solidarity problems, Mozambican schooling 209

Somerset Thinking Skills 252–7
South Africa
  effects of adversity 6
  sex education 104
special school exclusions 111, *113*
specialist training, lack of 38–9
staff
  exclusion units 119–21, *120*
  support for 37, 38, 39–40
strengths, child's internal 28
stress, Japanese children 11–12
structure, child's need for 27
subject material, Greenstreet Project 221, 222–4
substance abuse 13
  avoidance project 187–94
  Mexican child workers 70
suburban Mozambican schools 200
Sue, mothers' group case study 162–6
suicide rates 172, 181
supervised contact with parents 143–4
supervision, staff 38, 39–40
support
  children 42
  staff 37, 38, 39–40
  terminally ill children 241, 244
  witnesses 129–30
  Youth Trust 191–2
survival strategies
  domestic violence 139
  work as 65–6, 67, 71–2
suspect identification 126
systems abuse 8, 33–45
  complaint mechanisms 44
  definitions 34–5

forms and examples
35–6
monitoring 43
preventing 41–2
reasons for 36–41
Systems Abuse Report 33,
34–5, 41

teacher training colleges,
Mozambique 211
teachers, Mozambique
primary 210–13
teaching methods,
Greenstreet Project
219–22
teenage sexuality 98–106
terminally ill children,
treatment decisions
238–45
therapy needs
abused children 149–58
child witnesses 127, 130
excluded children 116
mothers of abused
children 160–7
truancy children 221,
224–5, 229
thinking skills course
250–7
time delays, child
witnesses 127–8, 130,
131, 132
timing
responding to child's 42
working with abused
children 153–4
toys, abused children work
155
trafficking for sexual
purposes 10–11
ng
of 38–9
health educators

h refugees

ion,
ties 61

'treatment' information,
child soldier studies
58–9
truancy project 217–30
trust building 9, 27, 28,
29, 154

unaccompanied refugee
children 77–84, 86–7
British legislation 80–2
international standards
80
needs 79–80
protection of rights 82–4
UK 78–9
UN Convention on the
Rights of the Child
7–14, 43, 74–6, 247,
258
armed conflict 52
contact with parents
135–6, 144
refugee children 80, 83
school exclusions 110,
123
UN Convention Relating
to the Status of
Refugees 80
UNICAMP 91, 94, 96
understanding disease,
terminally ill children
241, 244–5
understanding problems,
Mozambican
schooling 197–9
Urban Child Project 7
urban Mozambican
schools 200
urbanisation 6–7

Victim Support 129, 130
victims of violence 178–9
of bullying 177–8
video facilities
child witnesses 129,
130, 131–2
student self-reflection
work 249–50
working with abused
children 157
violence 9, 13

see also domestic
violence; mental
health and violence;
sexual abuse
Violence and Young
Minds campaign 173
visas 80–1, 87
voice for children, lack of
40–1
voluntary combat
recruitment 53, 54, 56

waiting time
classrooms 196
courts 127–8, 131, 132
trials 127, 130, 131,
132
wartime children 5, 14
see also soldiers, children
as
welfare checklist, Children
Act 136, 144
welfare (well-being)
policy, Brazil 90–1,
93–7
'well-being' information,
child soldier studies 61
'whole-school' approach
to bullying 176–7
witnesses, children as
9–10, 39, 126–32
changes since 1985
128–30
further improvements
131–2
problems 127–8
working children see child
labour
World Conference on
Human Rights 54

Young Management Team
188, 189–90, 192,
194
Young Minds 173, 183
youth exchange,
Greenstreet Project
218, 223–4
Youth Trust 187–94
aims and objectives
188–9
emergence 187–8

examples of actions
190–3
role of young people
189
Young Management
Team 189–90
Yugoslavia, former 5

Author Index

Adler, Z. 181
Ahmad, Y. 174
Ainsworth, M.D.S. 42
Alvim, R. 90, 92
Aristotle 12–13
Arita, M. 12
Association of Educational
Psychologists 122

Baker, R. 214
Baloi, O. 210
Barron, J. 137
Baudrillard, J. 260
Bauman, Z. 260
Beitchmann, J.H. 180, 181
Bentovim, A. 179
Berno 92, 95
Berridge, D. 39
Bifulco, A. 181
Binney, V. 137
Blagg, N. 252
Borkowski, M. 138
Boswell, G. 178
Boulton, M. 174
Bray, M. 157
Brennan, D. 35, 36, 38,
41, 42, 43, 44, 45
Bridge Child Care
Consultancy Service
138
Briere, J. 152, 165, 181
British Crime Survey
137–8
Brizzio 68
Brophy, J. 141
Brown, G.W. 181
Browne, K. 165, 182

Cambridge Partnership for
Record of
Achievement 254
Carey, K. 42
Carter, R. 257
Casey, M. 138

Cashmore, J. 35, 36, 38,
40, 41, 42, 43, 44, 45
Castanhar, J.C. 93, 95, 96
Castell-McGregor, S. 36
Cavanagh, J. 39
Chiau, S. 200, 201, 203
Child Psychotherapy Trust
173
Christensen, E. 138, 139
Cleaver, H. 39
Cockcroft, W.H. 248
Cohn, I. 53
Conte, J.R. 154
Criminal Statistics 138
Cupitt, D. 124

Davies, G.E. 179
Dawes, A. 6
Debbonaire, T. 146
Dent, H. 9
de Oliviera, S. 11
Department of Health
184, 247
Department of Health
Social Services
Inspectorate 83
Dingwall, R. 136
Dobash, R.E. 137, 138
Dobash, R.P. 137, 138
Dolby, R. 35, 36, 38, 41,
42, 43, 44, 45
Donald, D. 6
Duncan, S. 39

Eekelaar, J. 136
Eliasson, Y. 201
Erikson, E.H. 243
Eskeland, K. 259
Evason, E. 137

Farrington, D. 177
Feuerstein, R. 250–1, 252
Field, N. 11, 12
Finkelhor, D. 158
Flin, R. 9, 37
Flood, S. 179, 180, 182,
183
Freire, P. 258
Freud, A. 42
Fromuth, M.E. 182
Fukuyama, F. 12

Fullan, M. 124

Gil, E. 34
Geffray, C. 207, 208, 209
Gelles, R. 137, 165
Goldstein, J. 42
Goleman, D. 259
Goncalves, J.M.F. 89, 94, 123
Goodwin-Gill, G. 53
Graham, P. 172
Gray. M. 39
Gretz, S. 155
Griffiths, R. 258
Grundy, S. 258

Hall, S. 258
Hallett, C. 38
Hammarberg, T. 52
Hankin, J. 173, 183
Hanmer, J. 138
Harkell, G. 137
Harne, L. 141
Hawker, D. 174
Herbert, M.D. 34
Hester, M. 135, 136, 137, 138, 139, 140, 143, 144, 145, 146
Hewson, M. 202
Hewson, P. 202
Higgins, G. 146
Hogan, R. 244
Holman, R. 124
Homans, H. 99
Hooper, C.A. 141
Horton, R. 213
House of Commons Home Affairs Committee 137, 140
˙hes, C. 172
˙hreys, C. 42
˙am, K. 199

˙4

Jeff, T. 248
Johnston, J. 137, 138, 141

Kabir, S. 99
Kelly, L. 137, 138
Kirkwood, C. 137
Kurtz, Z. 183

Lane, D.A. 177
Lansdown 245
Law Commission 141
Leitenberg, H. 179
Levering, B. 9
Lindsay, M.J. 40
Linha, C. 201, 202
Lloyd, C. 179
Luis, M. 199

MacKinnon, L. 39
Magorian, M. 155
Mama, A. 137
McDowell, H. 181
McManus, M. 114
Meiselman, K.C. 181
Mellor, A. 174, 176
Minayo 93, 95
Minow, M. 41
Miringoff, M. 6
Mirlees-Black, C. 138
Mooney, A. 34, 38
Mooney, J. 138
Morley, R. 138
Morrison, T. 36, 37, 38, 39
Mould, J.W. 34
Mulgan, G. 3
Mullen, P.E. 181
Mullender, A. 138
Murch, M. 138

NAHT (National Association of Headteachers) 111
National Children's Bureau 5
NCH Action for Children 137, 138
NEPPI 93, 94, 95
Newell, P 44
Newman, K. 99

NHS Health Advisory Service 184
Nixon, J. 137
Nunn, J. 89
Nunno, M. 34, 38
Nuttall, D. 254

Oates, K. 181
Olweus, D. 175, 176, 177, 178
Opdycke, S. 6
Overton, J. 36

PAI (Population Action International) 98
Palin, W. 123
Palme, M. 195, 201, 202, 204, 210
Parfitt, G. 248
Parsons, C. 123
Paxman, M. 40
Pearson, C. 140
Perry, N.W. 39
Peters, S.D. 152, 165
Pines, A.M. 181
Plotnikoff, J. 131
Powers, J.L. 34, 38
Proudford, C. 214

Rabb, J. 36
Radford, L. 135, 136, 137, 138, 139, 140, 141, 143, 144, 145
Ramos, L. 95
Ramphele, M.A. 6
Reder, P. 39
Riesmann, P. 199
Rindfleisch, N. 36
Roland, E. 177
Rose, N. 6
Rosenbaum, M. 44
Rouf, K. 154
Rowntree, D. 257
Runtz, M. 152, 165, 181
Russell, D.E.H. 180
Rutter, M. 177

Sabóia, J. 95
Salama, P. 95
Samaritans Annual Review 172

Santos, W.G. 95
Sartre, J-P. 3
Saunders, A. 138
Scarman, Lord 247
Schofield, G. 9
Schuerman, J.R. 154
Senn, C.Y. 158
Serpell, R. 199, 214
Sharp, S. 175, 177
Sharron, H. 251
Shaughnessy, M.F. 38
Silbert, M.H. 181
Sivard, R.L. 5
Smart, C. 136, 141
Smith, D. 176
Smith, M. 179
Smith, P.K. 174, 175, 177
Snow, B. 38
Social Trends 173
Solnit, A.J. 42
Sorensen, T. 38
Spencer, J.R. 37
Spiecker, B. 260
Stein, M. 42
Steinhauer, P.D. 39
Steinmetz, S.K. 137
Stephenson, P. 176
Straus, M.A. 137, 165
Stroud, C. 199
Szanton Blank, C. 7

Tattum, D. 177
Thomas, G. 34
Thorburn, J. 9
Thornes, R. 183
Tong, L. 181

UN (United Nations) 98
UNFPA 98
UNHCR (United Nations
    High Commissioner
    for Refugees) 83
Uniacke, P. 238
UNICAMP 93, 94
US Advisory Board on
    Child Abuse 36

van Manen, M. 9
Vedder, P. 214
Vianna 96
Victim Support 140

Waddell, M. 155
Walker, A.G. 39
Walker, V. 138
Walmsley, R. 179
Watson, G. 158
Weinberg, S.K. 179
Westcott, H.L. 36, 38
Whitcomb, D. 37
Whitney, I. 175
Wilkinson, H. 3
Williams, M. 180
Williamson, L. 77
Winnicott, D.W. 243
Wolking, S. 183
Woolfson, R. 131
World Health
    Organisation 101–2,
    103
Wragg, E. 123

Xerinda, C. 195, 201, 202

Yamaoka, S. 12
Young, R. 258
Young Minds 165

Children in Charge Series

This new series concentrates on the theme of children's rights, reflecting the increasing knowledge in the area. The perspectives of empowerment and of 'voice' run through the series and the United Nations' Convention on the Rights of the Child is used as a benchmark. The editor, Mary John, is a developmental psychologist, holding a Chair in Education at the University of Exeter. She has worked in the field of disability rehabilitation and independent living and has researched with minority rights groups.

Children in Charge
The Child's Right to aFair Hearing
Edited by Mary John
1996 288 pages ISBN 1 85302 368 X pb
Children in Charge 1

Emerging clearly from the first volume in this new series is the importance of the voice of the child. With their emphasis on the twin themes of participation and empowerment, the contributors present the active role of children as autonomous individuals with a stake in the decision-making process. Contributions from many different perspectives - including chapters by children - examine the liberation of the voice of the child, addressing the need to listen to children and to act on their thoughts in order to transform traditional power relationships.

'This is the first volume of the new series called Children in Charge, with two other titles shortly to be published, both edited by Mary John. The focus of this particular volume is children's thoughts - how we can know them and act on them, how we honour the thinking and the thinker in our research, interventions and relationships with children and how these thoughts shape us. This book, and I suspect the series, is an important development and a significant contribution to the literature and ways of thinking and more particularly, to ways of organising and practising. This book poses a major challenge to professionals and organisations in all areas where children are, or should be, significant actors.'   – Community Care

Children in Our Charge
The Child's Right to Resources
Edited by Mary John
1996 256 pages ISBN 1 85302 369 8 pb
Children in Charge 2

This second book in this new series concentrates on the theme of providing for children in child-centred ways. It includes the philosophical background to thinking about children's rights *vis-à-vis* society's responsibilities and examines the effectiveness and dilemmas associated with the concept of the 'Best Interest of the Child'. Article three of the Convention of the Right of the Child states that all actions concerning children, whether undertaken by public or private social welfare organisations, courts of law, administrative authorities or legislative bodies, must hold the best interests of the child as the primary consideration. Rarely, however, does a child have a say in what those interests are.

This volume redresses the balance and looks at provision and redistribution of resources as far as possible from the child's perspective. It looks at children in very disadvantaged circumstances such as in Romania but also at some of the issues arising from developments in the 'developed' world. In addition to established areas this volume looks at two new issues as they concern the rights of the young: the possibilities of the information super highway and the rights of children born as a result of reproductive technologies.

of related interest

A Voice for Children
Speaking Out as Their Ombudsman
Målfrid Grude Flekkøy
1991 1280 pages ISBN 1 85302 118 0 paperback
ISBN 1 85302 119 9 hardback
Published with UNICEF

'this publication is especially timely. It sets out clear principles and practice
of children's rights... This book is compelling... Politicians and adminis-
trators...should...inform their opinions by reading this book. It could also
inform many practices and assumptions of social work.' – Community Care

In this century there has been a growing recognition that children's special
needs and life circumstances require a special – an extra – response from society,
in law and in practice. The new United Nations Convention on the Rights of
the Child represents a turning point in the international movement on behalf
of children's rights. Many nations will now find it useful to develop a
mechanism to serve as watchdog for children's rights and to monitor the
evolving situation of their children against the international standards laid down
in the Convention. The Norwegian Ombudsman for Children experience offers
one approach. Målfrid Grude Flekkøy was the first – and until 1988 the only
– Ombudsman for Children in the world. This analytical evaluation of the
Norwegian experience covers administrative and practical issues and shares the
knowledge gained from eight years' work. The author covers in depth the range
of cases that came up and discusses the ethical and practical questions these
raised. One chapter describes alternative ways of working, leading to tentative
conclusions on what makes such models work. The final chapter takes a closer
look at the Convention on the Rights of the Child and its importance both in
countries that ratify and those that do not.